HOW TO SELL
DISABILITY INCOME INSURANCE

Your Guide to Becoming a Top Producer in a Revitalized Market

Jeff Sadler

PO Box 14367 • Cincinnati, OH 45250-0367
1-800-543-0874 • **www.NationalUnderwriter.com**

Cover and layout design: Jason T. Williams

This publication is designed to provide accurate and authoritative information in regard to the subject matter covered. It is sold with the understanding that the publisher is not engaged in rendering legal, accounting or other professional service. If legal advice or other expert assistance is required, the services of a competent professional should be sought. **– From a Declaration of Principles jointly adopted by a Committee of the American Bar Association and a Committee of Publishers and Associations.**

ISBN: 0-87218-636-9

Library of Congress Control Number: 2005925851

1st Edition

Copyright © 2005
The National Underwriter Company
P.O. Box 14367, Cincinnati, Ohio 45250-0367

All rights reserved.
No part of this publication may be reproduced, stored in a retrieval system, or transmitted, in any form or by any means, electronic, mechanical, photocopying, recording, or otherwise, without prior written permission of the publisher.

Printed in U. S. A.

Dedication

This book is dedicated to the memory of my father, DI specialist Raymond A. Sadler, who would be surprised to know that I've now exceeded the number of years he was in the insurance business; and to all of those agents who opted to persevere during the more difficult recent times in the DI industry by putting their clients first.

> *"Still out here in the wind and rain, I look a little older, but I feel no pain."*
>
> – **the late Warren Zevon**

Acknowledgements

This book was some time in the making and my thanks go to out to my wife Eileen who kept encouraging it to the finish line—mostly by saying, "Aren't you finished with it yet?" —and to a number of DI agents around the country who offered numerous suggestions on what was working for them in the 21st Century. Let me also thank my long-time editor and friend Deborah A. Miner, J.D., CLU, ChFC, for always believing in these projects.

ABOUT THE AUTHOR

Jeff Sadler began his career as an underwriter in the disability income brokerage division of the Paul Revere Life Insurance Company following his graduation from the University of Vermont in 1975. Disability income and long-term care insurance have been the primary focus of his career, leading to the founding of Sadler Disability Services, Inc. with his father, Raymond Sadler, in 1989.

Over the last several years, Jeff has authored a number of insurance books, including *The Long Term Care Handbook* (3 editions—1996, 1998, and 2003), *How To Sell Long Term Care Insurance* (2001), *Disability Income: The Sale, The Product, The Market* (2 editions—1991 and 1995), and *The Managed Care and Group Health Handbook* (1997), all published by the National Underwriter Company. Other books include *Business Disability Income* (1993) and *Understanding LTC Insurance* (1992).

Jeff has been very active in the industry throughout his career, currently serving as a member of the National Association of Health Underwriters' Long-Term Care Working Group. He is a past president of the Central Florida Association of Health Underwriters, the Florida Association of Health Underwriters, and the Central Florida General Agents and Managers Association. He is a past winner of the Stanley Greenspun Health Insurance Person of the Year Award and the NAHU Distinguished Service Award.

TABLE OF CONTENTS

Dedication iii
Acknowledgment v
About the Author vii

PART ONE: THE DISABILITY INCOME NEED 1
   The Financial Planning Gap 4
   The Checkbook Story 6
   Today's Hot Prospects 8
      The Middle Income Worker 8
      Women 10
      Home-Based Businesses 12
      Boomers 15
   Small Business Prospects 18
   What About the ADA? 22
   9 – 11 – 01 25
   D.I. in a Down Economy 26
      Uncovering Need For Worksite DI Coverage 28
   Critical Illness 30
   Identifying the Need: The Tried and True Methods 31
      Waiver of Living Costs 32
      Two Kinds of Lost Income 33
      The Business Card 33

PART TWO: WORKING WITH A CLIENT 37
   Preparing for the Sales Interview 41
   Preparing for the Interview 41
   It's the Income, Stupid 43
   Disability Income Needs Analysis 44
      Part 1: Financial 44
      Part 2: Occupation 51
      Disability Income Fact-Finding Sheet 58
      Completing this Fact-Finding Form 60
         Proposed Insured Information 60
         Desired Coverage 61
         Existing Coverage 64
         Public Disability Coverage 68
      Cash Sickness 69
      Workers' Compensation 70

Railroad Retirement Act 76
Social Security 77
Public Program Summary 84
    State-Specific Disability Programs 84
    Workers' Compensation 85
    Railroad Retirement 85
    Social Security 86
A Programming Example 86
Making A Sales Presentation 89
    Disability Income Sales Principles 91
        Existing Coverage 99
        To Your Health 103
    Key Benefit Components 107
The Business Propsect 109
    Request for Business Disability Income Proposal 110
    Completing This Proposal Form 112
        Proposed Insured Information 112
        Desired Coverage 113
    A Taxing Issue 115
    The Employer-Employee Disconnect 117
    Business Overhead Expense 124
    Disability Buy-Sell 126
    Key Person DI 128
    Closing the Sale 129
    Underwriting 133
        Tools of the Trade 134
    Claims 140
    Placing the Policy 145

PART THREE: WHICH PRODUCT SHOULD I CHOOSE? 153
DI Unbundled 157
The Money Provisions 157
The Major Product Features 159
    Renewability 159
    Definitions of Injury or Sickness 162
    Definitions of Disability 163
        Total Disability 164
        Residual Disability 167
    Other Policy Provisions 172
        Regular Care and Attendance of a Physician 172

  Elimination Period 174
  Presumptive Total Disability..................................174
  Automatic Indexing..175
  Rehabilitation 177
  Benefit Limitation for Mental/Nervous Disorders............178
  Waiver of Premium 179
  Recurrent Disability 179
  Treatment of Injuries 180
  LTC Conversion..180
  Exclusions 181
 Optional Benefits..182
  Own Occupation/Residual 183
  Guarantee of Insurability......................................183
  Social Insurance Offset Rider 185
  Cost of Living Rider 188
  Retirement Benefit Protection 190
Business Overhead Expense 192
 Reimbursable Contract 193
 Maximum Total Benefit 193
 Carryover Account 194
 Summary of Differences 195
 Renewal Provision 197
 Definition of Total Disability..197
 Residual Disability..198
 Covered Expenses 199
  Examples of Covered Expenses 199
  Expenses Not Covered 200
 Conversion Privilege 200
 Death Benefit 201
 Legal/Accounting Fee Benefit 201
 Other Policy Provisions..202
 Optional Benefits..203
Disability Buy-Sell 204
 Ownership Interest 204
 Elimination Period 206
 Payment of the Policy Proceeds...................................206
 Minimum Ownership 208
 Valuation...208
 Renewability..208
 Conversion 209

Definition of Disability 209
　　　Transfer Privilege 209
　　　Professional Fee Reimbursement 210
　　　Waiver of Premium 210
　　　Exclusions 210
　　　Optional Benefits 210
　Key Person DI 211
　　　Who is a Key Person? 212
　　　Key Person Benefits 213
　　　Elimination Period 213
　　　Benefit Period 214
　　　Renewability 214
　　　Definition of Disability 214
　　　Conversion 215
　　　Waiver of Premium 215
　　　Optional Benefits 215
　　　Taxation 215
　Worksite Disability Programs 216
　　　Voluntary DI Plans 216
　　　Group Disability Products 219
　Critical Illness 222
　Critical Illness Prospects 223

PART FOUR: KNOWLEDGE IS POWER 229
　History of the Disability Income World, Part 1 231
　History of the Disability Income World, Part 2 235
　　　Stop Making Sense 235
　　　Small Craft Warnings 237
　　　Die Another Day 239
　DI Market Info Update 243
　　　Women 245
　　　Asian-Americans 245
　　　Home-Based Businesses 246
　　　The Professional Market 247
　Statistics to Work By 248
　　　Impairments by Percentage of Claim 248
　　　Obesity Leading to Increased Disability Among the Young 249
　　　Disability Sales Surpass Life Insurance 250
　More on the ADA 251
　Taxation 252

DI Product Info, Part 1 255
DI Product Info, Part 2 257
DI Product Info, Part 3 259
Transferable Skills Analysis 261
Claims-Related Information 268

GLOSSARY 273

INDEX 283

PART ONE:
THE DISABILITY INCOME NEED

"Money cannot buy health, but I'd settle for a diamond-studded wheelchair."

– Dorothy Parker

Key Concepts

1. Consumers are generally unaware of the disability risk.

    - There is a greater chance each year of a disability than death.

    - One out of 18 mortgages is not being paid because of a disability to the mortgage holder.

2. Disability is money going out, no dollars coming in.

3. Today's hot DI prospects are middle income earners, women, home-based businesses, boomers, and small businesses.

4. The Americans with Disabilities Act has been narrowed by the U.S. Supreme Court, elevating the importance of private disability insurance protection.

5. Selling DI in a down economy can be simpler because it's easier for the consumer to see the effect of lost income.

6. Diversify your DI prospects just as you would diversify your financial portfolio.

7. Critical illness insurance is another way to insure the risk of disability.

PART ONE: THE DISABILITY INCOME NEED

If I Were A Carpenter ...

"John Doe" was a carpenter, married with a wife and child, and finding more work than he could possibly handle in building-mad Orlando, Florida. Despite time away from his family, he often worked weekends, knowing in the back of his mind that it's better to earn it now as this kind of work could dry up at some point. He and his wife had talked about a second child, and he wanted to make sure there was enough money in the bank for this next step in their lifestyle. What John didn't count on was the back injury, when he fell from his own ladder while cleaning out the eaves along his home. The pain was excruciating for weeks; he was unable to work for any length of time. The carpenter work on various job sites began to go to someone else, who could be counted on to show up and meet the building deadlines. The money John had put away eventually dwindled down. Frustrated with John's inability to recover and his deep depression as a result, his wife took their child and moved to Ohio to live with her mother. John stayed in the house until it was repossessed, then began living on the streets, joining a group of homeless people, just trying to get by day to day. He sometimes thinks about what could have been, and what one unexpected back injury had taken from him.

... And You Were A Lady

"You think cancer won't happen to you," said a 40-year-old quality-testing analyst for a computer firm in Columbia, S.C. "But sometimes it does, and you have to get from that nightmare point, where they say you have it, to a point where you accept it and move on." In this case, it was a malignant lump in her breast that had spread to the lymph nodes. She was out of work for nearly a year. During her illness, her employer paid her sick leave benefits for 90 days. She then began receiving long-term disability insurance benefits that she had taken out at work. Even though her income was secure, she was anxious to get back to her job. Doctors did not want her to hurry back to work, and the insurance carrier was wary of too early a return. But they constructed a work schedule for her, graduating from part-time, as little as 10 hours a week – to full-time work in just over six months. Said the claims examiner who worked with the computer analyst, "Many of the disabled people I deal with want to work because it helps them stay focused on something other than the illness or injury." The claimant said, "I didn't feel I had to go back to work. I wanted to go back." The disability benefits made the economic part of the recovery easier, so she could focus on her physical improvement.[1]

The Financial Planning Gap

"It amazes me that most people spend more time planning next summer's vacation then they do planning the rest of their lives."

— Patricia Fripp

You spend weeks, months and years trying to build up your income, putting in the extra time, taking the promotions that come along, all focused on some financial goal: a house, a new car, the kids' college education, a retirement cottage on the beach. The spotlight shines so bright on these financial objectives that it is easy to overlook the one key element that makes it all possible—the ability to work and earn an income.

Have you ever passed a homeless person on the street and wondered where this individual came from? What sort of bad hand they were dealt that placed them in this unenviable position? There are a number a stories out there like the carpenter's, people who led a normal life until an unforeseen occurrence turned their lives upside down. Disability is just that kind of life-changing event.

In today's performance-based economy, few Americans feel any sense of security. Bruce Springsteen sang about vanished dreams due to the country's floundering financial times in his legendary song "The River." But disability can be permanent unemployment: when no earned income is projected for the future. Imagine the bills, the loss of a home, of savings, of college funds, of prom gowns, and wedding dresses. No more trips to McDonald's after little league games. The stress on a marriage and a family is overwhelming.[2] A lifestyle can be altered overnight.

Consumers simply aren't aware of the disability risk. They receive their medical benefit booklets from work, take them home, may or may not look at them, and assume they have adequate coverage. Individuals are conditioned to think about medical insurance benefits, but not about what happens to income should an injury or illness extend for a protracted period of time.

> Nearly half of the 1 million Americans who filed for bankruptcy protection in 1999 did so after being sidelined by an unexpected injury or illness.[3]

Despite this relative lack of urgency about the issue, the risk is real. A Conning Research study found that 30-year-old women have a 57% chance of becoming disabled, and only a 16% chance of dying before age 65.[4] Yet the focus of most people when they discuss employee benefits with their employer is health and life insurance.

Insurance coverage that can supply a significant portion of an individual's pay during a disability is *not* a mandated coverage. As such, people don't think to ask for it. They know they need health insurance (although this isn't mandated, either.) They understand they have to secure auto insurance to put a car on the road. They accept that they must obtain homeowner's coverage if they want to be assured of obtaining a mortgage from a lender. But if they do not protect their income, there are no immediate consequences—until a disability happens.

Conditions that used to kill people have evolved into "disablers," thanks to the wonders of modern medical technology. This would not necessarily be an issue if everyone had enough cash on hand to cover the disability contingency. But the typical U.S. citizen over the past 13 years has had a decline in personal savings rate and an increase in percent of debt when compared to disposable personal income.[5]

Disability or Death Before Age 65: What Are Your Chances?

Age	MALE Disability	Death	FEMALE Disability	Death
30	33.1%	23.5%	56.6%	16.2%
35	31.3	22.8	51.7	15.6
40	29.1	21.8	45.2	14.8
45	26.3	20.4	37.5	13.6
50	22.6	18.3	29.3	11.8
55	17.6	14.9	21.0	9.2
60	10.6	9.3	11.9	5.5

Source: Conning & Company, Guardian Life Insurance Company

"In a two income family, the odds are two in three that one of the earners will be put out of work temporarily or permanently. Working couples with no disability coverage should consider putting money into a disability package before they buy more stocks."

– Peter Lynch, Manager,
Fidelity Investments Magellan Fund,
during the height of the bull market, 1999

"Being a two-income family is the best disability income protection you'll ever need, because if one of you is disabled, the other can work and make up the money lost."

– Charles Givens,
from his best-selling book,
Wealth Without Risk

THE CHECKBOOK STORY

Who should consider disability income insurance? Everyone that works and earns an income should become acquainted with the concept. We're all vulnerable. It just isn't easy for healthy people to think seriously about a possible unhealthy future.

> One of out 18 mortgages is not being paid because of the disability of the mortgage holder.[6]

One way to illustrate the potential financial disaster that could lie ahead is to take out a checkbook. I know, I know, these are much harder to find these days. Perhaps you can pick one up at a garage sale or an antique store for illustrative purposes only. Many people do their banking online today. So whether you use a checkbook or pull up a sample *Quicken* page on the computer, the idea is the same.

Flip through the pages of the checkbook. Whom do you pay the mortgage or rent to? Who is the utility company? Who is the phone carrier? Whom do you pay for the car each month? Chances are the consumer may have some of the same bill payments and creditors as you do. It's then easy to go down the respective columns: income goes on the credit side of the ledger, and the bills on the debit line.

Ask the person if you started to erase or delete the credit numbers coming in, how long could the bills be paid? How much time before the money in the plus column runs out? Will the bills stop coming just because the paychecks do not? Most people can relate to paying bills and grumping about it. Just think how loud the complaints would be if there was a declining balance to try and make ends meet.

This is the story of disability. Money going out, nothing coming in.

In today's changeable, volatile economy, employees are often being asked to take pay cuts to avoid layoffs.[7] They can see the income going down quickly – and this is in a situation where they are healthy. But it is similar to disability in some respects – both the decline in earnings and the lack of control in keeping this from happening. The key difference is that the healthy worker with a pay cut can still work, perhaps even find another job. But the disabled worker has few work prospects and a bleak future without financial help.

> According to the Health Insurance Association of America, on any given day 17 million Americans are disabled and unable to work.

This recent stock market instability would seem to underscore the importance to consumers of income earned and invested for retirement. If that person's ability to earn an income is interrupted by prolonged illness or injury, the regular deferral of income made into the retirement vehicle(s) generally stops. The result could be, in addition to a struggle to pay regular monthly expenses, a shortfall in the retirement income nest egg. Disability insurance coverage can help workers continue to make contributions into a retirement plan during the disability.[8] Why should an injury or illness also take out the retirement accounts? Advances in medical science mean that the career-threatening disabilities of the past are replaced with recoveries, complete or partial, with some able to go back to full-time work. If there is a chance of eventually returning to the job, wouldn't it be beneficial not to have lost ground in one's savings for the future?

Most people are concerned with their investing today. Should I hang on to my stocks because I just know the market is going to go back up? Or should I move it into bonds and stop the bleeding for now? Or should I take it all out and put it under my mattress?

While the person is mulling over his financial future, you can assist with at least protecting the ability to make future contributions. If you work with anyone on his investments, he should hear about disability income insurance protection.

TODAY'S HOT PROSPECTS

For years, the disability income industry primarily sought out the high income earners to offer disability income coverage, with substantial benefits and policies rich with lucrative features. That strategy ultimately backfired, and missed a lion's share of prospects in the process.

> Don Hanson was once at the top of his game. A top salesman making $70,000 a year at a Minneapolis-based printing firm, he was an enthusiastic skier, an avid power boater, and fit enough to referee weekend soccer games. So when an insurance agent offered disability insurance to supplement his employer's coverage, Hanson declined. 'I thought, I'm in sales. I can't imagine anything that would keep me from being able to do this,' he recalls. Today, at age 47, Hanson is out of work: a victim of autoimmune hepatitis that has left him suffering from fatigue, joint pains, and short-term memory loss. A long wait before he could collect the first disability payments from his employer's policy forced Hanson to declare bankruptcy. And even with the $2,000 monthly payment he now collects, his family cannot cover all of its bills. Hanson maintains his salesman's optimism, but he worries how he's going to meet looming college costs for three teenage kids. 'It makes a difficult situation even more difficult,' he says. Each year, an average of more than 380,000 working-age Americans suffer a disability grave enough to face the kind of upheaval the Hansons experienced. Indeed, a 27-year-old worker is 50% more likely to suffer a disability before reaching age 65 than to die.[9]

The Middle Income Worker

According to the Federal Reserve, half of U.S. families with incomes between $25,000 and $50,000 had less than $2,000 in their checking accounts. That's not much to fall back on should a disability occur. The financial support is neither wide nor deep, and that's a problem that needs solving.

Today's middle income worker rarely has the chance to talk to a financial advisor about what plans are in place should disability strike. Those earning $50-60,000 or less seem to fly in under the insurance agent/stockbroker radar, yet they are arguably the most susceptible when it comes to an extended injury or illness. It's time to seek these prospects out and talk to them about their plans for the future if paychecks were not forthcoming.

These were not individuals who had a substantial stake in the stock market frenzy of the 1990s. Less than 15% of this group had invested in either stocks or mutual funds. What they did have were certificates of deposit, savings bonds, and some contributory retirement accounts.[10] They deserve the opportunity to protect the assets they do have.

Many of these middle income workers are single parents. The number of single parent households has more than doubled since 1970. How does a family survive financially when the sole breadwinner no longer is earning an income, or has incurred a substantial reduction in the money coming home? In addition, about 60% of today's U.S. households depend on a dual income. What happens when one income or a portion of one income is lost?[12]

> Barely 1% of middle income workers have individual disability coverage that supplements a group income protection plan.[11]

Many middle-income earners are located in mid-to-small businesses and often don't have much in the way of even group disability coverage. Quite simply, no one is approaching this group of prospects. It's often easier to see the decision-maker in this business size. Even if a group disability program is in place, does the worker understand it is replacing only 60% of gross income and the benefit, if the employer is paying, will be taxed? How will they make up the balance? If a reasonable portion of the income is in the form of a bonus, this isn't typically included in the group LTD calculation, meaning a further shortfall in what the individual thought was adequate coverage.[13]

COBRA, the legislation that allows employees to continue their health insurance coverage after leaving a firm, does *not* apply to disability coverage. Group DI programs will probably stay behind (as portability provisions usually aren't that attractive) and the individual has to start all over again. Many middle-income earners switch jobs in an effort to get ahead. Some leave and go out on their own. Either way, there will not be the same opportunity to continue disability benefits.

The middle income worker is perhaps in the weakest position to financially combat a disability. The great majority lack coverage. That's a scenario made in heaven for the financial advisor who wants to truly help these prospects.

Women

"There is nothing wrong in this world that a sensible woman can't set right in the course of an afternoon."

– Giraudoux

For the last several years, women have been starting new businesses at a faster rate than any other segment of the economy. They are also becoming the decision-makers in terms of finances both for their businesses and their families.[14]

Women are the wild cards in today's financial environment. While they are working more and more, taking charge in many cases, financial planning is still an elusive task for these pioneers. Women are more flexible, adapting their working careers to specific family lifestyles. As a result, they are in and out of the workforce, facing varying income levels depending on how much work they can perform, mostly due to caregiving responsibilities for children and/or aging adults. So they've increased their presence, but they are still susceptible to an extended injury or illness and they may not have had the opportunity to build up their financial safety net.

Female business owners are multiplying in a hurry. Since 1992, the number of people employed nationwide at female-owned firms grew 107%, while overall small company employment grew by only 12%. Substantial growth for women-owned businesses can be found in non-traditional areas such as manufacturing, construction, and wholesale distribution.[15]

In general, the number of women in the workforce is growing at twice the rate of men and, on average, women contribute 30 to 40% of all household incomes. Yet a recent survey by the Health Insurance Association of America indicates that women are much less likely than men to have insurance against the loss of income due to illness or injury.[16]

Without question, women have closed the gap on men in the working world. While there is much to be done yet to equalize income opportunities, many financial advisors have not been talking to women about their disability insurance needs. The Women's Institute for a Secure Retirement reports that many women either have no disability income coverage or are under-insured. Some of the reasons, the report says, that women lack disability coverage are that they leave jobs, get divorced and lose their spouse's benefits or are unable to afford the insurance. The executive director of the organization says, " A good case can be made that disability insurance ought to be at least as high a priority as life insurance, especially if you are a single mother or you are bringing home a substantial chunk of total household income."[17]

> Seventy-three percent of single parents are women who must balance job and family responsibilities with little outside support. Source: Watson Wyatt Worldwide and U.S. Dept. of Labor

According to a LIMRA International study, in marriages where both spouses work, 1 in 5 women earn more than their husbands. This translates to more than 7 million wives who are the primary earners in the family.

Part of the difficulty lies in the types of employment women are in. Today, at least 4 million women are "alternative" workers, meaning independent contractors, on-call workers, and those who work for temporary agencies, according to this same LIMRA report, "The Women's Market: Myth and Reality." This indicates some job areas where benefits could slip through the cracks. Many of these situations are ones where women are not going to have an opportunity to learn about and purchase disability insurance coverage.

So what do we have here? A market full of prospects, earning money, unprotected with disability insurance, many primary breadwinners, many willing to listen to financial advisors as long as that individual takes them seriously. Translation: plenty of work for the DI salesperson (especially female agents) who will take the time to talk with these upwardly mobile workers. I know it seems obvious, but there is a good reason this market is underserved—nobody is contacting these people about their needs.

Arguably, disability is a more important coverage to address given the statistics cited earlier in this section. Women are more likely to be disabled prior to age 65 than men, and many of these women have substantially more to lose. Not only could it cost them a business they worked hard to create, but the spillover negative consequences to the family is going to be a motivating influence for them. There are many people who depend on women today—from children to aging parents to a spouse to employees. They are earning more money today than they ever have. Protecting their ability to work and earn an income is a task we must thoroughly undertake.

> **Wealthy Women: A Profile**[18]
>
> Affluent women actively invest and manage their money, devoting 8.5 hours per month, on average, to overseeing their finances.
>
> This affluent market is relatively young. The average age of the women in this study of affluent women and their personal finances is 46, with 43% being under age 45.
>
> Affluent women generally rate personal service and financial advice slightly ahead of financial performance. 65% said they are willing to pay slightly higher fees for better service. The desire to simplify their lives and keep financial affairs uncomplicated influences how affluent women choose financial advisers. This affluent market gathers information via the Internet and other sources, but prefers to purchase financial products and services face to face.

Home-Based Businesses

"Don't follow trends. Start trends!"

– Frank Capra

Every 11 seconds. That's how often it is estimated that a home-based business opens. What began as a mere blip on the demographic radar screen following the 1990s corporate downsizing has exploded into the fastest-growing segment of the U.S. economy.[19]

So many people are working out of a home office today that yesterday's rules need to be thrown out. The DI industry's long-standing concern with a self-employed worker at home was the inherent difficulty in tracking the course of the disability recovery, since the worker's places of recuperation and work are the same.

The industry seems to have moved past this hang-up. Using an income-replacement method for a disability claim, it is easy to track lost income through financial statements and tax returns. A doctor will still have to certify the physical disability as they would on any claim. There is policy language that cuts off benefits one year after a full ability to return to work has been certified. There are sufficient safeguards here to let agents and advisors connect to this market.

> According to the American Association for Home-Based Business, more than 24 million Americans run businesses from their home. Most of them are owned by women who want the time and freedom to juggle family and career pressures. The occupations range from accountants, planners, lawyers, and insurance agents to caterers, freelance writers, and artists.[20]

Most people understand that they will ultimately make more money working than they will being disabled, so the incentive is there to return to work. Many people, like the cancer patient mentioned at the outset of this section, can't wait to get back on the job. These home-based workers are ones that have decided—voluntarily or otherwise—to go out on their own, and they take a great pride in building a home-based business. Many students coming out of high school and college are *starting* their working careers this way, and disability is likely the single largest threat to their freedom to work in this type of desired environment.

It's easy, technologically speaking, to be on your own today. A computer, fax, DSL line, and you're in business. Hang that shingle—as long as you've checked your residential zoning requirements. Today, Fortune 500 companies and other large entities are outsourcing a large part of their work to home-based folks, growing the number of financially successful people who merely have to walk down the hallway to get to work.

Without a commute, there may be certain disabilities that are, well, non-disabling where the home worker is concerned. A broken leg, for instance, might keep someone who had to drive to work, immobile for a time. But the worker who merely has to move from one room to another can likely still actively work, meaning the claims experience, in some situations, will be improved over the average commuter.

Home-based businesses are at a great financial risk during a disability as often it is a sole business owner doing the work. In many cases, there is no back-up, no assistant or associate to pick up the slack until the disabled person can recover.

What about earnings? According to the Bureau of Labor Statistics, 20% of these home-based businesses grossed revenues of between $100,000 and $500,000 in 2001 and 14% reported annual salaries of $50,000 to $250,000. That two-thirds of these businesses have filed papers of incorporation would lead one to believe these are bona fide prospects, who are in for the long haul.[22]

The Top 10 Home-Based Businesses[21]
1. *Internet sales and marketing*
2. *Children's products and programs*
3. *Information researcher*
4. *Home inspector*
5. *Internet webmaster*
6. *Personal assistant*
7. *Event planner and organizer*
8. *Home repairs and landscaping*
9. *Personal coach*
10. *Technical support*

Financial advisors would do well to keep this group of people in mind in looking for new sources of disability income coverage. Check out home-based business associations on the web for potential prospects. Some, like the National Association of Home-Based Businesses, break down their membership by state. DI insurers have begun structuring their policies to be able to cover these workers today.

Jose's Story

At age 38, Jose Perez was the classic hard-working corporate sales manager, suburban homeowner, family man and kids' sports coach. Then, during a workout, his "left arm didn't keep up with his right arm." In most cases, this might just be a strain, ache, or perhaps a muscle pull. In Jose's case, it led to a diagnosis of amyotrophic lateral sclerosis (ALS).

ALS is a phenomenally expensive disease. It can easily cost hundreds of thousands of dollars a year in lost income, medical bills, and for home care. Not only is it difficult to work as it grabs deeper (with exceptions like author Stephen Hawking), but many victims are not set up with private disability income coverage and must wait two years for Medicare eligibility. Because the diagnosis is difficult and rarely immediate, it's common for patients to suffer motor deterioration for a while before they are eligible for Social Security disability payments.

But Jose Perez had long-term disability insurance coverage in the amount of $4,000/month, with a lifetime benefit period (back in the days when this was a standard option). He made $75,000 annually while working, and this personal DI coverage was able to replace a good portion of Jose's take home pay as the benefits were payable income tax-free.

Jose has been living successfully with his disability for several years, a rarity for ALS victims. His financial concerns alleviated, he has been able to focus more on his physical needs in addition to being an advocate and counselor for other ALS patients.[26]

Boomers

"Middle age is when you believe you'll feel better in the morning."

– Bob Hope

There are boomers and then there are ... other boomers. Those born between 1946 and 1964, some 77 million people (when you factor in immigration), who are the healthiest and wealthiest generation in this country's history, are endlessly promoted as financial planning prospects. They are earning more than their parents ever dreamed of, we hear, and still are way behind on retirement planning. Then, there are others:

Leonora and Humberto Vierra live in New Bedford, Massachusetts. The couple's house is paid off, and their two sons have grown up and left home, so expenses for necessities are limited. But the New Bedford economy, battered by foreign textile makers and the decline of New England fisheries, has made their life a little less comfortable. Their joint income was a reasonable $60,000 in 2000 and then dropped to $47,000 in 2001 as a layoff forced Lenora to find other work. Like many other aging boomers, the Vierras' prime concern is that a single major illness could wipe out their modest nest egg.[23]

The Vierras are a composite of one subset of the Baby Boomer generation today. These are the ones that have been working for about three decades, who have raised children that have either left or on the verge of adulthood, and who are finding their financial circumstances tenuous at best. Some have built up a little bit of savings, but these dollars are first in line to be spent when expenses outstrip income—the exact scenario in a disability situation.

Many boomers have put off thinking about disability. They simply couldn't relate to it, plus there were far more pressing priorities of concern. Now many of these classic boomers have found themselves open to losing that American dream they are barely clinging to from day to unpredictable day.

Boomers are so significant a group (and make up the majority of the workforce today – your essential DI prospects) that they have even influenced future generations.[24]

BOOMERS: According to the 2000 U.S. Census, about 70% of them own their own homes and have median household incomes that are $10,000 to $15,000 higher than other age groups.

SHADOW BOOMERS: Otherwise known as Generation X, they are settling into midlives, setting career paths, having families, and buying homes. They are typically the first generation of consistent two-income families, and have shown a distinct tendency to move around in their careers.

ECHO BOOMERS: Those born after 1980, made up largely of children born to the original baby boomers. They are just now entering the workforce, poised to take over for retiring boomers and going to work for the shadow boomers.

All of these groups are candidates to discuss disability income protection. Sure, the older Boomers, like the Vierras are in their 50s, but there is still a need for disability income protection, made even more important by the probable need for Boomers to work longer than any previous generation. Besides, as actress Helen Hayes once said, age is not important unless you're a cheese. Older Boomers seem more focused on long-term care. But LTC will generally only reimburse expenses, not pay benefits to help meet basic expenses, making it a mistake to overlook DI protection.

Financial advisors are focusing on younger affluent boomers—highly paid employees in their 30s and 40s, who are at risk for a disability event. They have money, know they need to protect it, but aren't quite sure how to go about it.[25]

The Xers understand that the financial world is a slippery slope, and one not to be counted on from one day to the next. They should understand the need for disability insurance. They are young, with a large exposure period of working years ahead, and need to ensure their ability to work and earn. They know a lot of money will be required by the time they get to retirement age, and shouldn't need much encouragement to protect their finances.

Echo kids have seen their parents go through some rough financial patches, and may have seen grandparents endure the problem of outliving what they built up in assets, especially if a long-term care event occurred. At a young age, entering the job market, what could be more essential to safeguard than one's health? Many of these youngsters are still single, with only family to fall back on if something happens. Depending on their situation, though, a parent Boomer layoff or a divorce may mean this fallback position isn't as strong a likelihood as it sounds.

Boomers and their offspring remain great potential DI policyholders, almost without regard to what stage of their careers they are now in. The workforce today is constantly adapting and transforming, and the rules will change many times over their working careers. But a DI plan can accompany the individual wherever that career path shall lead.

Rick's Story

Many agents say that disability income insurance is coverage every working person needs. Unfortunately, most resist buying it.

Rick Jacobs did. Jacobs, 46 and his wife Susie, 41, were the working co-owners of Simply the Best Cleaners in a Memphis, Tennessee suburb. The business (it opened in January 2000) cleaned smoke- and water-damaged clothing in addition to the normal dry cleaning business. In addition to Rick and Susie, their four children and eight other employees worked at this successful new business. By the end of the first year, they were making $8,000 per week on the dry cleaning alone.

Rick had the opportunity to consider disability income insurance around this time for both he and Susie. Jacobs turned down the chance to get it, saying he didn't want to spend the money on something he thought he'd never need.

The business continued to flourish, to the point where the couple looked at upgrading their personal residence. On the evening prior to meeting with a builder to discuss this new home, Susie experienced chest pains. That next morning, she collapsed, suffering a heart attack. Her heart actually stopped beating, but paramedics revived her with a defibrillator. She stayed in the hospital's intensive care unit for eight days while a machine breathed for her. After her stay in ICU, she spent another three weeks in hospital and an additional two weeks in rehabilitation. But the time during her heart stoppage had caused some brain damage, an effect that was significant and irreversible.

The Jacobs' cleaning business suffered. The medical bills piled up. By February 2002, Rick had to sell the business. Although he had health insurance coverage, nearly $40,000 of the medical bills were not covered. The $1,600 Social Security disability check is not enough to keep pace with their regular bills. The couple had to sell a lakefront home that had been in the family for generations to help meet expenses. Eventually, they declared bankruptcy. Said Rick, "Had I listened to the insurance agent and purchased disability income coverage, our lives would have been so much easier after Susie's heart attack."[27]

SMALL BUSINESS PROSPECTS

The American Council of Life Insurers recently completed a study on the small-employer market and attitudes towards disability. The result? It's conclusion was that small employers greatly underestimate the risk that an employee between the ages of 35 and 65 will suffer a serious disability. Over 80% of the small business respondents to the study said they have no disability coverage. With the majority of U.S. workers being employed by smaller firms, this just multiplies the number of people who do not have the chance to look at disability income insurance.

The good news? More than half of small businesses said they would consider adding the coverage if it was affordable.[28]

"Six months earlier, John Palko was a poster child for hard-driving entrepreneurs, a man who climbed steps two at a time and sprinted through airports. Today, he gets winded walking to his car. Palko's Orlando, Florida office is filled with blueprints, files and reminders everywhere of his illness. Oxygen tanks. An intravenous drug pump hooked to his heart. Bottles filled with the 20 pills he takes each day. Palko, who needs a lung transplant, can no longer travel to meet his clients. His warehouse consulting business is suffering. So would his family if not for disability insurance."

Palko thought the DI policy to be too expensive when he looked at it seven years ago. It was $1,800 annually and some colleagues finally talked him into it. Now he never tires of telling others about the importance of this coverage, especially for small business owners. Palko has an autoimmune disorder called scleroderma, and his medical expenses are heavy enough, if he had to worry about other bills, too. Fortunately, the disability insurance has been worth every penny he initially didn't want to pay.[29]

"A ship in harbor is safe, but that is not what ships are built for."

– John A. Shedd

Being a small business owner has always been a risky proposition. Yet it was what this country was founded on—people wanting to carve out a niche of their own, beholden to nobody. It is just this spirit that keeps people optimistic enough to continue opening new ventures every day, and it should be our job as a risk manager to help them minimize the disruption a disability can cause.

Once again, this is a market overloaded with individuals who are unaware of the disability risk, as was noted in the above survey. Today's economy, a Wall Street version of "Mr. Toad's Wild Ride," has many small business owners hanging by a thin financial thread, needing to personally stay productive and have their employees do the same.

On the employee benefit side, small business is barely holding its head above water, having to pass more fiscal responsibility along to the employee with medical insurance changes. But perhaps this is a good time to step in with a group disability plan for the firm, a low premium outlay for coverage that can be viewed as a positive and balance out the inevitable rate increases on the health insurance side. In these bear market days, some employers are likely to be more enthusiastic about beefing up the employee benefit packages than raising salaries.[30]

Questions that arise during an owner's or employee's disability:[31]

- How long will the disability last?

- How long can the business afford to continue to pay the salary of the disabled partner?

- How long does the business keep the position open and when does it look for a replacement?

- When will creditors and customers begin to lose confidence in the future viability of the firm?

- How can the healthy owners continue to include the disabled owner in business discussions when the disabled owner can no longer participate in the ongoing functions of the business?

- At what point does a discussion begin about what to do with the disabled person's interest?

- Are sick pay benefits or salaries paid to disabled owner/employees tax deductible?

- What happens to the outstanding business loans made to healthy owners where all signed personally?

- Will the business have to get a new owner? Will it be the spouse or child(ren)?

- Will the disabled owner sell his or her interest to a competitor because the money is needed?

These are tough questions that have no easy answers. But every single one of these queries is valid—and should be discussed and planned for well in advance of a disability occurrence. It is the financial advisor's responsibility to raise these important issues. If you don't, who will?

It's safe to say that very few small business people have sat down to plan for the loss of either an owner or a key employee. The need clearly is there to initiate these discussions. Merely by asking the small business person any of the aforementioned questions, one can begin to do a risk analysis for the firm, and help prevent what many owners fear from time to time, and sometimes day to day—the loss of the business opportunity for which they sacrificed to create. And it's not just owners who aren't prepared.

> 2001 Nonfatal illnesses and injuries, private industry:
>
> - 5,215,600 recordable cases
> - 1,537,600 cases involving days lost from work
> - 669,889 cases involving sprains, strains and tears[32]

A recent survey by MetLife confirmed that disability income insurance and what it covered remained a mystery to many full-time employees. More than half of full-time employees had done no specific planning for their financial security and protection in the event of a disability. Of employees who actually had coverage, only 52% believed their coverage provided adequate protection, and far fewer female employees were confident about the sufficiency of their plans.[33]

There are many who feel comfortable that Workers' Compensation will be enough coverage, but most of the disabilities, especially illness, occur away from the job where this insurance will not extend. It's easy to dismiss private disability income coverage as the Jacobs' family had done in the story noted earlier. The need may be easily seen, but a plan to

> According to the National Health Interview Survey, 16.2 million working-age people have a work limitation, representing 10.5% of the 18-64 year-old population.[34]

put DI coverage into play still has to happen. One of the many advantages of properly illustrating the need for DI with a business is that there are multiple prospects under the same roof for the coverage. Plus, there are many ways to provide the coverage with group, individual or some combination of these insurance plans.

States with the Highest Percentage of People with a Work Disability:

12.6 %	West Virginia	11.4%	Kentucky
11.2 %	Arkansas	11.0%	Mississippi
10.3 %	Louisiana	10.2 %	Maine
10.2 %	Oklahoma	10.0 %	Oregon

Source: National Institute on Disability and Rehabilitation Research

The small business market continues to represent an important source of prospects for financial advisors who recommend disability income insurance. As we will see, there are more DI needs within the business entity than simply personal disability coverage.

WHAT ABOUT THE ADA?

In 1990, the Federal government passed wide-sweeping legislation to benefit the more than 40 million Americans considered disabled in this country: The Americans with Disabilities Act (ADA). It was intended to open opportunities for the disabled in the workplace, give them rights if disability happened while employed, and prohibit employers from discriminating against a qualified individual with a disability because of that impairment.

Disability income carriers adjusted, re-writing some policy language of group LTD plans to include some coverage to reimburse the employer for expenses incurred in complying with this law. New types of coverage, such as paying for "reasonable accommodation" that must be made to allow a disabled worker to return to the job, were born into this fresh environment.

This law, as many enacted by government, had good intentions. What it wrought was a flood of lawsuits directed at employers accusing them of violating rights under this legislation. It may also have led some employees to believe the protections afforded under this law were an acceptable substitute to disability income insurance.

As former Presidential candidate Ross Perot put it "the devil's in the details." What Congress passes is often sent through the court system to interpret certain passages of any law. Court rulings are often the last word on legislation, unless Congress decides to change it. The ADA is no different and the key element of the language to be decided was who exactly is considered "disabled" under this law. This has brought cases, some of which are noted to the left, by a circuitous route all the way to the Supreme Court.

In 1999, the Court ruled that people with correctable impairments generally cannot rely on the ADA to sue employers over alleged discrimination.

The vote was 7-2, and Justice Sandra Day O'Connor, writing for the majority, said that Congress estimated the ADA to apply to some 43 million disabled people and if correctable impairments were to be part of the law, then the Congress would have used an estimate about 100 million higher. She concluded by saying the 43 million number reflects an understanding that those whose impairments are largely corrected by medication or other devices are not 'disabled' within the meaning of the ADA.[36]

Round One had gone to the employers, handing them their first victory since prior to Workers' Compensation laws being passed at the beginning of the 20th Century.

The U.S. Supreme Court wasn't through. In January 2002, they further whittled down the meaning of "disabled" in this legislation with regard to carpal tunnel cases. Carpal tunnel syndrome has asserted itself in the computer age as a sometimes painful injury brought on by repetitive motion, very likely (but not always) from keyboard work.

Sutton v. United Airlines: Twin sister pilots sued the airline after it rejected their job applications because they are extremely nearsighted, corrected by glasses/contacts.

Murphy v. UPS: Man sued the shipping firm after he was fired from his job as a truck mechanic because he had high blood pressure.

Kirkingburg v. Albertson's: A man who worked as a truck driver for this supermarket chain was fired after he failed a vision test, being almost blind in one eye, even though he had an excellent driving record.[35]

A Toyota assembly line worker named Ella Williams claimed that her carpal tunnel syndrome and tendonitis warranted a job transfer. The Court disagreed, saying she had to show that the impairment also interfered with major life activities, such as bathing. Justice Sandra Day O'Connor again wrote the opinion for the Court, stating that the impact of the disability must also be permanent or long-term. She said Congress did not intend for everyone with an impairment that barred "the performance of some isolated, unimportant or particularly difficult manual task" to be covered by ADA. The Court's decision was unanimous.[37]

In reaction, one leading advocate of the ADA called it "the incredible shrinking law." A lawyer for a consortium of employers praised the Supreme Court for looking at who the law was actually intended to cover. Mostly, these types of rulings should provide some relief to the court system, as more than 140,000 claims of disability discrimination had been filed since the ADA began in 1992. The ruling was expected to spur reluctance on the part of employers to make some accommodations to employees with ergonomic difficulties, and it was also believed employees would be less likely to complain about any such accommodations that would be made.[38]

An HIAA Public Opinion Survey revealed that 7% of respondents had their DI insurance premiums either fully or partially paid for by their employer. Company size is critical, though. Only 20% of those working for companies employing 11 to 100 people had disability coverage.[39]

The narrowing of the ADA law should help to motivate employees to look elsewhere for financial solutions to disability problems. Some of the situations where ADA is not responsible may be serious enough for people to collect private disability benefits, when they are unable to perform duties of their occupation. This would also provide relief for the employer, who could satisfy an impaired employee without having to get involved. Most employers are quite content to pass the chore of determining disability to a third party like an insurance company.

It is one more way the need for protection against disability can be easily seen by those who have the greatest need for it. Employers, particularly those in a small business environment, need the planning help financial advisors can give with this vital coverage.

9 – 11 – 01

In 1988, Mark Norden, then age 48, a personal injury attorney, was persuaded by an insurance agent to buy disability insurance on himself. With a thriving law practice, it seemed like good business sense. In June 1997, in the middle of a mediation, he felt a tingle in his jaw and left arm. Dizziness was immediately followed by a fainting spell and he was taken to the hospital. When the tests were all run, he had lost partial vision in both eyes, and had difficulty with memory, equilibrium, problem solving and other cognitive tasks. Short-term memory loss was significant and took a toll on his business. When his long-term memory suffered, too, he was forced to close his practice. Doctors told him the damage to the body is permanent, and that there are no real rehabilitative exercises or medication that could help. Thankfully, the DI policy has paid benefits, and continues to do so, helping to relieve, at least, the financial burden of this disability.[40]

In the space of a morning, the world changed forever on September 11, 2001. If there was ever a thought about taking security and freedom for granted, it was dispelled that fateful day. While the nation remarkably pulled together in a hurry, the sense of vulnerability is one that will stay with most Americans into the future. No longer is it far-fetched to think about death or disability, as millions of Americans were connected to those directly affected by terrorism on our own shores.

The tragic events of 9-11-01 also dealt a sudden financial setback to the insurance industry. While the property and casualty sector received the brunt of the blow, with estimated claims reaching into the tens of billions of dollars, the life and health industry also incurred substantial losses. It is projected that losses directly resulting from the terrorist attacks will cost life and health insurers roughly $3 billion - $2.5 billion in death claims and $500 million in disability income claims. While disability income is typically one of the lesser-publicized products offered by life and health insurers, it has received much more attention since that September day.[41]

A persistent cough and burning, irritated eyes constantly remind Jason and Joanna Schlossberg of the lingering clouds of dust and smoke that blanketed their New York City apartment for several months following September 11. The Schlossbergs, like thousands of people whose homes were near ground zero, are experiencing a variety of health problems as a result of the World Trade Center collapse.

A survey by the New York City Department of Health and the Centers for Disease Control and Prevention found that half of the surveyed residents living near the World Trade Center site continue to experience physical symptoms – such as nose, throat, and eye irritations – that are likely related to the attacks.

In addition, researchers predict that many residents, employees working near ground zero and people throughout the country who were traumatized by the events may experience behavioral health conditions, such as post-traumatic stress disorder, in the coming months and years.[42]

The disability claims have been coming in—for those fortunate enough to have coverage. Asthma conditions have manifested locally in New York City. But everywhere across the U.S. were mental reactions. People were afraid to fly. Those that were in the air on September 11 have experienced emotional problems. There are people who are fearful of tall buildings now, and some that used to work in them find themselves unable to enter a structure higher than three stories.

People I know that lived in Manhattan and had to leave because of damage to their apartments were initially frightened about returning. It took a number of weeks to fight off those feelings, and work loss was suffered by many.

Some individuals were reimbursed for their income loss through disability insurance, either group or individual. Given the financial help, these folks could concentrate on their counseling sessions and other ways to deal with these monumental events.

D.I. IN A DOWN ECONOMY

Even before the 9-11-01 attacks, the economy was teetering on the brink of a fall. News of below average earnings, corporate layoffs, 401(k) losses, Enron accounting practices, and disappearing retirement funds brought a new type of economic schizophrenia to the markets before and after September 11. Down days started to outpace positive returns, and consumers lost millions of dollars.

During an economic downturn, as has been pointed out earlier, the need for disability seems abundantly clear. Disability insurance is a replacement of lost wages. Wages and retirement dollars saw decimal points change for the worse in a frighteningly short period of time.

People affected directly by September 11 and those who are working in surroundings of cutbacks and downsizing can all too clearly see a future that has no paycheck in it. How will they replace it? How will they pay for rock-bottom necessities? Some will be affected by medical conditions and some will not. A post-traumatic stress disorder will interfere not only

> 72% of Americans say they will be adversely affected financially if they could not work for a year or longer, according to the American Council of Life Insurers and the Consumer Federation of America.[43]

with a person's ability to work, but to even seek other wage sources. A disability income check and a rehabilitation specialist working with you can alleviate the great majority of this problem. The one hitch is the coverage must be purchased before any of this happens.

People are focused today on protecting their wealth. They see it sailing backward after a rapid growth phase. They are, in essence, trying to put a brake on financial disaster. You can transfer this situation to one where a breadwinner has a disability event and is unable to work.

The same kind of monetary slippage will occur. It is a down economy for one person, one family. They need help to plan for this possible contingency so that all that is necessary is to follow the directions of what to do should one become disabled. It's like being prepared for a twister in Kansas as Dorothy found out in *The Wizard of Oz* when Auntie Em and the gang headed for the shelter and survived a nasty tornado. No dreams, no flying monkeys, no Wicked Witch. That's what we want for our clients should disability strike.

> The National Safety Council reports that the total cost of unintentional injuries in 1999 was $489 billion. The costs of treating these injuries are higher than many families expect.[44]

There is belt-tightening going on everywhere. This does not mean people won't buy disability insurance coverage during this time. Historically, in a recession or economic slowdown, disability claims tend to rise. Thus, more people may encounter a disability situation—of a friend, associate or family member—that forces them to think about what their situation would be like should the same medical thing happen to them.

During this time, businesses are doing plenty of re-tooling to survive. One of the key ways you can help is to set up a DI plan (likely group) to help the employer beef up the employee benefit package, without much direct economic impact to the business. The result can be the retention of key employees, vital during this economic struggle. Without a high-quality workforce, managing costs and maximizing productivity are difficult objectives to attain.[45]

Thus, employers thinking about key employees are one avenue to explore for implementing more disability insurance in days of a troubled economy. Employees, as noted, are the other natural source to think about DI sales. The Bureau of Labor Statistics reports that there were more than 21,000 mass layoffs (50 or more from a single company) in 2001, affecting 2.5 million workers. Manufacturing was the hardest hit, accounting for 46% of these layoffs, but all industries have been affected.[46]

Uncovering Need For Worksite DI Coverage[48]

What to ask employees in fast-changing industries:

- Is any of your current coverage portable; that is, can you keep it if you change jobs or retire?

- For coverage you can keep, will the premiums increase?

- Would the amount or type of your current coverage change if you switched jobs?

- Does your spouse have coverage?

- Has your family situation changed in the past year?

- How would your family be affected if you or your spouse lost your income for a period of time?

- Is your DI coverage currently all in a group product, or do you personally own some individual DI?

The number one reason employees are not offered disability insurance through their employers is that financial advisors have not mentioned it.[47] Yet, situations like 9-11-01 sent many people to their agents asking about DI coverage or, if they had a proposal pending, finishing the deal by signing an application. While DI claims increased in that September aftermath, DI sales did, too.

Employees often feel reassured if they have group disability coverage. But that's usually a great deal for employers, and only as good for employees if they stay with the same job. But group DI may not have attractive portability arrangements, meaning the loss of

> Payroll employment fell by 101,000 in December 2002, following a decline of 88,000 in November 2002.
>
> *Source: U.S. Bureau of Labor Statistics*[49]

a job is also the loss of DI coverage. That is one of the more significant advantages of individual disability coverage. You can cart that around with you wherever you go, because you own it. I've had individual disability clients change jobs as quickly as they change cars, and their personal coverage stays intact—no muss, no fuss, no change in benefits.

Diversification: Working with different types of firms today is a solid strategy for the DI salesperson. During turbulent economic times, everyone has learned the importance of diversification of portfolio. Don't load up with aggressive stock portfolios, or place your money only in bond and/or money market accounts. A little of each works wonders when volatility reigns, and it can also minimize your losses.

The same is true with your DI work. Don't concentrate only in one market sector. White collar, blue collar, gray collar, manufacturing, professional services—branch out into each of these areas, so when one end of the business is in turmoil, another will do well.[50] Look at fields you think will thrive without regard to future economic changes. Many people are still investing in health stocks, for example, believing that as the country ages, this industry will prosper.

Approach health professionals about disability insurance, too. Doctor's incomes may be heading south, but there has been a slow, steady march towards the use of second-tier health professionals like nurses, physician's assistants and therapists of all kinds. These people will likely be in demand no matter what happens to the hospital or practice they currently work for, and they are also exposed daily to the repercussions of disability.

Down market or not, these folks are always great candidates for DI because they are exposed to it regularly. But you have to ask them about it, not assume because they are immersed in it every day, they will be seeking out an insurance agent or financial advisor.

There's much ground to be made up after September 11. The economy will ultimately bounce back, that much is historically certain. How fast and how far are different questions to answer. But selling disability insurance during these uncertain times is a must, and far easier than you will expect it to be.

CRITICAL ILLNESS

"I've got all the money I'll ever need if I die by 4 o'clock."

– Henny Youngman

In 1967, South Africa's Dr. Christiaan Barnard performed the first heart transplant on a human being, a 53-year-old dentist, who survived about three weeks before his body ultimately rejected the donation. This procedure changed medicine forever, and transplants today, while far from routine, are more plentiful and successful with each passing year.

In 1980, Dr. Marius Barnard, Christiaan's brother, performed the first financial transplant on behalf of a patient with his creation of critical illness insurance. He had realized over the course of time that while he and his brother and their associates could help save someone medically, the expenses associated with these procedures were causing a financial death for the patient and family. As medical science was progressing, Dr. Barnard reasoned, so, too, should financial science. If doctors healed the sick, what ultimate good did it do if the result was still negative due to the stress over financial circumstances?

> **Top 5 causes of long-term disability in 2001:51**
> - Cancer
> - Depression
> - Back conditions
> - Cardiovascular conditions
> - Complications from pregnancy

Critical illness coverage has sold well in South Africa and Europe and, to a certain extent in Canada, but has not done well in the U.S. Why not? It's a type of disability protection and one that many people can relate to since benefits trigger upon diagnosis of a serious illness or injury. Conditions like heart attacks, stroke, cancer, and other major disablers will create an indemnity payment of a face amount of coverage, such as $200,000. No questions asked. No need for continuing disability claim forms. There is the built-in assumption that this type of medical problem will create financial problems for the patient and family.

Condition	Death	Disability
Hypertension	-73%	+70%
Heart diseases	-29%	+44%
Cerebrovascular	-48%	+36%
Diabetes	-27%	+36%
All Four	-32%	+55%

Source: National Center for Health Statistics, 1999[52]

This money can be used to replace wages, cover un-reimbursed medical expenses, pay for family members as caregivers, or to hire a private duty nurse, among other possibilities. It is an idea that fewer people have heard about than a traditional individual DI policy.

> "I've always considered myself a healthy person. At 33, I was in the best shape of my life – eating right, exercising regularly, enjoying my great family, and I loved my job as an insurance agent. So when I was diagnosed with leukemia, it was a shock. I'm an agent who works on commission. If I can't sell, I don't get paid. Beating leukemia was going to take me away from work for months. I never doubted my ability to survive. But I still had concerns: How would I support my family with no income? Would we have to move to a smaller house? Would my wife have to find a job? Who would take care of the kids? While I was mulling over these issues, I remembered that I had purchased a critical illness policy. As it turned out, that contract made a huge difference in my life and that of my family. Because the diagnosis was one of the covered illnesses, the policy paid a benefit of $130,000 – enough to keep my family financially secure while I spent 25 straight days in the hospital, on the road to recovery. That lump-sum check kept us from having to make all of those painful decisions I was worried about. The bottom line? A serious illness can happen to anyone. If it does, you need to be prepared for the financial impact. You need to have a way to make up that income. Critical illness insurance may be the answer. It certainly was for me."[53]

While critical illness coverage is a different approach to insuring lost income during a disability, it is a valid planning tool, whether you use it to supplement individual DI coverage or write it as a stand-alone product.

Consumers are most concerned about the major illnesses or injuries. Cancer, leukemia, stroke—these are all conditions one can see would precipitate a long road to recovery. The critical illness policy lists the medical conditions it covers and can be an excellent sales tool when explaining the importance of a "financial bypass" (as Dr. Marius Barnard might say) during this difficult period of time. Heart bypasses are changing mortality into morbidity, but the recovering periods of disability need to be financed.

IDENTIFYING THE NEED: THE TRIED AND TRUE METHODS

"How far would Moses have gone if he had taken a poll in Egypt?"

– Harry S. Truman

This opening section has illustrated a number of ways to break into the disability income market, re-start a career with this coverage, break out of a sales slump, or figure ways to demonstrate the need in a down economy. But these pages will not be worth anything if you don't take them and start doing something with these concepts.

There are other tried and true methods of working in the DI market. These ideas have as much relevance today as they did years ago when agents successfully employed them to market this valuable coverage.

In 1982, when I opened a disability income brokerage office in Orlando, I was contacted by a retired insurance agent, who lived locally and had worked for the same insurer. He encouraged me to visit so we could talk about the old days of selling disability insurance.

I had thought my "old days" to be quite different from his "old days" (he'd retired in 1959), but nothing could be further from the truth. I was using ways to stimulate interest in disability income that he had utilized decades before I entered the business.

Waiver of Living Costs

Most life insurance agents add waiver of premium or waiver of mortality costs or a similar provision to a life insurance policy. If the policyholder becomes disabled, there is no reason to be forced to continue paying for the life insurance premium in place of other, more imminent expenses. When delivering the life insurance policy, save the explanation of waiver of premium for last. Discuss disability and the purpose of the provision, to waive this premium expense while recovering.

Then, bring out the DI proposal you ran on this client prior to your policy delivery interview. Ask, "How would you like to have a waiver of living costs, too? I have a plan I'd like to show you that would also waive your mortgage payment, grocery bills, car payments, phone bill, clothing costs and other necessities during a disability. Would you be interested in this type of protection?"

It's a simple, but effective segue to the importance of planning financially for the disability contingency. And it leads into another way to bring up a discussion of disability for the life insurance specialist.

Two Kinds of Lost Income

When talking to a prospect about life insurance, you are generally discussing the replacement of lost income, necessary because of the person's death. The family's lives will go on, but they will need to survive financially for many years. If, say, the prospect is married with two children, you would be working on a calculation of a face amount that could generate dollars for the three survivors.

But there is also another type of lost income. What if the prospect doesn't die from the illness or injury? This is more likely, given the nature of medical science today. If the client was alive, but unable to work for a time (or maybe ever), wouldn't the family need money in that event, too? The family of four hasn't dwindled, either. It's still a family of four going forward with income needs, and when you factor in out-of-pocket medical costs, there could be substantially more dollars necessary to survive than if the person has simply died.

With a life insurance sale only, the person is just half-insured. There are two kinds of lost income, and two ways that must be used to address these future financial concerns. If you are comfortable calculating lost income to arrive at a life insurance face amount through needs analysis, then it's a small step for mankind to perform the same kind of mathematics for a disability.

The Business Card

After delivery and review of a life insurance (or any other type of) policy, you will normally hand over your business card to the client, asking the individual to contact you if there are ever any questions or life changes to discuss, and that you will be in touch with them in any event to do an annual review.

While the person is holding the business card, ask him or her to turn the card over (assuming it is blank on the back), and write down the names of two or three individuals or entities who would help pay the rent or mortgage, car payments, and other bills if the individual was disabled and unable to work.

Wait for the answer. It's highly unlikely the person will be able to jot down any sources of income. After an appropriate interval, or following his protest that no one is going to do that for him, ask him to turn the card back over and say, "I can." (Hint: Try to resist saying, Presto!) The stage is set to discuss disability income, and you can now bring out the DI proposal you've been saving.

This is the challenge. Consumers don't, as a rule, think about disability *first*. There are other priorities in their employee benefit packages, primarily because the exposure can be almost immediate. Health insurance can be accessed quickly and often, even through a wellness visit to a physician for an annual exam.

Disability is not that easy to see, feel, or touch—until something happens. By then, it could be too late to perform the type of financial acrobatics that a DI policy can easily achieve. What's left is a family ready to vote the disabled provider off their island for neglecting to plan ahead in case this type of medical event occurs. Easily avoidable, and yet this type of unhappy ending is written more often than the reverse.

In a 2001 survey of workers by the Health Insurance Association of America, 58% of respondents said they were "very concerned" about "having sufficient income if injured and unable to work for an extended period of time." However, respondents placed a greater emphasis on five other concerns, including the cost of medical care (66%) and losing health insurance and other benefits upon job loss or change.[54]

To help make this a "happily ever after" story, you must be proactive. Financial early intervention is called for in the form of a disability sales presentation to as many people as you can tell. The gauntlet has been officially dropped; the remainder of this book will detail how best to accomplish this worthy labor.

FOOTNOTES

1. "How 'Working' through her Illness Helped One Woman's Recovery," *PR Newswire*, October 10, 2000.
2. Matthew Tassey, CLU, CHFC, LUTCF, " It's a Great Time to Sell DI!" *Advisor Today*, July 2002, p. 24.
3. Christopher Francescani, "There's No Insuring You Won't Go Bankrupt," *New York Post*, April 3, 2000.
4. Lucretia DiSanto Jones, "Consumers Unaware of DI Need," *Advisor Today*, August 2002, p. 30.
5. Mark W. Anthione, RHU, CLU, ChFC, "Disability Insurance: Middle Market Multi-Life Opportunities," *Life Insurance Selling*, August 2002, p. 90.
6. Source: Department of Housing and Urban Development – FHA Loans.
7. David Brauer, "How To Play The Pay-Cut Game," *My Generation*, July-August 2002, p. 10.
8. Dennis P. Mullen, "Sell DI Insurance To Protect Savings In Retirement Plans," *National Underwriter*, Life & Health/Financial Services Edition, Cincinnati, OH, April 30, 2001, p. 14.
9. "Disability Insurance: What to Know about this Crucial Protection," *Consumer Reports*, July 1999, pp. 64-65.
10. Cherie Tibbetts, "Disability and Middle Income Workers," *HIU Magazine*, April 1999, pp. 12-14.
11. Brad Weir, "Reaching the Middle Market by Voluntary DI," *Advisor Today*, February 2000.
12. Mark W. Anthione, RHU, CLU, ChFC, "Disability Insurance: Middle Market Multi-Life Opportunities," *Life Insurance Selling*, August 2002, p. 90.
13. Howard Hanger, RHU, "Think Selling DI is Difficult? Think Again!" *Advisor Today*, May 2001, p. 60.
14. Michelle Swanda, "Women Hold More Sway Over Family and Business Finances," *National Underwriter*, Life & Health/Financial Services Edition, Cincinnati, OH, April 22, 2002, p. 11.
15. Bill Meyers, "Women Increase Standing as Business Owners," *USA Today*, June 29, 1999, p. 1B.
16. Brittawni Lee Olson, "Have You Sold DI to Any Women Lately?" *National Underwriter*, Life & Health/Financial Services Edition, Cincinnati, OH, March 5, 2001, p. 7.
17. "Many Working Women Lack Disability Income Protection," *Best's Review*, December 2001, p. 92.
18. Carole Ann King, "Survey Explodes Myths about Affluent Women," *National Underwriter*, Life & Health/Financial Services Edition, Cincinnati, OH, April 12, 1999, p. 7, 10.
19. Matthew P. Berard, "There's No Place Like Home for DI Sales," *Life Insurance Selling*, April 2002, pp. 58-66.
20. "Home-Based Businesses," *Life Association News*, April 1999, p. 62.
21. Monte Enbysk, "10 Ideas for Starting Your Home-Based Business," *Microsoft bCentral*, April 15, 2003.
22. Matthew P. Berard, "There's No Place Like Home For DI Sales," *Life Insurance Selling*, April 2002, pp. 58-66.
23. Joseph Pereira, "Can We Afford to Retire?" *Wall Street Journal*, August 22, 2002, pp. B1, B3.
24. Drew King & Mary Beth Carion, "Catching the Next Wave," *HIU Magazine*, November 2002, pp. 59-62.
25. Linda Koco, "Think Needs When Targeting Aging Boomers," *National Underwriter*, Life & Health/Financial Services Edition, Cincinnati, OH, April 29, 2002, pp. 6-7.
26. Jeffrey R. Kosnett, "Left Leg, Right Arm, Right Leg, Left Arm," *Life Association News*, July 1999, pp. 72-76.
27. Chuck Jones, "Taken to the Cleaners," *Advisor Today*, April 2003, p. 26.
28. Marcella De Simone, "Small Employers Misjudge DI Risk, Survey Finds," *National Underwriter*, Life & Health/Financial Services Edition, Cincinnati, OH, March 3, 2003, p. 32.
29. Susan G. Strother, "Ill Entrepreneur Thankful He's Insured," *Orlando Sentinel*: Central Florida Business section, February 22-28, 1999, p. 30.

30. Allison Bell, "Agents Can Help Employers with DI Risk Assessment," *National Underwriter*, Life & Health/Financial Services Edition, Cincinnati, OH, January 8, 2001, p. 31.
31. Michael J. Eskra, "Don't Miss the Disability Income Succession Plan," *National Underwriter*, Life & Health/Financial Services Edition, Cincinnati, OH, February 11, 2002, p. 12.
32. Source: U.S. Department of Labor, Bureau of Labor Statistics.
33. Marcella De Simone, "Disability Coverage: a Mystery to Many," *National Underwriter*, Life & Health/Financial Services Edition, Cincinnati, OH, December 9, 2002, p. 23.
34. Source: National Institute on Disability and Rehabilitation Research: Chartbook on Work and Disability in the United States, 1998 .
35. Richard Carelli, "High Court Redefines Disability," *Orlando Sentinel*, June 23, 1999, pp. A-1, A-4.
36. Richard Carelli, "High Court Redefines Disability," *Orlando Sentinel*, June 23, 1999, pp. A-1, A-4.
37. Joan Biskupic, "Carpal Tunnel Cases Limited," *USA Today*, January 9, 2002, p. 1A.
38. Joan Biskupic, "High Court Raises Bar for ADA," *USA Today*, January 9, 2002, p. 3A.
39. "Disability Insurance: A Public Opinion Survey," *HIU Magazine*, November 2000, pp. 59-60.
40. Mark Norden, "Keeping the Boat Afloat," *Life Association News*, July 1999, pp. 78-82.
41. Source: Conning & Company, 2002 report: "Disability Income: The Long Voyage to Profitability."
42. Lori Chordas, "When the Dust Settles," *Best's Review*, June 2002, p. 77.
43. Steven Brostoff, "ACLI and Consumer Group in DI Education Drive," *National Underwriter*, Life & Health/Financial Services Edition, Cincinnati, OH, May 7, 2001, p. 32.
44. "New Accident Product From Colonial Supplemental Insurance Offers Affordable Family Protection," *Business Wire*, March 7, 2002.
45. Steven Hulbert, "Ability-Focused Sales," *Life Insurance Selling*, November 2001, pp. 132-140.
46. David Rather, "Uncertain Job Market Makes Case for Worksite Coverage," *National Underwriter*, Life & Health/Financial Services Edition, Cincinnati, OH, June 17, 2002, pp. 4-5.
47. John Roberts, "Prescription for DI Sales Success in a Down Economy," *National Underwriter*, Life & Health/Financial Services Edition, Cincinnati, OH, February 24, 2003, p. 11.
48. David Rather, "Uncertain Job Market Makes Case for Worksite Coverage," *National Underwriter*, Life & Health/Financial Services Edition, Cincinnati, OH, June 17, 2002, pp. 4-5.
49. Betsy Robinson, "Return-to-Work Programs Make Sense in a Recession," *National Underwriter*, Life & Health/Financial Services Edition, Cincinnati, OH, February 24, 2003, p. 18.
50. John Roberts, "Prescription for DI Sales Success in a Down Economy," *National Underwriter*, Life & Health/Financial Services Edition, Cincinnati, OH, February 24, 2003, p. 11.
51. "Sales Brisk in 2001," *Advisor Today*, September 2002, pp. 37, 40.
52. Timothy J. Nicholson, "How to Sell Critical Illness Insurance? Demonstrate the Need?" *National Underwriter*, Life & Health/Financial Services Edition, Cincinnati, OH, May 20, 2002, pp. 12, 14.
53. Jack Perry, "One Agent's Own Story with Critical Illness Insurance," *National Underwriter*, Life & Health/Financial Services Edition, Cincinnati, OH, April 22, 2002, p. 17
54. "HIAA Surveys Workers on Disability Insurance," *Employee Benefit Plan Review*, February 2001, p. 16

PART TWO:
WORKING WITH A CLIENT

"A good listener is not only popular everywhere, but after awhile he gets to know something."

– Wilson Mizner

KEY CONCEPTS

1. Distinguish between insuring the disability risk and self-insuring it for a client.

2. Perform a complete disability income needs analysis to properly identify this financial issue and its suitable solution.

3. Understand your DI insurer's income limits chart, occupational guide, and medical underwriting parameters.

4. Ask your clients about the probable course their disability might take to determine if total or residual disability (or both) is appropriate for them.

5. Know what type of income statements a DI insurer will request during a residual DI claim to properly prepare your client before a disability occurs.

6. Know how to program around existing coverage to be sure the client has the proper and adequate amount of protection.

7. Public disability coverage, like Workers' Compensation and Social Security, provide benefits but should not be relied on as the primary source of dollars during a disability.

8. Disability can be permanent unemployment.

9. A client's greatest asset is the ability to work and earn an income.

10. Proper financial preparation can ease the physical recovery.

11. You can't sell a policy the day of your sales presentation, merely assist the individual in making an offer to an insurance company with an application.

12. Express the policy premium as a percentage of gross income.

13. Indicate the total amount of disability coverage the client would be buying, not juts the monthly benefit amount.

14. Make sure you have looked into disability insurance for yourself before you begin making any disability sales presentations.

15. Business products available to fill business DI needs include business overhead expense, disability buy-sell, and key person coverage.

16. An employer without a formal sick pay plan may have a large tax liability in the future.

17. New Health Savings Accounts may free up discretionary dollars to help fill the DI need.

18. Be sure those individuals who decline to purchase DI to fill their need sign the Waiver of Liability form.

19. Insurers strictly use tax returns to verify income.

20. Find out your carrier's claims procedures—before a claim occurs.

P.D. owned a carpet installation business. Like most small business owners, work ebbed and flowed; for P.D. it depended largely on new business construction. When it was busy, he kept dozens of independent contractors in work, while he hopped from job to job, bid to bid. When it was slow, it was just P.D. and his assistant, as he struggled to put together enough work to keep him active. During one of his vigorous phases, his insurance agent R.M. sold him an individual disability income and business overhead expense plan. P.D. understood the need to protect his earning power if something unexpected happened. He had seen his income drop just in slow business periods. Months later, when work was slow and bills tough to pay, he considered dropping his DI policies, as it seemed like an extravagant expense he could ill afford at the time. R.M. convinced P.D. to keep the policies, stressing the importance of having a source of money when P.D. might be physically unable to solicit business for his firm. It took some convincing, but P.D. trusted R.M.'s judgment and continued making the premium payments. Not long after, business picked up again, with several major projects emerging at once. P.D. assigned out all the actual work, and kept tabs by visiting each job regularly in addition to bidding for more work. One such worksite check took him to a new hotel construction where his foreman was putting in carpet. The contractor had decided to also put carpet down in the balcony areas, so P.D. needed to measure the space involved to order the right amount of product for this additional work. After hours, as the skies darkened, he went from floor to floor, and on the seventh floor, disaster struck. After taking the measurements of one balcony, he leaned against a railing he thought was sturdy to jot down the specifications, and went right through it, falling from the spot and landing on his back in a pile of dirt. Unconscious for a time and then alone without help until the early morning crew found him, P.D.'s prognosis was not great when he was wheeled into the hospital emergency room. He could not feel his lower extremities and wondered if he would ever be able to walk again. Doctors went to work and when P.D. next woke, his wife was at his side. They spoke briefly about the number of bones that were broken, and the long road back to recovery that doctors felt would be complete. The initial paralysis was gone, replaced by a pain P.D. knew would stay on for some time. He asked his wife to call R.M., but she had already contacted him and he was driving over to visit. When P.D. saw R.M., he smiled and said, "I kept the policies and I owe you." R.M. shook his head and replied, "You don't owe me anything. I've placed a call to the claims department and paperwork has already been started. That's what the plans are for—to pay your bills when you can't." P.D. laid his hand on R.M.'s arm. "I'm going to be back to work faster than you think." R.M. smiled. "I have no doubt about that, buddy."

Preparing for the Sales Interview

Disability News You Can Use ...[1]

Every 2 seconds	someone is injured in an accident.
Every 4 seconds	someone is injured in an accident at home.
Every 5 seconds	a worker is injured off the job.
Every 5 seconds	someone is injured in a traffic accident.

Source: Northwestern Mutual

Preparing for the Interview

"There's no such thing as a person that nothing has happened to, and each person's story is as different as his fingerprints."

– Elsa Lanchester

P.D.'s story is real. He had to learn to walk all over again. Doctors gave him only a small chance to return to normal activity and that would be months away. His DI policies started paying after a 30-day elimination period, both personal and business overhead expense. His office stayed open, the jobs he had started were completed, and dollars from the DI plans paid for the majority of his expenses. Freed from worrying about his financial situation, he worked harder than ever at his physical recovery. Not only did he recover, he did so months before the medical specialists predicted.

P.D. also knew that his agent had spared him a life in financial turmoil. That interview, when R.M. convinced him to pay the DI premium, noting if it was hard to pay this premium when he was working how tough would it be to pay the mortgage when he wasn't able to work, likely saved P.D. from a larger disaster. R.M.'s reward was being able to deliver claim checks to a client that had trusted him to know the right thing to do in this financial matter.

This agent had a great relationship with his client. Can everyone say the same? How many of these situations occur all the time, where the policies are dropped, and then a disability occurs? How many times does the agent find out only when an overdue premium notice hits the desk?

People can easily understand what disability insurance is intended to do. The difficult part is in motivating the healthy individual to purchase the DI policy (and keep it) while that person is capable of qualifying medically for the coverage. You can cite all the statistics that exist; yet it is often only a *real story* that hits home for the prospect—somebody they know that has a disability and is now in financial trouble. Someone like P.D., who could have seen his small business that he took pride in disappear under the inability to keep it financially afloat.

R.M. was able to motivate P.D. (and then convince him to stay the course) because he believed that disability can—and does—happen. He owns the coverage himself—the first primary step in becoming a successful DI producer. You have to believe that this unexpected event could happen to you—before you can inspire someone else to consider this possibility. Once you have determined that disability income insurance can serve you and your family well, you are on your way to mastering the sale of this needed product.

IT'S THE *INCOME*, STUPID

"We can try to avoid making choices by doing nothing, but even that is a decision."

– Gary Collins

Governor Bill Clinton waged a successful 1992 campaign for the Presidency with the now-famous slogan, "It's the Economy, Stupid." By maintaining his focus on this simple phrase, he stayed on message all the way to the Chief Executive Office.

For insurance agents and financial advisors, the spotlight should be on *income*. Whether the planning concerns death, disability, or retirement, it's "all about the Benjamins." At death, survivors need money to keep up the accustomed standard of living. During a disability, the dollars are necessary to help pay both living and medical expenses. For retirement, it's a need for cash to enjoy a more leisurely lifestyle.

> **SURVEY SAYS:**[2]
>
> How financially prepared are your clients to deal with a financial setback such as a serious illness, accident or death?
>
> 43% Somewhat prepared
> 24% Very prepared
> 14% Somewhat unprepared
> 10% Very unprepared
> 6% Did not respond
> 4% Don't know
>
> Source: Allianz Life Insurance

Many planners sell life insurance to address a variety of needs, but many fail to fill a key necessity that also requires an income: the individual who doesn't die from an illness or injury but instead is significantly impaired to the point of affecting earning ability. If a prospect understands the need for income should he or she die, how large a leap of thought is it to recognize the potential problem of needing this same money (if not more) during one's disability?

It all starts with the insurance agent/financial advisor. If that person believes in the need for income during a disability, a more convincing argument can be made to the prospect. How many agents have looked at their personal income protection plan? How many planners could pro-

INSURE	SELF-INSURE
Transfers risk to a third party who will provide a regular cash benefit to help replace lost income and pay for living expenses during a disability.	Utilizes savings to replace lost earnings during a disability. Liquidate stock and bond portfolios if savings are not sufficient. Begin selling off assets if unable to convince family and/or friends or a bank to loan money to pay living expenses. Convert child's education fund to cash. Sell the business.
Cost: Policy premium (1-4% of income) and self-insuring own expenses during a short period (usually 60-90 days) prior to the start of cash payments.	
Gamble: Money spent and disability does not occur.	Cost: Loss of cash flow, net worth, lifestyle, self-worth, and (maybe) family
	Gamble: A serious disability will occur.

duce their DI policy should a prospect ask? Success in this market won't come easy for those who don't "practice what they preach."

Which of the two scenarios listed above makes more sense to you? Seems obvious doesn't it? But unless you have discussed the threat of a disability with a prospect, the less desirable choice (by omission) will likely be made. Do your services to your clients include helping them liquidate their portfolios and assets in an effort to raise mortgage money?

Not everyone will be disabled. But for those who do, all will feel the financial impact, as well as the physical trauma. They will walk the lonely road of fiscal stress, a path that will lead them away from their physical recovery. Agents should not let this stand.

DISABILITY INCOME NEEDS ANALYSIS

What's involved? If the prospect understands the risk, how do you insure it? What must be considered? What are the components of a disability income needs analysis?

Part 1: Financial

"A nickel isn't worth a dime today."

– Yogi Berra

One of the many reasons why disability income coverage can be easily worked into an overall sales presentation is that much of the data you'll need is available when you first collect information on your prospect. The essential income worksheet identifies earnings and expenses that are vital to proper DI planning.

Income

Enter your annual taxable income from wages and salaries for all jobs you hold: $_____

Add your annual contributions to a tax-deferred payroll savings plan such as a 401(k) or 403(b): $_____

Add any pre-tax annual contributions made to a flexible spending account for medical or child-care expenses: $_____

Add any bonuses, commissions or free-lance income: $_____

TOTAL INCOME: $_____

Source: *Consumer Reports*[3]

Disability insurance programs are based on total income. The chart above should collect all of the dollars one brings in, even if some of the money is spent right away. Should one be disabled, wouldn't it be great to have enough money to keep making 401(k) contributions? That's why it's important to look beyond taxable income, since that amount will be reduced by pre-tax contributions whose continuance would be vital to the future of the disabled individual and family.

This brings us to a critical point of understanding in insuring the disability income risk. You can't buy 100% coverage of your gross earnings. Insurers contend that this could provide a disincentive to return to work, as one would be as well off disabled (financially) as when working and earning a living. The insurer wants the policyholder and family to maintain their standard of living, but not to the point where recovery motivation is diminished.

Most individuals would want to rehabilitate successfully so they can return to work, even if they were fully paid if they stayed home. But to avoid the potential of abusing the process, only a percentage of gross pay is used to calculate the amount of DI coverage that can be purchased. For individual disability income policies, that percentage will vary based on income. The higher the income, the higher the benefit that can be purchased, but the *lower* the percentage of gross income covered. The lower the income, the lower the benefit amount, but the higher the percentage of gross income replaced.

The chart below will give you a sense of these varying amounts and percentages. The insurer will verify income from the applicant's tax returns.

Individual Pay Limits[4]

Annual Earned Income	Monthly Earned Income	Basic Monthly Indemnity	Social Security Rider	Total Monthly Indemnity
$20,000	$1,667	$ 550	$ 750	$1,300
$30,000	2,500	1,020	830	1,850
$40,000	3,333	1,440	910	2,350
$60,000	5,000	2,270	1,080	3,350
$80,000	6,667	2,900	1,200	4,100
$100,000	8,333	3,600	1,200	4,800
$120,000	10,000	4,000	1,200	5,200
$150,000	12,500	4,900	1,200	6,100
$180,000	15,000	5,850	1,200	7,050
$240,000	20,000	6,900	1,200	8,100
$300,000	25,000	8,000	1,200	9,200
$360,000	30,000	8,850	1,200	10,050
$420,000	35,000	9,650	1,200	10,850
$480,000	40,000	10,250	1,200	11,450
$500,000	41,667	10,400	1,200	11,600

As previously noted, coverage will not be 100% of earned income. However, it is worth noting that these are individual pay limits. Disability insurance premiums are not typically deductible by an individual, and benefits, when received, are not taxable. The annual earned income figures insured above represent income, after business expenses, but before taxes. Thus, the tax-free total monthly indemnity amount should be considered as a percentage of take-home pay, since benefits are not taxable.

Also included in this table is a Social Security rider amount. This portion of the coverage integrates with Social Security (and, often, Worker's Compensation) so as to not duplicate benefits that might be received under these programs and create a situation where more than 100% of earned income is insured. Later in this section, it will become more obvious why insurers have this type of offset coverage in their benefit design when one sees the potential payment amounts under these government social programs.

Now, since the percentage of income covered is not 100%, this means your DI financial analysis must also review expenses, to ensure that the benefit being bought for disability protection is sufficient to handle the *necessary* or must-pay expenses.

Once this list is complete and all expenses accounted for, it can be compared to the income amount already identified. One would hope that income would be higher than expenses, or at least even since you've given consideration to savings contributions under the "Expense" chart. If income is higher than expenses, you've already identified a smaller percentage of earnings necessary to pay these living costs.

A paring down of expenses that can be considered more luxury than necessary will further reduce this percentage needed to sustain the general standard of living for an individual (and family) during a disability. Recreational expenses, vacation and charitable contributions can be casualties of this extra analysis. Help the prospect truly focus on what is important here. This is an exercise that is best done now, ahead of a disability, rather than during what will otherwise be a traumatic time.

Thus, mortgage (or rent), utilities, food, clothing, and car payments will be going to the head of this list. Once the final necessities are calculated, you will be able to compute that amount as a percentage of income

EXPENSES

Mortgage or rent	$_____
Automobile payment(s)	_____
Food	_____
Utilities (heat, a/c, electric)	_____
Telephone	_____
Child care	_____
Elder care	_____
Credit card payments	_____
Personal care (clothing, cosmetics, hair)	_____
Insurance (auto, home, health, etc.)	_____
Alimony, child support	_____
Other loan payments	_____
Cable TV	_____
Medical (out-of-pocket spending)	_____
Education expenses	_____
Recreation (dining out, movies, books, etc.)	_____
Vacation expenses	_____
Charitable contributions	_____
Savings contributions	_____
Other expenses	_____
TOTAL EXPENSES	$_____

that must be insured. As noted earlier, this is not an empty exercise. Perhaps you've already done this with a client when you were estimating the income needed for survivors in the event of a breadwinner's death. If so, the numbers will already be available. If not, this same calculation can be used for life insurance purposes.[5] The need for income is the driving force behind this work.

This exercise has fulfilled the first component of insuring the disability risk. How much coverage can one buy? What percentage of income can be insured? It's easier to see now, and the prospect has a clear understanding of the amount selected since it was based on numbers he or she supplied.

There are some other factors that will be used to evaluate the income benefit that can be purchased.

Group disability income: In group LTD coverage, a set percentage is generally selected rather than a varied one based on actual income. It can be 50, 60, 66 2/3, or another flat percentage. A further review will be done later in this portion of the book.

Unearned income: This is a number that could reduce the amount of coverage a prospect might buy. Unearned income is, simply defined, money that will likely be paid to an individual on a regular basis *without regard* to a disability. Where earned income depends on the ability of the person to work, unearned income will come in without the same effort. It might be rental income from properties owned, payments from a trust fund, regular dividends from an investment, or a similar arrangement. That number should be calculated and it will reduce the need for disability insurance somewhat. Be sure to factor in any expenses here. For example, rental income received should be net of any regular expenses associated with this property.

Net worth: A substantial net worth may also reduce the need for disability insurance. Wealthier individuals (multi-millionaires) may be able to self-insure this risk if a disability occurs. Again, it is important to analyze this net worth to identify its composition. Perhaps a large part of it is the value of one's business, a firm that may be in jeopardy and not worth the same value should a disability happen to its owner. A net worth consisting primarily of property and real estate may be discounted because of the time factor in selling these assets to convert to cash when needed. Just know that there may be some net worth limits that when exceeded may make it difficult to obtain DI coverage.

Income track record: Most individual disability insurers will be looking at the track record of earnings over the past couple of years in order to properly gauge current income and potential earnings in deciding the amount of coverage to offer to the prospect. Let's examine three such individual's earnings histories below:

	Earner #1	Earner #2	Earner #3
Most recent tax year	$115,000	$ 82,000	$127,000
Two years ago	102,000	100,500	77,000
Three years ago	91,000	111,200	121,000

Earner #1 would seem to be following a progressively positive income path. The insurer would likely issue coverage based on $115,000, the most recent substantiated earnings. Earner #2 would seem to be going backward. A disability underwriter is going to be looking for cause of income decline and, providing there is not a medical reason for this downward financial trend, or a potential job loss, may use either the most recent tax year number ($82,000) or average the last three years based on the income outlook for the person. Finally, Earner #3 has one aberrant year. The underwriter might check both the reason for the income drop that year, and earnings from even earlier years. If there is a consistent track record of earnings around $120,000 and a reasonable explanation for the income drop in the one year, then the most recent tax year earnings may again be used to calculate the amount of coverage the prospect can buy.

Pension and profit-sharing contributions: There are many firms that contribute to their employees' pension or profit-sharing accounts. This is income, too; it's just not income you take home in your paycheck. Most insurers consider these contributions when calculating earned income for the purposes of issuing coverage. Up to 25% of income can be added to an individual's earnings based on the actual pension or profit-sharing contribution. For example, an individual earning $100,000 annually whose employer puts another $20,000 into a pension plan on behalf of the employee can use $120,000 as earnings to compute the maximum amount of DI coverage that can be obtained. This will help your client buy a more representative coverage amount commensurate with total compensation.

Employer-paid issue limits: DI insurers generally have a separate issue and participation limits table when the employer is buying the disability insurance on behalf of an employee. The reason is that because the employer will pay the premium and deduct it as a business expense, the benefits when received during a claim are taxable to the employee. To offset this, insurers issue higher amounts of coverage in this situation. The end result is a higher gross DI benefit that, after taxes, closely approximates what an individual buying coverage would have received. The following table illustrates the relationship between individual limits and employer-paid limits:[6]

Liquid resources: It may be important to single out savings account numbers, Certificate of Deposits, stocks, and other items easily changed into dollars. Calculate that number and set it aside for the moment. This

INCOME	MAX. INDIVIDUAL PAY	MAX. EMPLOYER PAY
$30,000	$1,800	$2,000
40,000	2,300	2,700
60,000	3,300	4,000
70,000	3,700	4,600
80,000	4,100	5,000
100,000	4,800	5,950
120,000	5,350	6,700
150,000	6,150	7,700
180,000	7,100	8,850
200,000	7,500	9,500
250,000	8,300	10,500
300,000	9,200	11,700

total may be revisited when selecting an *elimination period*—the number of days one will self-insure prior to policy benefits being paid.

The first part of your DI analysis is complete. The next phase is identification of the occupation and duties of the individual.

Part 2: Occupation

"In the spider-web of facts, many a truth is strangled."

– Paul Eldridge

An individual's income dictates the amount of coverage one is eligible to purchase. But one's occupation has even farther-reaching effects on benefit and policy choices. Occupation will determine the individual's rate class and the type of policy disability definition one should seek and may also have an effect on the maximum amount of coverage the person can buy.

It's easy to take this portion of the DI analysis for granted, but it's arguably the most crucial portion of your fact-finding. Details of one's work are vital in helping the underwriter and insurer place your prospect in the right classification.

Why is this important? The nature of disability is such that each individual will handle a disability differently. Much of this effect is due to the type of job the person is trying to return to full-time. A broken arm may not mean significant time-loss for a CPA, but could keep a physical therapist out of work until full healing and rehabilitation takes place. Thus, a CPA, working in a sedentary occupation, will enjoy a better premium rate than the physical therapist since there are fewer disabilities that would have a lasting impact on the ability of this professional to work.

When conducting the DI analysis, provide as many specifics as one can about the occupation. A job title alone does not explain what someone does on a daily basis.[7] Let's look at the Vice President of Acme, Inc. The title sounds like an executive, and it's easy to simply assume that the position keeps the prospect out of harm's way in an office setting.

Kill those assumptions. What is Acme, Inc. exactly, and what does the VP of this company do specifically? This will better help you classify this risk in the appropriate occupation. Acme, Inc. could be the manufacturer of computer equipment, for example, and your client's position is in Marketing spending the day mostly on the phone dealing with small businesses and trying to sell desktops by the bunch. This is more executive in nature, and your next questions will be to find out how this VP is paid. Salary only? Salary plus bonus? What happens to the income if a disability occurs? Is it guaranteed? Or will there be a significant loss because the sales VP is not writing any orders?

Acme, Inc. may also be the company that manufactures explosives designed for key enforcer Wily Coyote to take out the Road Runner. In this case, the V.P. of Acme, Inc. handles oversight of the various jobs Acme, Inc. contracts, such as razing a building or clearing a hill for a new highway. There is very little office work and far more hazards than would be the case for the computer sales VP.

Two risks. Both Vice Presidents. Both of Acme, Inc. By seeking more details, you can see the difference in classification. One position is generally office-bound, while the other is out in the field in a marginally dangerous environment. One will pay a lower premium for the same coverage because of a lesser risk in the nature of the work performed.

What about the relationship between income and occupation? Why the questions on how one is paid?

Here, you are trying to isolate the best disability definition that would fit an individual's situation should an illness or injury strike. There are two primary definitions that are incorporated into disability income insurance policies: total disability and residual (sometimes called partial or proportionate) disability.

Total disability: This definition measures ability: can a person perform the duties of his occupation following an accident or sickness? The type of work and employer can help indicate if this definition is the right one for the prospect. How the person is paid *after* a disability strikes is also significant. If the person returns to work in any capacity, will earnings be adjusted or will the individual be entitled to full earned income even if only working a few hours a week? A return to full income would mean that this definition-based DI policy is appropriate for the risk since the disabled person will either be totally disabled and needing income or be back at work without an income loss. There are sub-sets of this definition that also are important in identifying the proper product for the individual, and those will be discussed in detail in Part 3.

Residual disability: This definition measures income: will the disability affect earnings adversely? If the person's limited capacity means a drop in income, then policies with this definition of disability may better serve the prospect. This policy calculates income loss. If there is one, there is a portion of the total disability benefit that will be paid to help make up for this lost income. The VP of Acme, Inc. who sells computers may need this type of coverage if a decent portion of income is based on how many units he can move. A reduced time at work will likely cause a dip in earnings that this type of benefit can assist in making up.

> A 2002 survey states that workers do not understand their disability benefits as well as other work-sponsored benefits. 43% of workers do not know what their basic long-term disability benefit is.[8]

The *residual* definition is more often the choice of those self-employed individuals or workers whose income is performance-based. The *total* disability definition can be used for employees whose income is not altered by a time or duty loss, or for a professional in a highly trained, specialized form of work.

Many policies build both definitions into a comprehensive-type contract. Today's DI contracts offer a broad range of incentive-based return to work features that do not penalize a disabled insured from returning to work in some capacity.[9] This measurement of income loss means a fair reimbursement of the actual income loss the individual (and family) is undergoing.

Specific occupational duties are a must in the field underwriting process. It will help you properly classify a prospect's risk for the insurer and help ensure that you quote both the right premium amount and the suitable policy definition for the individual.

Generally, to qualify for disability income coverage the prospect must be working full-time, defined as at least 30 or more hours per week. There are other considerations as well.

Home-based business: This was a gray area for several years as DI insurers struggled to figure out how to cover this risk. But with a growing number of new workers *starting out* in a home-based business, and a likewise increasing number of down-sized employees going out on their own to take advantage of company outsourcing, this is now too large a market to simply ignore for this vital coverage. There will be limitations, however. Individuals that work out of their home but spend a significant amount of time away from it calling on clients or consulting for various entities will find an easier path towards qualification for DI coverage. If the individual has frequent contact with clients, patients, or customers, a home office location becomes less of an issue. Income documentation will be required in full, including all the schedules that are filed as part of the tax return for the individual and business. Some companies may limit the benefit period, depending on circumstances, or have a maximum issue limit, but there are many more ways to write this risk than existed, say, five years ago.

Business owners: There are all types of business owners, even within the same field. Insurers have long recognized there is a risk difference between the self-employed sales person, for example, who works out of his car, has bounced around selling for various firms, and averages about $40,000 in compensation, from the sales person who has been highly successful financially ($100,000+ for several years), has worked in the same product field during that time, and has built up a number of high-profile clients. This latter business owner might rate the company's first or second best occupational classification, meaning better coverage at lower rates, while the former might qualify for the third-best occupational rating or lower. Carriers use risk factors—income, percentage and length of business ownership, limited or no manual labor, and the presence of other employees—to potentially upgrade a risk from its standard classification. This again emphasizes why the *details* of the job are so important. Utilization of this data generally ensures that the higher quality business owner will be singled out and rewarded as a better risk for the insurer.

Short-time on the job: Individuals who have been working in their occupations for less than a year cause insurers to wonder about *stability*, a vital factor in DI risk classification. If there is a less than 12 month job situation, you should be prepared to solicit more information from the client, such as plans for the future in this position, past work that may have been the same or similar that indicates the individual has just changed employers within the same field, and a track record of income over the last 2-3 years. Self-employed individuals in their new business less than a year will be especially scrutinized, and it will be helpful to their cause if they are coming out of the same field when starting their new venture.

Government employee: Government workers are generally eligible for disability coverage through their federal, state, or municipal employer, and may not have a need for individual DI coverage to supplement it. Federal workers are typically not eligible for private individual DI benefits. State and municipal workers *might* have room to add coverage. If you have an individual in a state or municipal job, the best practice is to obtain a copy of their benefits booklet. The insurance company underwriter can review and make a specific offer as to eligibility for individual DI to supplement their employer coverage. It is important to this worker to add some outside, personally-owned DI coverage, if possible, as termination from employment in the state or municipal employment position means leaving that company DI program behind. With deficits beginning to soar, budget cuts have necessitated wholesale layoffs among government workers. The individual may then be fortunate to find work in the private sector with a business that may not have DI coverage, or has a lesser program, and this individual worker can then build up coverage under one's previously-owned personal DI plan.

Foreign-born: Generally, insurers won't accept an applicant for DI coverage who does not speak or read the English language. Carriers want to be certain of an individual's intent to stay in the United States on a permanent basis. This is important, as the DI policy issued may be either non-cancelable or guaranteed renewable. This typically means that as long as the insured continues to pay premiums on a timely basis once a policy is issued, they are covered without regard to where they are living. If a laid-off 50-year-old decides to chuck it and head to the Bahamas to become a fishing guide, continues to pay disability insurance premiums, and then puts a hook through his hand and can't operate the boat, he is disabled and may be eligible for policy benefits. A more likely scenario is a very recent immigrant to this country who works for a while, sending money home, and then chooses to return to the country of his or her birth. Thus the insurer will be checking how long the individual has been in the country—6-12 months minimum is a likely requirement—what the individual's profession is, and what his intentions are. If the person's situation makes it appear that he or she is here to stay, there is a better chance of acquiring individual DI coverage.

Young professionals: There are certain occupations that have sizable earnings potential. Twenty years ago I worked with an agent who had an in with an anesthesiology practice. Young anesthesiologists who had finished their residencies in this specialty were hired by this firm at $200,000 annually *to start*. Recognizing this, disability insurers would suspend the normal income tables and publish a special chart allowing certain young professionals just starting out or still in school to buy more coverage than would normally be offered. This way they could lock in low rates and their insurability, and the insurer was fairly safe in knowing these individuals would achieve the income for which these benefit levels were intended. Of course, managed care has whittled away the $200,000 starting salary for anesthesiologists, but the principle still applies.

For example, the chart below will give you an idea of who these professionals are who can qualify under special income rules, and how much they can purchase.[10] It also shows you who some of the professionals are that have potentially large incomes to protect, giving you a head start on your prospecting list.

STUDENTS	MAX. MONTHLY BENEFIT
Medical	
Physician, starting or in first 2 years of practice	$4,500
Resident, Fellowship	3,500
Intern	2,500
Medical student—in 3rd or 4th year	2,000
Dental	
Dentist in specialty, starting or in first 2 years	3,000
Other dentist, starting or in first 2 years	2,500
Resident	2,500
Dental student, in 3rd or 4th year	2,000
Accounting	
CPA, starting or in first 2 years of practice	3,000
Student in last year of school	1,000
Architect	
Registered, starting or in first 2 years of practice	2,000
Student—last year	1,000
Computer Science	
Student—last year or first year working in field of degree	1,000
Engineer	
Working in field of degree, starting or in first 2 years	2,000
Student in last year of school	1,000
Legal	
Attorney, starting or in first 2 years in practice	2,000
Student in last year of school	1,000
Optometry	
Optometrist, starting or in first 2 years of practice	2,000
Student in last year of school	1,000
Pharmacist	
Registered, starting or in first 2 years of practice	2,000
Pharmacy student in last year of school	1,000
Podiatrist or Chiropodist	
Starting or in first 2 years of practice	2,000
Veterinary Medicine	
Starting or in first two years of practice	2,000
Student—in 3rd or 4th year	1,000

Disability insurers publish underwriting guides detailing much of the information noted above. There are many considerations as you prepare to begin meeting with prospects. While you won't be able to learn all of the many aspects of financial and occupational underwriting, you should study this material to have a general sense of what you can and can't do in designing an insurance solution to a potential income problem due to a disability. Then, keep the underwriting guide handy when you meet with a prospect to refer to if necessary.

Figure 2.1

Disability Income Fact-Finding Sheet[1]
Personal Individual Disability Coverage

PROPOSED INSURED INFORMATION

Name:_____ Degree_____ DOB___/___/___ Age_____

Male _____ Female _____   Tobacco Use : _____No _____ Yes

Occupation _____ Since_____
Industry_____
    (If MD, specify type. If nurse, specify type and workplace.)

New business? _____Yes _____ No Since _____ Home-based? _____Yes _____ No
% of time spent in office? _____% in field? _____% # of employees? _____ State _____

Duties: Breakdown by percentage and add details to a separate sheet with full description.

Sales/Marketing _____% Travel (Local _____% Abroad _____%) Student _____Y _____N
Administration _____% Supervisor of _____Manual _____ Administration
Manual _____ (If manual, describe with %) _____
Type of business _____Sole Prop_____Part_____LLC_____S Corp_____C Corp

Government employee? _____ Federal (if so, _____FERS or _____SERS)
    _____ State _____ County

Income: (include bonus, if regular, and retirement contributions)
    Note: Minimum income must be $20,000 to obtain DI proposal.

If employee $_____ This year (annualized) $_____ Last Year (from W-2)

If self-employed: $_____ (net income from Sched. C/P&L, last filed tax year)

Net unearned income: $_____(e.g., alimony, investment interest, passive income)

Health: Problems? HBP_____ Diabetes _____ Counseling _____
Overweight? Specify _____ Height and _____ Weight. Other _____.
If yes, provide details: onset age, medication, duration, prognosis, surgery, etc. *A printed cover sheet would help.*

_____
_____
_____

Ever denied coverage? _____Y_____N   Ever had coverage rated? _____Y_____N
Details: (Why? Who?)
_____

Figure 2.1 (cont'd)

DESIRED COVERAGE

Agent's Statement: For prospects with incomes around $20,000-$30,000, please initial below that the client understands DI policy cost will run about 2-4% of income.

Initials: _____

_____Budget (fewer guarantees, options, lower cost)   _____Best (better definitions, more $)

Benefit amount: $_____Specified   or ___Maximum allowed

Specified monthly premium $_____

_____Base only   or   _____Base + Social Security rider (lower premium $)

Elimination period _____days   Benefit period_____

Options: ___Residual   ___COLA ___%   ___FIO $_____
              ___Own Occ   ___Return of Premium

Premium paid by: Corp: ___S ___C   Non-Corp.: ___Sole Prop. ___ Employee
                                                    ___ Employer ___ Other

EXISTING COVERAGE

____None ____Individual: Benefit Amt. $_____ Soc. Sec. Amount $_____
EP_____BP_____)

____Group LTD $_____ Benefit Amt or _____% $_____Cap
____Association $_____ Benefit Amt. EP_____ BP_____

Options? ____Residual ____ COLA (%____) ____ AIR ____ FIO ____ ROP ____ Step-rate

To be replaced? ___Y___N Insurer:_____ Date Issued __/__/__ Mode: _____

If yes, please submit by mail a complete copy of the policy to determine if replacement is realistic. If not, a proposal will be prepared for the remaining amount of coverage for which the client is eligible.

Note: The purchase of disability income coverage involves securing information and specific details that can best determine the type of policy for which the individual is eligible and the cost of this coverage. Be sure to answer all questions on the proposal form. This may also speed up the ultimate underwriting of the application.

Completing this Fact-Finding Form

Important: If your client is earning $30,000 or less, verify that the premium (2-4% of annual income) is affordable. If this range does not seem affordable, secure a specific premium dollar commitment from the client and indicate it on the form under "Desired Coverage."

Proposed Insured Information

Note: Some of this information may already have been taken if a financial analysis has already been completed.

Degree: PhD, Masters, MD, DDS, etc.

Date of birth/Age: Some companies rate on actual age, so give both for best rate.

Occupation: Be as specific as possible about duties. Describe and break down by percentage what manual duties are (if any are performed). This helps place an individual accurately in an occupational classification, an important factor as it affects the rate being charged and the coverage that can be purchased. The term "Business owner" is **not** an occupation, but "electrician" is.

Government employee: Individuals employed by government generally are entitled to some disability benefits through work, so be specific about what retirement system they are under and for how long.

Income: DI insurers require the submission of tax forms to validate income, so this is the best source for this information. Be sure to include bonuses and retirement plan contributions as this can help increase the benefit allowed. W-2 employees can use their W-2s or current pay stub as evidence of income. Self-employed individuals should provide the Schedule C of their tax return. Net unearned income is income from investments, real estate, alimony, or any other type of income that will likely come in regardless of whether the individual is working or not. Remember that expenses can reduce this unearned income figure. For example, rental income may be offset by the expenses associated with owning the real estate from which this income comes.

Health: Good health is a necessity when applying for DI coverage. This section lets you identify potential health problems early. Details will help determine if the individual is an insurable risk before you spend time presenting and writing coverage. Even if they are normally uninsurable, it may still be possible to obtain an offer. If they have ever been denied or had insurance coverage rated, find out the details and how long ago it occurred.

Any form of counseling will require full details as to when commenced, number of visits, current status, any medication, etc.

Desired Coverage

Budget: Check this box if the client has a small amount of discretionary income to spend. Normally, a male will pay 1-3% of income as a cost for coverage, while a female will spend 2-4% of income on her DI coverage. The budget proposal might keep the cost closer to a 1-2% range, but might include fewer options, fewer guarantees, shorter benefit period, etc.

Best: Check this box for better coverage that includes better policy definitions and features, more guarantees, but at a higher cost. Individuals earning more than $30,000 annually are the best candidates here.

Benefit amount: Either specify a monthly amount that the person is seeking or check the box entitled "*Max. allowed*" to secure the highest possible benefit amount the person can qualify for based on earned income. Each DI carrier is somewhat different in terms of the amount of coverage they will write depending on the individual's income, occupation, and other forms of coverage. Generally, it's between 40 and 55% of gross earnings.

Specified monthly premium: Indicate a specific dollar amount that an individual can afford to set aside to pay for coverage, such as $50/month. The proposal will be prepared to offer the most and best coverage within the desired budget guidelines. If this number is closer to 1-2% of income, remember that this proposal might be a budget type plan. This is especially important when the prospect makes less than $30,000 annually, due to the high cost of providing maximum coverage. A specified premium amount gives some flexibility in developing a quote that has a chance to be placed.

Base only or Base + Social Insurance coverage: This determines whether the individual wants all base coverage (plus whatever Social Security pays, if approved) or a *lower* cost approach where a portion of the total monthly coverage is written on a Social Insurance rider, meaning that the rider amount will reduce on a dollar-for-dollar basis if the person collects Social Security benefits as a result of the disability.

Elimination period: The number of days before any benefits are payable. The longer the elimination period selected, the lower the premium cost. Ninety days is today's most economical elimination period, although there are other EPs with some smaller savings as well.

Benefit period: The length of time benefits are payable. The longer benefit periods typically pay to age 65 or 67 and are the highest priced. Shorter benefit periods like 2 or 5 years can save some premium dollars while still providing reasonable coverage.

Options: Disability coverage can be tailored to specific individual needs through the use of optional benefits. The basic disability policy often comes with some type of "own occupation" total disability definition. White collar workers will usually get a full benefit period own occupation policy, while blue collar workers might have an own occupation period of a shorter duration.

 Residual: This option can be added to a base policy that has a total disability definition and pays a portion of the total disability monthly benefit if the insured is back to work at a reduced earnings level. There are also policies that pay only residual benefits and do not use a total disability definition at all, meaning benefits are based strictly on earnings loss following an accident or illness.

 COLA: or, the Cost-of-Living Adjustment rider can increase benefits at claim time by either the CPI or a specified %.

 FIO: or, the Future Income Option benefit offers the ability to increase the monthly benefit in the future *without* having to answer any medical underwriting questions. Current income is all that is needed to justify the increase. For a small extra premium, this is a very worthwhile benefit as you are guaranteeing your client's future insurability—something that is very fragile when the acquisition of disability insurance is involved—in the purchase of more coverage.

ROP: or, the Return of Premium option is a high priced way of getting 80-100% of the money paid for the policy back in later years, usually reduced by any claims paid. It will significantly add to the premium (it is usually about 50% higher and definitely only found when indicating a "Best" coverage), but does answer the question about what happens to the premium paid in if little or no claims result.

Premium paid by?: A C-Corporation can pay for and deduct the premium for an individual disability policy. When the premium for the policy is paid for on behalf of any employee, a higher benefit amount can be issued. The individual is then taxed on the benefits when they are received at claim time. **Note:** all other types of business firms can purchase coverage on behalf of employees and deduct the premium. However, on coverage purchased for the S-Corp. owner, a partner or a sole proprietor, the deductibility of the premium is limited and may not be allowed at all.

Existing coverage: There is a limit on the amount of coverage one can buy. For an employee, it is a percentage of gross income. For the self-employed, it is limited to a percentage of net income before taxes. For this reason, details about existing coverage should be given. Existing coverage may not be a candidate for replacement *especially* if it is a few years old, due to lower premiums and possibly better benefits. There is always the possibility additional coverage can be written to ensure adequate benefits commensurate with income when disabled. If the existing coverage is more recent, review benefits and provisions carefully as there may be a possibility of improvement.

Group LTD covers a percentage of income (for example, 60% up to $5,000 per month cap). Some people are eligible for benefits through their professional association and you should indicate the monthly amount. In all cases, indicate the elimination and benefit periods, any optional benefits, and whether coverage should be replaced. Note: If an individual has group LTD coverage in force, they will only be eligible for Base only coverage and not Base plus Social Security rider as the group LTD coverage already is integrated with Social Security. To secure a proposal, you must specify the percentage of income coverage and the cap, if any.

This form and its explanations should be helpful in both preparing to meet with a client and in acquiring sufficient information to run an accurate proposal for coverage. There are many moving parts in the disability income coverage world, and it is important to complete this type of proposal form in full. It is vital that you properly design the right coverage for each prospect, and this requires comprehension of the cause and effect a disability will have on the individual's ability to earn an income.

This is, to me, what makes disability income insurance fun to work on. Every client is different and has a unique situation, so each disability proposal and design is diverse. While it also presents challenges, keep your eye on the prize: that you will be the one providing income when it will be dearly needed. It's easy to forget that when bogged down in the intricacies of the proposal and the policy definitions.

> "John has a progressive disability due to Multiple Sclerosis. Over the past six years he has worked as much as he has been able. Within the past year he had found this has become much more difficult. He found that it was taking him several hours to get ready to go to work and another hour to get into his office. He changed his lifestyle and work habits to accommodate his progressive disability but he no longer has the energy to get to and from his office and work effectively for any period of time." John's after-tax income is approximately 70 percent replaced by his disability insurance coverage and is enough to maintain his family's expenses.[12]

Every once in a while, it's good to remind yourself of what the positive consequences are in the time spent properly designing a disability income program. In the above example, John was adequately taken care of financially. Almost every disability has psychological implications (not just physical and financial issues) and John is struggling with his steadily downhill physical condition. The strong financial planning work here that included disability income coverage helps significantly (especially for the family) in maintaining as much of the previous lifestyle to retain some level of normalcy and connection to life before the disability occurred. It is because of agents like you that this is possible.

Existing Coverage

One of the juggling acts that is involved in writing disability income coverage is keeping the amount of disability insurance benefits below (or no more than equal to) normal income levels when combining it with all other sources of income that will continue to come in whether the individual is working or not. The presence of other coverage is not bad news; it merely means that adjustments will have to be made in the amount of coverage that can be written.

There are several types of existing coverage that could come up in this portion of your analysis. In general terms, there is private and public coverage.

Private coverage will consist of any in-force individual, group, or association benefits already owned by the insured. Let's review each one separately.

Individual: If a prospect owns individual coverage, obtain a copy of it. Establish the year it was purchased, the monthly benefit amounts, elimination period, benefit period, types of disability coverage—total or residual or both—and any optional features. It is also important to check the policy's renewability. Non-cancelable policies mean the insurer cannot cancel the policy (prior to age 65) and cannot raise the premium rates, a crucial point for the insured. The presence of this provision can mean that it is best to consider adding on more coverage either through the present carrier or by means of an additional policy through another insurer.

Existing coverage more than two years old means the insured has passed the incontestability period of the policy. Any claims filed after two years are more routine than otherwise due to the expiration of this time period when claims are more thoroughly investigated. Policy replacement will establish a new two-year period that may or may not be in the best interests of the individual insured. Often, it is better to compare existing benefit levels with the insured's present income to see if additional coverage is warranted. There may have been a lengthy time that has passed since the initial coverage was written and benefits may be largely inadequate due to a significant rise in the person's income since then. Calculate the difference in what currently exists and what the individual is now eligible for and you may have a nice sale of add-on coverage to bring the potential need to replace income up to date.

Group LTD: Many insurers have a separate income limits table when group coverage is present. That's because, unlike individual insurance, group coverage integrates with a variety of sources, meaning the amount of the monthly benefit should not be taken at face value. Thus, insurers

> **Disability Insurance 2002**[13]
>
> **Individual:** $3.3 billion in-force premiums, 3.3 million covered lives
>
> **Group STD:** $2.5 billion in-force premiums, 14.6 million covered lives
>
> **Group LTD:** $6.9 billion in-force premium and 33.8 million covered lives.

will allow individual coverage to be written in addition to group coverage and generally publish a separate table to provide a guide as to how additional coverage is available. One of the keys to these available amounts is the percentage level at which the group LTD has been designed. Group LTD usually specifies a percentage of covered income along with a maximum benefit amount allowable. For example, group LTD policies may cover 60% of income up to a maximum of $5,000/month. Based on the individual's gross income, there will be a corresponding amount of individual coverage that can be written to supplement the group plan. Agents that come across group LTD coverage in force should not abandon hope of writing any benefits. Even if it amounts to only a small additional sale, the effort is well worth it. Why? Because group disability coverage will not be in the insured's control. If the employer cuts back on benefits and eliminates the DI program, the individual employee may now be out of luck if there are medical conditions that prevent qualification for individual insurance. If the employee is terminated (or decides to leave), the DI coverage stays right where it is—it's not a COBRA benefit. If there is a conversion privilege offered to individual coverage, it is likely to be highly priced, anticipating that the individual exercising this privilege is not healthy enough to qualify for individual coverage otherwise.

But if a small supplemental individual policy is written when group LTD is present, and a future insurability option—where ability to buy more coverage in the future is guaranteed—is added, then the loss of group LTD coverage is not a financial disaster. The individual policy will always go with the person regardless of the change(s) in jobs that happen through the years, and the insurability option means coverage can be increased. As many people do move more often from employer to employer, and from self-employment to employment (and maybe back and forth over the years), the individual plan remains part of the solid financial foundation the individual is building over time.

The presence of group short-term disability (STD) offers other options. If the STD benefit period is 13 or 26 or (less often) 52 weeks, you can design an individual plan that can start after the group policy benefits have completed their run. Elimination periods in individual policies of 90, 180, and 365 days can accomplish this objective. There is no need for a special income limits table, either, since you are only coordinating the start and finish of benefits, not supplementing coverage that will be paying benefits at the same time.

Don't let the presence of group LTD derail the sale. Congratulate the individual on signing up for the DI coverage at work and demonstrate the gaps that still exist that can be easily bridged with individual DI coverage. Employees often relate to COBRA; the knowledge that COBRA does not apply to disability coverage helps to emphasize the importance of owning an individual DI plan that can both ensure complete coverage and provide a base of new coverage should the individual's work situation change.

Association coverage: Many professionals belong to their own associations, local, state and national. Insurance agents specializing in disability insurance may be members of the National Association of Health Underwriters (NAHU), and as a result, their local and state chapters. There are dues to be paid for which the member benefits from a wide number of services and programs exclusive for them. In addition, they have a powerful lobbying force in Washington, D.C., fighting for those issues relevant to the association. The individual voice has become a crescendo of thousands of voices represented by this one association—far more likely to attract the necessary attention on Capitol Hill to air their views.

Other professions from physicians to electrical engineers have associations as well. Many of these associations also offer insurance coverage to their members, as it can often be attained at lower rates due to the volume purchasing potential. Disability insurance can be one of those insurance options and your prospect may well have signed up if they received a members-only flyer offering them coverage.

When association coverage is in force, review the policy specifics. It may well contain better definitions than group coverage, but it will still retain some of its same properties. The coverage could be canceled by the insurer and thus the conversion privilege should be read carefully. If the individual decides to not renew his or her association membership, it may have the same effect as termination of employment has to group LTD, so there are important reasons to supplement the association coverage with an individual DI plan. Check your underwriting guide to see how association coverage affects the amount of coverage the individual can purchase. It could involve sending a copy of the benefit booklet into the underwriting department to determine the benefits available, since association coverage has a far wider range in design than does group LTD.

Private existing disability insurance will affect the amount of DI benefits you can write on an individual. But even if no private existing coverage is in effect, there are still public disability programs that must be acknowledged and understood, as these sources of DI benefits do affect the design of your prospect's individual DI plan.

Public Disability Coverage

"This used to be a government of checks and balances. Now it's all checks and no balances."

– Gracie Allen

You are almost ready for your DI sales interview. You understand the importance of a financial analysis to identify the need for disability income. You have seen the importance of occupation in the securing of a DI plan. You know that income has a direct relationship to the amount of benefits that may be purchased. These benefits that may be bought are reduced by the presence of other sources of income, including other existing disability coverage.

There is public money available for disbursement during a disability, too. Yes, your taxes at work! There are both state and federal programs, and insurers are well aware of these. You should be, too; as it helps you better understand both the income limits table and the Social Security or Social Insurance offset riders offered by DI carriers.

Cash Sickness

Five states (and Puerto Rico) have temporary disability insurance programs that pay a disability benefit for a temporary non-occupational disability. These laws followed the development of the Social Security program enacted in the 1930s during the Depression.

STATE	LEGISLATION PASSED
Rhode Island	1942
California	1946
New Jersey	1948
New York	1949
Hawaii	1969

Source: Lord Bissell Brook

Most privately employed wage earners in these states are eligible for this temporary DI coverage. Prominent exclusions are for self-employed individuals, except in California. To be eligible for coverage, an individual must have a certain level of earnings. Benefits are payable on a weekly basis, with minimum and maximum benefits payable as follows:

CASH SICKNESS BENEFITS[14]

California: Replaces 55% of average weekly wage with benefits a minimum of $50/week and a maximum of $728/week. Pays for up to 52 weeks. Elimination period: 7 consecutive days, waived from the date of confinement in a hospital.

Hawaii: Replaces 58% of average weekly wage, up to a maximum benefit of $418/week ($14 minimum). Pays for up to 26 weeks. Elimination period is 7 consecutive days.

New Jersey: Replaces 66-2/3% of covered employee's average weekly wage, up to a maximum weekly benefit of $459. Pays for up to 26 weeks. Elimination period: 7 consecutive days (on 1st day if disability lasts at least 21 days).

New York: Replaces 50% of the covered worker's average weekly wage up to $170/week (minimum $20). Pays for up to 26 weeks. Elimination period is 7 consecutive days.

Rhode Island: Benefit calculation based upon 4.62% of earnings in the Base quarter, up to a maximum weekly benefit of $543 (minimum $57). In addition, a dependency allowance of $10 per week is payable for each dependent to a maximum of five children. Pays for up to 26 weeks. Elimination period is 7 consecutive days, applied only to the first sickness in a benefit year.

The benefit potential under these plans is significant enough (it is intended to replace at least one-half of the individual's weekly wage) to affect issue limit tables in these states. This helps to avoid writing more disability coverage than income earned, thus providing a disincentive to return to work. These benefit levels and components are subject to alteration and should be periodically reviewed to evaluate for changes.

For example, in California, legislation was enacted in 2002, effective July 1, 2004, expanding the cash sickness program to pay 55% of wages up to $728/week for workers needing to take time off to care for a newborn, newly adopted child, or ill family member.[15] An individual qualifying under this provision would not be eligible for regular private DI benefits.

These are the only states with this specific reimbursement for disabilities.

Workers' Compensation

"If we knew what we were doing, it wouldn't be called research, would it?"

– Albert Einstein

There was a history book published in 2003 entitled *Murdering McKinley*. It analyzes at length the assassination of President William McKinley in 1901 by professed anarchist Leon Czolgosz, and the effect of this death on the Vice President who was sworn into office as a result: Teddy Roosevelt. McKinley stood for capitalism with a capital "C", and was chummy with big business and the millionaires of the day: a stance that drove people like Czolgosz to terrorist acts. Roosevelt understood that there was a wide divide between employer and employee, and that the plight of common labor in the U.S. had to be rectified in the new 20th Century.

For the U.S., the 19th Century had been about changing from an agricultural economy to an industrial one, a painful process that helped to ignite a civil war. But change we did, and the new industries and the machinery that produced goods also made the new workplace a dangerous area to be. Industrial accidents were far too common, and the laws in place at that time forced the injured *employee* to prove employer liability to receive any type of compensation for the injuries (and sometimes death) sustained. Employees couldn't afford attorneys (even then) to fight the far-wealthier employers, and many lost their jobs and much more as a result of their accident. The dice, in essence, were loaded, and the employer was rolling the cubes.

In that first decade of the 20th Century, with President Roosevelt's encouragement, new employer liability laws began to turn this accountability issue towards the employer. Negligence on the part of the employee was no longer assumed, and the safety of the worksite was called into question. There was still the problem of compensation in lost wages and medical bills, and the matter of litigation that needed to be resolved. This finally came about in 1911 with the passage of the country's first Workers' Compensation laws.

The objectives of these laws were simple:

1. to provide medical and income benefits to the employee;

2. to reduce court costs and delays;

3. to relieve public and private charities, who often came to the assistance of a disabled individual and/or a surviving family;

4. to eliminate lawyers' fees and time-consuming trials;

5. to encourage employer interest in safety and rehabilitation; and

6. to promote studies of accident causes to create a safer workplace.

The essence of modern Workers' Compensation laws was that employers had to assume the cost of occupational disability, death, or disease without regard to fault. As a result, this has done away with the issue of negligence. In exchange for this protection, injured workers gave up the right to sue their employers.

Workers' Compensation benefits vary by state, but generally involve the following reimbursements: (1) cash benefits for income loss; (2) medical expense coverage; (3) rehabilitation benefits intended to return the disabled employee to work; and (4) death benefits to a surviving family. Disability income coverage is impacted by (1) and (3), and this is why the total private DI benefit that can be written comes with a high amount of Social Insurance rider that can potentially be reduced by dollars paid under Workers' Compensation laws for an employee's disability. It's all about not <u>over-insuring</u> the client, and creating a situation where one collects more in disability benefits than regular wages.

Workers' Compensation covers injuries or illnesses that are *work-related* only. Disability insurance, of course, is 24/7 coverage for the most part, less any offsets due primarily to payments made under Workers' Compensation, State Cash Sickness, or Social Security. Workers' Compensation covered 127 million workers in 2001 with total wages of $4.6 trillion.[16]

Employers carry Workers' Compensation coverage to insure the risk they now assume when an employee gets hurt on the job. Most states require all employers to carry this insurance, with a few minor exceptions. The cost of these benefits has risen over the years and made it difficult for smaller businesses to afford. Workers' Compensation costs was one of the "hot-button" issues in the 2003 recall election in the state of California, with the more than 130 candidates generally weighing in with an opinion, including the then-future Governor Arnold Schwarzenegger: he believes the costs are too high and aid in driving businesses out of the state.

> Workers' Compensation costs as a percentage of payroll were 2.19% nationwide in March, 2003 compared to 1.96% in March, 2002.
>
> *Source: Bureau of Labor Statistics*

Workers' Compensation laws extend coverage to sole proprietors and partners (in 37 states), agricultural workers in various manners (in 40 states), and domestic workers to some degree (in 25 states).[17] And, despite the efforts to keep the majority of these matters out of the court system, there are still lawsuits that are filed when a worker feels that not enough has been done. A court case in New York concluded that plaintiffs may recover medical costs if they suffer a needle stick in circumstances "that would cause a reasonable person to develop a fear of AIDS."[18] Thus, the need for DI insurers to have some offset in the event of an employee's qualification for lost wage indemnification under these laws is obvious.

Common injuries experienced by workers include back sprains, where data shows return-to-work averages following this type of injury to range from 25 to 130 days, and carpal tunnel syndrome, with recoveries ranging from 35 to 171 days.[19] The nature of disability makes it difficult to measure the length of loss simply by the type of claim. This variance is another reason DI insurers are wary of Workers' Compensation benefits when evaluating coverage amounts to approve for issue.

Employers today face far different issues in the Workers' Compensation arena than was true nearly a century ago. Today, most are dealing with an aging workforce and the increasing presence of chronic health conditions. Orthopedic impairment, intervertebral disk disorders, hearing impairments, and cardiac conditions are all disorders that increase with age. These conditions present a problem for workers' compensation cases because they are often indistinguishable from work injuries. The severity of work-related injuries also increases with age. While a 20-year old spends an average of 3 days in bed for a work injury, a 50-year-old spends 35 days in bed for the same injury.[20]

The future promises to be even more difficult for employers and Workers' Compensation coverage. A 2003 survey by AARP showed that 7 in 10 Americans plan to work past the once-typical retirement age of 65 and nearly half expect to work well into their 70s and even 80s, with a need for money being the primary motivator.[21] This will present challenges for employers and insurers to determine how best to cover the older (and perhaps more vulnerable) worker for disability.

Number of workers covered under Workers' Comp. Programs & total covered wages

Year	Workers (millions)	Total Wages (billions)
1990	105.5	$2,442
1991	103.7	2,553
1992	104.6	2,711
1993	106.5	2,810
1994	109.6	2,955
1995	112.4	3,132
1996	114.8	3,328
1997	118.1	3,591
1998	121.5	3,885
1999	124.3	4,151
2000	127.1	4,495
2001	127.0	4,604

Source: National Academy of Social Insurance, July 2003, (www.nasi.org)

In 2001, 130 million work days were lost due to disabling work injuries, costing $132.1 billion dollars. This exceeds the combined profits of the top 15 Fortune 500 companies in 2001.

Source: National Safety Council

Figure 2.2

Jurisdiction	% of Worker's Wage	Weekly Payment Minimum	Weekly Payment Maximum	Maximum Period Payable
Alabama	66 2/3	$146	$531	Duration of disability
Alaska	80	110	762	Duration of disability
Arizona	66 2/3	-	374	Life or duration of dis.
Arkansas	66 2/3	20	410	Duration of disability
California	66 2/3	126	490	Life
Colorado	66 2/3	-	594	Life
Connecticut	75	168	838	Duration of disability
Delaware	66 2/3	150	450	Duration of disability
D.C.	66 2/3	237	949	Duration of disability
Florida	66 2/3	20	571	Duration of disability
Georgia	66 2/3	38	375	Duration of disability
Hawaii	66 2/3	137	547	Duration of disability
Idaho	67	223	446	52 weeks, then 60% of state's average weekly wage for duration of dis.
Illinois	66 2/3	359	956	Life
Indiana	66 2/3	50	508	500 weeks
Iowa	80	121	1,031	Duration of disability
Kansas	66 2/3	25	401	Duration of disability
Kentucky	66 2/3	106	530	Duration of disability
Louisiana	66 2/3	104	388	Duration of disability
Maine	80	-	459	Duration of disability
Maryland	66 2/3	50	668	Duration of disability
Massachusetts	66 2/3	166	831	Duration of disability
Michigan	80	179	644	Duration of disability
Minnesota	66 2/3	377	750	Until age 67
Mississippi	66 2/3	25	316	450 weeks
Missouri	66 2/3	40	600	Duration of disability
Montana	66 2/3	-	439	Duration of disability
Nebraska	66 2/3	49	508	Duration of disability
Nevada	66 2/3	-	581	Life
New Hampshire	60	185	923	Duration of disability
New Jersey	70	158	591	450 weeks
New Mexico	66 2/3	36	493	Life
New York	66 2/3	40	400	Duration of disability
North Carolina	66 2/3	30	620	Duration of disability
North Dakota	66 2/3	271	497	Duration of disability or until age 65
Ohio	66 2/3	309	618	Life
Oklahoma	70	30	473	Duration of disability
Oregon	66 2/3	50	629	Duration of disability
Pennsylvania	66 2/3	358	644	Duration of disability
Puerto Rico	66 2/3	65	200	Duration of disability
Rhode Island	75	-	653	Duration of disability
South Carolina	66 2/3	75	533	500 weeks
South Dakota	66 2/3	224	448	Duration of disability
Tennessee	66 2/3	84	562	400 weeks

Figure 2.2 (cont'd)

Jurisdiction	% of Worker's Wage	Weekly Payment Minimum	Weekly Payment Maximum	Maximum Period Payable
Texas	75	80	533	Life
Utah	66 2/3	45	450	Life; 312 weeks if rehab. possible
Vermont	66 2/3	263	790	Duration of disability
Virginia	66 2/3	152	606	Duration of disability
Virgin Islands	66 2/3	60	340	Duration of disability
Washington	60-75	43	822	Life
West Virginia	66 2/3	164	491	Life
Wisconsin	66 2/3	30	582	Life
Wyoming	66 2/3	-	505	80 months; extensions possible

How much in benefits can a disabled-on-the-job individual expect to collect? The chart below reflects the minimum and maximum benefits by state.[22] As you can see, the benefit levels can be sizable, thus necessitating the need for an offset rider as part of the private disability insurance plan an individual can acquire.

Workers' compensation benefits can add up to a substantial percentage of take-home pay, and this is why DI insurers will offer offsets, especially at lower income levels. In recent years, there has been some movement toward combining workers' compensation benefits with medical or disability insurance for true 24-hour coverage. For now, some familiarity with your state's specific amounts is all that is necessary to detail this possible source of coverage for your client.

It is also important to emphasize that workers' compensation only covers on the job injuries and illnesses. This will be more relevant for some workers than others, depending on the type of job. Remember the Acme, Inc. VPs? The individual with sales duties would be much less likely to incur an on-the-job disability than would the explosives executive. This doesn't mean that workers' compensation benefits alone are sufficient. The majority of disabilities are off-the-job illnesses, underscoring the critical need for private DI insurance to cover this risk.

Railroad Retirement Act

When I was a kid, I always thought Randolph Scott had built the railroads, or at least the Santa Fe line. It looked like hard work on television: long hours of back-breaking work that always met with some calamity from landslides to robberies to Indian attacks. Only later, after first learning about the Railroad Retirement Act, did I realize what they were working for all this time. When my 7-year-old nephew first asked me what I thought about a career with the railroad, the first word I said to him was "benefits."

Railroad workers have two types of disability benefit potential, and thus are often treated separately when reviewing a DI insurer's income limit tables and guidelines. The first is a cash sickness type short-term benefit, and the other is a remarkable facsimile to the Social Security system.

In the cash sickness program, there is a 7-day elimination period (similar to the 5 state programs reviewed earlier in this section) and benefits payable up to 26 weeks. There is the possibility of extended benefits if the disabled railroad employee has 10 years or more of service. Benefit levels max out at $1,421/month (in 2002).

The Railroad Retirement Act also provides retirement, disability, and survivors' benefits under rules approximately the same as for Social Security. There are two types of disability benefits under the Railroad Retirement Act: occupational and total disability. Both require a 5-month waiting period before the benefits will begin.

Occupational disability benefits are available at age 60 if the worker has at least 10 years of railroad service, or at any age with at least 20 years of service. An occupational disability is one that prevents the railroad worker from performing one's job with the railroad. It does not necessarily prevent that person from working at some other kind of job. This is a more liberal definition than that of the Social Security system.

If unable to meet that definition, total disability benefits are available at any age if the worker has become permanently disabled and has at least 10 years of railroad service. Total disability means that the railroad worker must be unable to perform any kind of substantial gainful employment.[23]

If the railroad employee has worked enough years in jobs covered by Social Security to qualify for Social Security disability benefits, that person may apply for both Railroad and Social Security disability benefits. This is one of the many reasons railroad workers can generally purchase only a smaller supplemental personal DI policy, due to the existing coverage they hold.

Social Security

"Research: the process of going up alleys to see if they are blind."

— **Barstow Bates**

The Social Security system may have been established in 1935, but the disability income portion of this legislation was not added until 1956. At the time, a number of insurance agents thought it would severely jeopardize the sale of private disability income insurance. In actuality, the opposite proved to be true.

The more enterprising agents, who viewed a major social change like the addition of a Social Security disability benefit as an opportunity rather than an impassable obstacle, took the offensive. They made calls to everyone they could think of, offering to go out and explain the new Social Security disability benefit at no charge. In the process of educating the consumer, it was a chance to demonstrate the need for some income at disability. Surely, they explained, the government wouldn't waste their time developing this program if there wasn't a legitimate need for the coverage. And, once this point was clarified and agreed upon, the actual amount of income benefits Social Security could pay didn't amount to as much as the person would actual need in reality. Magically, disability insurance sales rose to *supplement* Social Security's effort in this regard.

Over time, it became clear that not only was the Social Security disability benefit inadequate, you couldn't count on receiving the benefit at all. To be eligible for Social Security disability benefits, an individual had to meet the following definition:

> "Disability is defined as the inability to engage in any substantial gainful activity by reason of any medically determinable physical or mental impairment that can be expected to result in death or that has lasted or can be expected to last for a continuous period of not less than 12 months.
>
> "A person must be not only unable to do his previous work or work commensurate with the previous work in amount of earnings and utilization of capacities but cannot, considering age, education and work experience, engage in any other kind of substantial work that exists in the national economy.
>
> "It is immaterial whether such work exists in the immediate area, or whether a specific job vacancy exists, or whether the worker would be hired if he applied for work."

Whew! If a private disability insurance policy had that kind of lengthy language in it for its definition of disability, chances are you wouldn't buy it. Despite this onerous description, people do qualify for Social Security disability benefits. Some 7.4 million disabled workers and their families accounted for about 17% of all Social Security beneficiaries in 1999, according to the General Accounting Office, Congress' investigative arm.[24]

In addition to meeting the stringent disability definition outlined above, the individual must be Social Security-eligible; that is, they must have a sufficient number of *credits* to qualify for disability benefit consideration. You earn credits under Social Security based on wages earned in a calendar quarter (three month period). Wages are adjusted each year for inflation, and in 2005, the earnings requirement in a calendar quarter is $920. Therefore, if you earn $3,680 or more, you will be awarded with the full four possible credits for 2005.

To be considered "disability-insured" and eligible for Social Security disability benefits, the following table details the number of credits you must have earned, based on your year of birth, according to the Social Security Administration.

Once it is determined that you are "disability-insured" for purposes of eligibility, and that you have met the definition of disability, it is a five month waiting period from date of disability before benefits will begin to be paid. In reality, it is often well past the five month point before you even hear back from the Social Security Administration as to qualification for benefits. Disability benefits will be paid retroactively for up to 12 months from the end of the waiting period, so it's not a question of losing benefits as much as it is trying to pay bills while the Social Security reviewers are making up their mind about your claim. A disability insurer's Social Insurance Offset Rider will be paying benefits during this determination process since no money is coming in (providing the individual meets the insurer's less strict definition of disability). Even if Social Security benefits are eventually paid retroactively, the insurer will not require a return of benefits paid during this time of waiting. (See Part Three for more on the Social Insurance Offset Rider.)

Age	Credits Required to Qualify for Disability Benefits
Under 24	6 credits earned in last 3 years
24 to 31	2 credits for each year above age 21
31 to 42	20 earned in the last 10 years
44	22, with 20 earned in the last 10 years
46	24, with 20 earned in the last 10 years
48	26, with 20 earned in the last 10 years
50	28, with 20 earned in the last 10 years
52	30, with 20 earned in the last 10 years
54	32, with 20 earned in the last 10 years
56	34, with 20 earned in the last 10 years
58	36, with 20 earned in the last 10 years
60	38, with 20 earned in the last 10 years
62 or older	40, with 20 earned in the last 10 years

There is also an offset with any benefits paid out under Workers' Compensation laws, so Social Security will coordinate with this state benefit program, too. The total of all disability benefits received under federal, state, or local law may not exceed 80% of the most recent earnings prior to the disability that prompted the claim. Like disability insurers, the Social Security Administration is also cautious about over-insurance with a disability claim.

How much would be paid under Social Security's disability benefit program? Individuals are eligible for a Primary Insurance Amount (PIA) just as is true with the Social Security Retirement plan. In addition, if eligible family members are present, the PIA would be increased up to a Maximum Family Benefit (MFB) amount. While the Social Security Administration now mails an annual statement to those paying into the Social Security system, you can calculate your benefits online, using the "Benefit Calculators" shown on the Social Security website (www.ssa.gov). The calculator is currently found at www.ssa.gov/planners/calculators.htm.[25] This is an easy way to measure the potential amount of Social Security benefits that could be payable.

In addition, each year The National Underwriter Co. publishes the *Social Security Manual*, an excellent reference source. In this publication, there are easy reference tables to refer to that can be used to approximate Social Security disability benefits.[26]

Monthly Benefits at Disability

Your Age in 2005	Who Receives Benefits	$20,000 and up	$35,000	$50,000	$65,000	$90,000
			Your Present Annual Earnings			
61	Individual PIA	$ 691	$1,099	$1,371	$1,598	$1,988
	MFB	1,036	1,648	2,056	2,397	2,982
60	Individual PIA	691	1,099	1,371	1,602	2,014
	MFB	1,036	1,648	2,056	2,403	3,021
55	Individual PIA	699	1,107	1,379	1,609	2,063
	MFB	1,048	1,660	2,068	2,413	3,094
50	Individual PIA	699	1,115	1,395	1,617	2,086
	MFB	1,048	1,672	2,092	2,425	3,129
40	Individual PIA	723	1,163	1,459	1,658	2,119
	MFB	1,084	1,744	2,188	2,487	3,178
30	Individual PIA	747	1,227	1,539	1,707	2,131
	MFB	1,120	1,840	2,308	2,560	3,196

While the qualifications may not be easy, the benefits are high enough to be taken into consideration when writing individual disability insurance. Depending on income and presence of family members, benefits close in on $3,000/month and disability insurers must hedge their bet with offset riders that will reduce their own payouts. The higher the annual earnings, the less significance Social Security benefits have in the overall benefit picture.

As noted, qualifying under the Social Security definition is the largest hurdle to climb. In 2002, the U.S. Supreme Court upheld the authority of the Social Security Administration and granted considerable deference to the SSA's "expertise and administrative experience." The case was *Barnhart, Commissioner of Social Security v. Walton* and it involved a claimant who was diagnosed with schizophrenia and associated depression in March 1995. He had stopped working as a teacher on October 31, 1994 and resumed full-time work again at a local grocery store on December 10, 1995. An administrative law judge ruled him disabled by Social Security standards and entitled to benefits between the dates (after the waiting period) that the individual had ceased to work. The SSA appealed the decision, asserting that the claimant had gone back to work less than 12 months from the date of *diagnosis* (March 1995) and therefore did not meet the Social Security definition of disability. The case finally ended up with the U.S. Supreme Court, who agreed to hear it and ultimately ruled in favor of the SSA.[27]

Social Security Claims Approval Rates

Calendar Year	No. of Applications (thousands)	No. of Awards	% Awards Approval
1992	1,335.1	636.6	47.7%
1993	1,425.8	635.2	44.6%
1994	1,443.8	631.9	43.8%
1995	1,338.1	645.6	48.3%
1996	1,279.2	624.3	48.8%
1997	1,180.2	587.7	49.8%
1998	1,169.3	608.4	52.0%
1999	1,200.1	620.6	51.7%
2000	1,330.6	621.3	46.7%
2001	1,498.6	690.5	46.1%
2002	1,682.5	750.0	44.6%
2003	1,895.5	777.5	41.0%

Note: Calendar Year in thousands.

Source: *Social Security Administration, 2004 (www.ssa.gov)*

You might notice from the above awards figures that the percentage approvals are relatively consistent from year to year. However, notice the difference in number of new applications when the economy is sluggish. The early 1990s and the beginning of the 21st Century were both recession-like periods, and the number of applications increase accordingly. Tough economic times keep DI insurers up nights worrying as well.

Social Security does not lose many fights in these determinations. Back in the 1980s, the Reagan Administration ordered the SSA to review current Social Security disability claims to ensure the disabled individuals were, in fact, still meeting the definition. SSA did, and stopped paying benefits to several hundred cases where they felt the person was no longer disabled under Social Security's rules. This resulted in a class action lawsuit ultimately lost by the SSA that cost Social Security (and the taxpayers) much more than if they had not done the reviews at all. But this is a rarity. More often, the SSA is able to send the letter below to a claimant and make it stick. In this case, a urological surgeon who suffered a stroke and some paralysis as a result, received the following after filing a claim with Social Security.

Social Security Notice
From: Department of Health and Human Services
      Social Security Administration

Explanation of Determination

Name of Claimant: _____ SSN_____

The following reports were used to decide your claim.

        _____, MD—report of 5-23-85 and report of treatment of 6-84
        _____, MD - report of treatment from 6-84 to 4-85
        _____, MD - report of treatment from 1-83 to 4-85
        _____, Medical Center—report of hospitalization of 6-84

We have determined that your condition is not severe enough to keep you from working. We considered the medical and other information, your age, education, training, and work experience in determining how your condition affects your ability to work.

You said you are unable to work because of a stroke, decreasing motor function and coordination of the left upper extremity. The medical evidence shows that because of a stroke you have decreased strength in the left arm, decreased ability to pinch and grip and to make normal movements with the right hand. Your sense of feeling is normal.

We realize that your condition keeps you from doing your past work as a urological surgeon, but it does not keep you from doing other work requiring less dexterity of the hands. Based on your age, education and past work experience, you can do other work.

If your condition gets worse and keeps you from working, write, call or visit any Social Security office about filing another application.

Of course, perhaps the SSA didn't realize this claimant could not hold a pencil to write, a phone to call, or a steering wheel to drive and visit them about filing another application. At least they understood this doctor was not going to be able to operate on his patients any longer.

A letter like this can be so disheartening to a disabled individual and family. Financial difficulties coupled with the physical aspect of the medical condition can devastate even the strongest of families. In this particular case, the surgeon had individual disability coverage that paid benefits and helped this family maintain their standard of living in a difficult time.

Exploring other benefits like Social Security with a prospect or client often makes it easier to see the true value of private disability insurance, individually owned and less restrictive than the government programs that also are a potential source of coverage. The SSA has been given authority to administer claims as they believe their definition applies, and they rarely lose after declining a claim.

Sure, there's an appeals process, but the SSA's expansive and complex claims system that varies widely across the country makes it difficult for an individual to crack alone. The Social Security Administration itself reports that 40% of the consumers who bring claims on their own simply drop out of the system.[28] If there is a legitimate need to fight, the claimant's best strategy is to retain an attorney that specializes in Social Security claims. There's even an association of them: the National Organization of Social Security Claimants' Representatives (www.nosscr.org).

Each year, the Social Security trustees estimate the solvency expectancy of the Social Security funds. In 2003, the estimate was put at 2042, if no changes or reforms are made prior to that time.[29] That's down a year (2043) from the 2002 projection, when the trustees also forecast insolvency in the disability portion of the Social Security funds in the year 2028. This is obviously not expected to improve much with the anticipated retirement of the Boomers beginning in 2010, combined with a decline in the number of workers. The trustees routinely suggest as an offset to this to help the funds remain solvent, either a permanent 13% reduction in benefits or a 15% increase in payroll taxes.[30] Neither suggestion has been heartily endorsed by anyone.

The difficulty in qualification for Social Security benefits should not be construed as meaning that disability rarely occurs. It is still vital to reach the working age population and ensure that there are sufficient income sources in the event of a long-term disability. A recent study by the Social Security Administration showed an increase in the number of Boomers collecting Social Security disability insurance benefits. The 40-44 age group showed a 4.4% increase in number of claimants between 2000 and 2002, while the 45-49 and 50-54 age groupings increased claimants over the same period by 10.3% and 9.3% respectively.[31]

It is important to recognize and discuss with your client the existence of a potential source of benefits from Social Security. But as a solution or fallback position in place of considering private disability insurance coverage, this government program typically comes up short of need.

Public Program Summary

Consumers may be eligible for certain public disability benefit programs. The following is a summary of the most common of these available programs:

STATE-SPECIFIC DISABILITY PROGRAMS

Who: 5 states, plus Puerto Rico
What: % of average weekly earnings insured
Length: 26-52 weeks, depending on state (short-term)
Affects: issue limits on a short-term basis in those states

California: 55% of earnings up to $728/wk., 7 day EP, 52 weeks BP
Hawaii: 58% of earnings up to $418/wk., 7 day EP, 26 weeks BP
New Jersey: 66 2/3% of earnings up to $459/wk., 7 day EP, 26 weeks BP
New York: 50% up to $170/wk., 7 day EP, 26 weeks BP
Rhode Island, % of earnings up to $543/wk., 7 day EP, 30 weeks BP

Workers' Compensation

Who: Employees (state specific rules exclude some firms and occupations)
What: % of statewide average weekly wage
Length: Depends on classification of disability
Affects: Issue limits, may be insured with offset rider if insured receives benefits

Disability Classifications under Workers' Compensation:

Temporary Partial: Return to work before reaching maximum medical improvement with reduced responsibilities and a lower salary

Temporary Total: Benefits are paid when the workers' lost time exceeds the three-to-seven day waiting period

Permanent Partial: Benefits paid to workers with residual consequences of their injuries or disease that continue after reaching maximum medical improvement

Permanent Total: Benefits may be paid if a worker continues to have significant disability difficulties even after reaching maximum medical improvement

Railroad Retirement

Who: Railroad employees
What: % of earnings up to $1,421/month
Length: 26 weeks, after 7 day elimination period
Affects: Issue limits (short-term)

Disability Classifications under Railroad Retirement Act:

Occupational Disability: Eligible after 20 years of service (or 10 years and is at least age 60). Unable to perform regular work even if could work at another occupation as a result of disability.

Total Disability: Eligible after 10 years of service. Unable to perform any substantial gainful work as a result of disability.

Social Security

Who: Individuals considered "disability insured" with Social Security Administration
What: % of earnings
Length: To age 65, after 5 month EP
Affects: Issue limits, may be insured with offset rider if insured receives benefits

Average Monthly Benefit (2003): $861.70

Definition of Disability: Inability to engage in any substantial gainful activity due to mental or physical impairment that is expected to last at least 12 months or result in death.

Average age of disabled beneficiary: 51 (in 2003)

A Programming Example

"Gentlemen, it is better to have died a small boy than to fumble the football."

– John Heisman

As one can see, existing coverage whether it is private or public will affect the amount of disability insurance coverage for which your prospect is eligible. Again, it's all about over-insurance and a consumer seeing a *rise* in income after disability, providing little financial incentive to return to work.

Insurers want to help disabled people; they do not want to enable them so that they are in no hurry to make a normal recovery. Rates for policies are based on expected physical recuperation according to the type of injury or illness of the disabled individual. A bonanza of money coming in as a result may throw those numbers off considerably.

Some insurance agents tend to shy away from clients who possess existing forms of disability coverage. This does a potential disservice to the prospect for often the coverage is inadequate when compared with the amount of money the person is earning. Take the time to sift through the benefit booklets and policies and note the coverage in place. This is a decent service to provide anyway as it is unlikely the individual has done this already. But if you are about assisting an individual in understanding their financial plan, this is a must to do anyway.

Let's look at an example of analyzing existing coverage to see if there is any room for writing additional benefits to adequately insure the person.

Beyonce, age 40, earns $60,000 annually and is married with one child. In your financial fact gathering, you note the following key expenses that Beyonce and her family consider necessary:

Housing (mortgage, taxes, insurance)	$750
Utilities (oil, gas, electric, water, cable)	175
Food	700
Clothing	200
Transportation (car payments, insurance)	650
Health Insurance	350
Medical	100
Computer DSL line	50
Entertainment/Miscellaneous	150
TOTAL	$3,125

$3,125 is the amount of coverage Beyonce would like to have. Her husband earns $24,000 annually and they are putting that into retirement and educational funds. She wants to continue that even if she should become disabled.

Beyonce has some protection right now in the event of disability. She has

(a) short-term group DI up to $500/week for 13 weeks,

(b) individual DI policy of $1,000/month beginning on 91st day and paying to age 65, and

(c) eligibility for Social Security disability benefits: her estimated current Maximum Family Benefit DI amount is $2,400.

```
$3,125 ─────────────────────────────────────── $3,125
           expenses that must be covered
                                              GAP ($2,125)
$2,167 ──────────────────
         short-term DI

$1,000                    ──────────────────── $1,000
                          individual DI policy

$-0-                                                $-0-
       ┌─────────────────────────────────────────────┐
              Days                    Years
        0    30    60    90    1    2    5    Age 65
```

Not considering Social Security coverage—that is not guaranteed—there is a $2,125 gap to be filled between the 91st day and age 65. When you add in the full amount of Social Security benefits—should she qualify—she would seem to have this need satisfied.

Of course, the primary issue is taking a chance on meeting the serious disability definition under Social Security. This can be handled by proposing personal DI coverage with a base coverage amount and the balance in a Social Security offset rider. Also, remember that Beyonce will not always be eligible for the Maximum Family Benefit. Her 11-year-old daughter gives her seven years before benefits would be reduced to the Primary Insurance amount of $1,600/month.

Under private disability insurance, she would be eligible for a total of $3,300 based on her earnings. That is close to the $3,125 she needs and writing the full amount may make sense in the event other expenses arise that have not been planned for yet. Of this $3,300, $1,800 of it can be written as an offset rider.

Beyonce has $1,000 of private DI coverage now, reducing her need to $2,300. If she elects a $500/month guaranteed base benefit and a $1,800 social security offset rider, this will give her a total of $1,500 guaranteed and $1,800 based on whether she qualifies for Social Security. If she ultimately ends up receiving only $1,600 from Social Security (providing she qualifies), the offset rider can make up the $200 difference (if it is a dollar-for-dollar offset rider).

This effectively eliminates the $2,125 gap in coverage, and should give her family sufficient funds to meet basic living expenses (with a little extra at this point) while continuing to put the husband's income into the retirement and educational vehicles as desired. Beyonce earns $5,000/month that even after taxes is more than she would bring in from her DI coverage. Thus, the narrow tightrope between having enough DI benefits to make ends meet and not enough to provide disincentives to return to work has been neatly walked.

Insurers may not always be able to match the gaps exactly, but this gives you a general idea about programming around existing coverage. Do not walk away if other coverage exists! Obtain a copy of the benefit booklet or policy schedule page and review it. Since the insured has likely not studied it very closely, this will be a nice service to perform by identifying and mapping out the coverage that does exist compared to what is practically needed to survive a disability financially.

As noted earlier, each individual and family situation is different. That's what makes the business of insuring a disability interesting. Done properly, your client will have adequate protection and will also understand the meaning of all the numbers. This can help to provide some of the proverbial "peace of mind" we often refer to when stressing the need for DI.

MAKING A SALES PRESENTATION

"I believe in looking reality straight in the eye, and denying it."

– Garrison Keillor

Enough homework.

It's time to persuade someone to look at their future differently—when an injury or illness could destroy the "taken for granted" routine of a steady cash flow.[32] Believe me, this will not be easy to do. What is easy is to ignore the possibility of this type of health disaster happening to you.

"Before Deborah Krotenberg suffered a devastating car accident, she paid little attention to how she would cover costs in case of a catastrophe. 'I knew I had long-term disability insurance, but who ever thinks of it?'"[33]

Actually, very few, Deborah. The idea of a disability is as tangible to most people as scaling Mount Everest. It doesn't help when a financial advisor tells a couple—as happened to me earlier this year—that they don't need disability insurance. That's exactly what people want to hear: they already have too much insurance as it is, and this curt dismissal of yet another type of coverage is music to their overinsured ears.

Trying to get people to focus solely on a possible future disability is quite likely the wrong approach to solving the need to keep income rolling in—no matter what. Heaping statistic upon statistic further clouds the key issue for families—they are overloaded with numbers and polls on a daily basis. And what do all these numbers mean? A stand-up comedian once said that a survey found that 10% of Americans thought Joan of Arc was Noah's wife. Enough with the numbers.

The key to approaching this need successfully with clients today is to focus on the type of environment we live in every day: uncertainty. A fluctuating stock market, rising gas prices, a war with Iraq with the potential for more conflict, a job market where it takes months to find a new position, mergers, acquisitions, the potential bankruptcy of Medicare, Medicaid, and Social Security, and even the news that the 51-year-old marathon runner who created the Power Bar nutritional supplement had dropped dead of a heart attack all point to the insecure foundation we all walk on every day. The world is made of shifting sands and there are no substantial safety nets any more.

There are no guarantees.

It is this vagueness about what the future could bring that your sales presentation may use as a starting point. Today's winners are tomorrow's "where are they now?" poster children. Physical disability may be hard to see, but the threat of *financial* disability may linger long in everyone's mind.

> "Larry Prier is as smart as they come. After graduating from MIT, he quickly rose through the corporate ranks, securing a position that took him and his wife, Francie, around the world. When Larry returned to his company's headquarters in Indiana, he and Francie had two young children and knew it was time to review their finances." They met with an insurance agent who recommended, among other coverage, disability insurance. Before he made a decision on solving this income need for his family, Larry went to work for his former boss at Union Pacific Railroad in Omaha, Nebraska. The insurance agent did not give up. She flew to Omaha, helped Larry review the coverage available through Union Pacific and convinced him to take advantage of his new company's disability income plan that would replace 70% of his total compensation if he was unable to perform his job due to illness or injury. "Less than a year later, Larry, 39, noticed a deterioration in his penmanship. It was the first symptom of Multi-Systems Atrophy, a form of Parkinson's disease. Larry could still work, but over time he became unsteady, couldn't project his voice, and had trouble swallowing." At 46, Larry went on long-term disability. Disability benefits provided much-needed income and paid for private nurses while Francie worked. Larry's disability benefits remain the primary source of income for his family.[34]

Above all, you should remember as you present this coverage to people that stories like the one detailed above happen all the time. Unfortunately, not all who are disabled have insurance to cover this contingency. Families like the Priers appreciate its benefits and that they were able to maintain their standard of living despite Larry's unforeseen ill health. Not every disability story has this ending though, yet every disability insurance product you properly install within a client's financial portfolio has the potential to enhance a world that will be significantly altered by an injury or illness. You have the power to write a happier ending to a script.

Disability Income Sales Principles

> *"My problem lies in reconciling my gross habits with my net income."*
>
> – Errol Flynn

There are several educational precepts that should be stressed in a disability sales interview. For purposes of this discussion, let's assume that the individual prospect carries no disability coverage at all.

Your greatest asset is your ability to earn an income. If J.R.R. Tolkien had written about disability insurance instead of a golden ring, he would have called income "the precious." Most of what we do in life is predicated on the money we make. Very few people head off to Walden Pond. Instead they go to work, earn an income, and buy goods for themselves and their families. *And they often take for granted that this will continue uninterrupted by any health catastrophe.*

Your starting point is not just asking an individual what his or her most valuable asset is—but to envision a world without that income. In short, what would happen to one's own situation if income ceased? Some financial advisors today claim Boomers are interested in hearing concrete discussions analyzing what would happen to their own personal finances if they became disabled.[35]

What would happen if income stopped? This is the scenario you should ask your prospects to describe. Listen to what they have to say. Their answers will form the basis for your future close of this sale. It's a fair question. In my experience, people will give you varying responses to this, but rarely have a bona fide source of funds they can draw upon if they suddenly failed to bring the dollars in the door anymore.

It is often helpful to illustrate why income is such a valuable asset. The sheer dollar potential of earnings is, depending on one's age, overwhelming to most people. Millionaires are people you see on TV, yet most people will bring in at least that amount during the course of their working career—as long as nothing changes. The illustration below depicts the total potential earnings to age 65 of individuals at varying ages and incomes, assuming a 5% raise in salary each year:[36]

Age	$25,000	$50,000	$75,000	$100,000
30	$2,258,000	$4,516,000	$6,774,000	$9,032,000
35	1,661,000	3,322,000	4,983,000	6,644,000
40	1,193,000	2,386,000	3,580,000	4,773,000
45	827,000	1,653,000	2,480,000	3,307,000
50	539,000	1,079,000	1,618,000	2,158,000

Based on potential earnings from the age stated up to age 65, assuming 5% salary increases each year.

As you can see, the potential earnings power at stake is sizable and the risk of losing that is the difference between maintaining cash flow and standard of living and being unable to do so, potentially altering many more lives than just that of the disabled individual.

Loss of income is one thing, but perhaps Boomers and Xers can relate better to a loss of retirement dollars. Most know that a successful retirement future will likely be based on the value of one's portfolio by the time one is ready to stop working full-time. The illustration above shows the potential earnings one risks by being vulnerable to an accident or sickness. But you could run a smaller illustration showing the loss of portfolio value based on a specific annual contribution—perhaps $2,000/year with varying rates of return. The younger one is, the greater the potential loss of money that was earmarked to fund a retirement.

That hits some of today's financially savvy investors where it hurts. You can read up on all the investing strategies in the world, but there is little help for the portfolio during a time of disability and lost earnings.

Income makes all possible. It is income that breathes life into otherwise lifeless assets. No income, no home. No income, no retirement fund. Income is the foundation for everyone's total financial plan.[37] A mistake here has a severe rippling effect on the rest of the personal fiscal program.

Disability can be permanent unemployment. In the days of bear markets, the risk of losing one's job is paramount in the minds of many. Perhaps your prospect can relate better to someone who is out of work than a person who has become disabled. Maybe the experience has happened to them. Out of work means a stoppage of cash flow. How well-prepared is the prospect for this contingency? How much money is stashed away for that proverbial rainy day?

The answer to this question is the same as if a disability had occurred. Both events—unemployment and disability—mean a drastic change in income circumstances—with one significant difference. The unemployed person is probably still healthy and can physically look for work and take it if offered. What about the disabled individual? Can he or she look for work as easily? Would a job offer be forthcoming given the physical limitations of the person?

This is an extension of that what-if scenario that you should talk through with your prospect. It's the prospect's future you are discussing, not yours. See if they've thought through the potential loss of income situation and, if not, you can help them prepare for that possible uncertain future.

Disability can and does occur at any age. It's no secret that people are working longer today. The increasing life spans being experienced in this country have led to the necessity of working longer, to avoid possibly running out of money during a lengthy retirement period. Older Americans—those age 55 and older—make up 12% of the workforce today, and are *five* times more likely to be absent from the workplace due to a short- or long-term disability than their younger counterpart.[38] Agents often make the mistake today of concentrating on long-term care for the 55-year-old rather than both disability income and long-term care needs.

These needs are entirely separate: disability requires an indemnification of a percentage of income to help pay personal bills and maintain a reasonable standard of living, while long-term care reimburses actual expenses incurred for treatment, much like health insurance paying doctor and hospital bills. The graying workforce is here, and odds are that 55-year-olds do not own any DI protection even as they are reviewing long-term care insurance proposals. Chances are your prospects will be more interested in a policy whose money is being sent directly to them rather than to a medical provider.

Lest those younger prospects think it's too soon to be thinking about a possible future disability, there is news that occurrences of disability have actually *risen* in recent years for those ages 30-49. This growth in disability has occurred within all demographic and economic groups rather than within isolated segments of the population. The source of this alarming new trend is not necessarily clear although there is an increasing presence of obesity and diabetes among this younger age group.[39]

As already noted in this text, the chances of disability occurring at any age are greater that year than the odds of dying. The above information shows that to be true, and prospects of every age should be discussing what their plans are should their income drop or discontinue.

Greed is good. When you talk about life insurance with your prospects, they may be amenable to the conversation, but for some, a certain inner voice may be telling them, "if you don't buy enough life insurance, you won't be around to know it." The same cannot be said for a disability. As we're fond of saying, a family of four that suffers the death of an income earner has a family of three left with income needs. A family of four where one of the breadwinners is disabled is still a family of four with income needs going forward.

Simply put, if your prospects make a mistake about disability insurance coverage, it will directly affect them, too. Is the risk worth it to them to ignore the possibility? A gentle reminder that being around for the consequences is one of the many downsides of improper planning for a disability can help close some cases.

Sure, disability may never happen. But is there any reason to roll the dice with your (and your family's) financial future at stake? Which mistake is better? The one where you spent $200/month for a DI policy you never used, or the one where you gave up $60,000 in policy benefits annually and then became disabled? What would the prospect's family say?

Proper financial preparation can ease the physical recovery. Being disabled is not just a physical setback: it can be a difficult mental adjustment as well. One day, you are moving through your daily routine, and the next day it's all changed. You can no longer do the formerly simple tasks you once did. Every movement becomes a challenge. Getting out of bed, getting dressed, even eating may be problematic, never mind the types of physical rehabilitation that may be required to improve one's health.

Disability comes with not only a loss of one's health, but of one's self-respect. It's a treacherous mental journey one must take during recovery—if, indeed, recovery is possible—as the peace-of-mind associated with the routines of work and family are completely disrupted.

So, what happens when there are financial pressures in addition to the physical trauma? The worry about how the bills will get paid or how the kids' college education will now be funded will add an extra mental burden on someone already straining to cope with a new reality. This lack of financial preparedness can wreak havoc on the physical recovery. Only the best mental framework will create the opportunity for the optimum bodily recuperation. A disabled individual beset with money woes is not in a proper intellectual state for a quick return to normalcy. A disability policy with its source of funds can actually help the rehabilitation by relieving the individual of a significant concern: the loss of income.

Disability income is one part of an overall financial plan.

○ Auto	Car Insurance
○ Home	Mortgage Insurance
○ Family	Life and Health Insurance
○ Wealth	Life Insurance
○ Salary/Income	
○ Retirement Portfolio	LTC Insurance

As you can see, the various assets listed on the left have a corresponding insurance element connected to each on the left. Automobiles and the home are always taken care of, as these are mandated coverages. Life insurance solves income and estate needs for the family in the event of death. The retirement portfolio is generally the domain of long-term care insurance.

But income protection is often overlooked by a majority of people. Listing assets in this way at least exposes the salary/income asset as being unaddressed by the overall financial plan.

I can't sell you a policy today. This is always a reassuring factor to your prospects. You are free to discuss the future what-if scenarios without the burden of an insurance purchase that day. Why? The prospect would have to go through the underwriting process to be accepted for disability coverage. No matter how much of a sense of urgency you create in the individual, it is the insurance carrier's underwriters who will likely have the final say.

This has the effect of putting the possible client at ease and focusing on understanding the planning that is being discussed. You can't leave a policy with the person today, but you can make an offer to an insurance company via an application with a deposit in the event insurability is not an issue and the coverage can go into effect immediately.[40] A lot of cases are closed because of this natural ease of pressure.

Express the premium cost as a percentage of gross income. Disability insurance can often give people "sticker shock" even as they understand the importance of protecting their income. A $2,500 annual premium may sound out-of-reach to some, even as it provides several hundred thousand dollars of protection. There are two ways of expressing the premium as it should be seen.

First, quote the premium as a percentage of gross income. A $2,500 premium may be helping to replace $80,000 of income, a 3% investment. Spending 3% of your income to provide 50-60% of gross income at some future date is sound monetary practice.

Second, be sure the coverage is illustrated as the total potential dollars available as benefit. For example, a $5,000/month disability benefit bought at age 35 and potentially payable to age 65 is 30 possible years of $60,000, or $1,800,000. A $2,500 premium seems reasonable to buy that much potential coverage.

> A financial planner has a client that spends everything he makes and then some, about $13,000/month. He has disability coverage from his company, but the limit is $5,000/month and it is taxable because the company pays his premium. If he nets $3,000/month from his disability policy, he'd have a gap of $10,000, so he needs all the disability insurance he can get. The planner helped the client look for coverage, and the best quote cost $3,500 a year. He balked, deeming the extra coverage too expensive. The planner was frustrated, noting that the client spends over $150,000 annually but would not spend $3,500 a year to protect that lifestyle. He made the client sign off on his decision not to take the coverage. If he is disabled for six months, the planner noted, he'll lose his house.[41]

Some risks are not worth taking, but be sure your prospect has the proper perspective on the cost of disability income coverage. As you will see, there are a lot of opportunities to design the coverage to make it as affordable as it can be without sacrificing too much in coverage.

At the other end of the spectrum, there are high income, high net worth prospects who might not object to the premium of a policy with substantial benefits, but may question the need for the coverage at all. Once again, that will depend on the client's circumstances. "A married, 52-year-old neurologist in Manhattan with an ex-wife who collects alimony, a new wife with an irregular income, two older children attending private colleges, one young child who loves horseback riding and attends private school, two cars, and a summer house on Long Island might need as much as $40,000 per month of coverage just to keep up with what he thinks of as a comfortable, middle-class existence."[42] It may be difficult (but not impossible) to find $40,000 of coverage on the DI market today, but it's possible if your prospect or client can clearly see the risk involved. If there is a need (as there is in this example), it's your job to help the person understand what they may be facing if an injury or illness strikes, regardless of the amount of money they have or are making.

Do you believe? Veteran agents carry their disability insurance policies along with them when they are making a DI sales presentation. Can you say the same thing? Do you believe in the possibility of an accident or sickness disrupting your cash flow and income situation to the point where a source of funds would be helpful?

If not, you may not have the conviction and attitude you need to legitimately persuade a prospect that this is a potential situation that requires attention. Why should a person buy a DI policy from someone who doesn't deem the coverage significant enough to have in his or her own financial portfolio? If you were making a sales presentation to Tony Soprano and he asked to see your DI coverage that you are telling him you believe is so strongly necessary, and you don't have a DI policy with you, what do you do? Tell him the dog ate it? Or that it's in your other briefcase? That's an offer he can refuse.

To consistently sell disability insurance, you must have your own faith in the product. If you do, it will be obvious in your presentation. It will cause the prospect to consider it more seriously because that individual will sense the sincerity you truly possess.

A disability can happen. It will create income issues. It may not be easy for most people to see this without your sales presentation, however. If you live along the Southeast coast of the United States, you are legitimately concerned with a hurricane striking and the resultant damage you would have to pay for *in the absence of* strong homeowner's coverage. You will have accomplished your difficult task of demonstrating the need for DI coverage if the prospect reaches the same conclusion that you have and that there is a realistic concern that finances will be affected by a disability *in the absence of* strong disability income insurance.

Existing Coverage

Earlier in this section, we discussed at some length the variety of income sources an individual could draw upon to help finance personal expenses during a disability. After you have established the need for planning for a disability in advance of that event happening, it will be time to review these options with your client.

You have already seen that each person or couple is different—in their income, occupation, and knowledge of the need for planning for a disability event. You are about to see that the resources that may be tapped during such an event are also going to vary widely. (NOTE: If you have not already done so, this is the time to complete the personal DI fact finder detailed earlier in this section of the book.)

Chances Out of **1,000** of at least one long-term (90 days or longer) disability event occurring prior to age 65:

AGE (single earner)	To 1 person (dual earning couple)	To any 1 of 2
30	467	716
35	451	699
40	430	675
45	401	641
50	360	590

Source: The JHA Disability Fact Book, 2003/2004 Edition, p. 13

As you approached your prospect with respect to the disability need, you will have already asked if the individual or couple has any existing coverage. If they have said yes, then you may not have to spend as much time on the need for disability insurance. Instead, you will have utilized the programming ideas shared earlier in this section to see if additional coverage is warranted. (It often is.) If the prospect(s) do not have existing coverage, your initial interview time is spent on establishing the need.

Now, either prospect is ready to examine the potential sources of dollars that can be utilized during a disability. This is where some of the objections to buying private disability insurance may arise.

Cash: Savings and liquid investments are the first source of money to note. How much does the prospect have stored away? How long will it last? The financial fact finder will have identified the expense picture. Which of these expenses has to be continued during a disability? Mortgage or rent, utilities, food—these are the essentials. Compare that monthly number to what's in the savings account and you (and the prospect) can quickly see how long these expenses can be financed with prior savings. Usually, this amount won't last long, and generally these numbers can help you determine an elimination period (number of days of disability before the policy starts to pay benefits) for the plan. Investments are a touchier subject. Some people look at the large number inside their 401(k)s and feel this is sufficient to pay their bills during a disability. But remember that this money was designated for *retirement*, not to be used up during a disability. The money will also be *taxed as ordinary income* as it is taken out, so the amount available should be reduced to a net number that would be available during a disability. Again, compare this number to the expenses to see how long it would last. If it will only continue a few months, what does the disabled individual do after that? Seeing it in black and white places the certainty of thinking one can self-insure this risk on shakier ground. As Lily Tomlin once said, reality is the leading cause of stress amongst those in touch with it.

Borrow: One can also try to look for help if disabled, although this is not usually a practical plan. Where does one turn to, when desperate, for financial aid? Parents, siblings, other relatives may be able to furnish some help, but what kind of position are they in? Do they have a cache of money set aside for your prospect's potential disability? Friends? Same question. What about going to a bank? Will they have much success completing paperwork for a loan when a key income earner in the family is out of commission? How about one's employer? Are these sensible ideas, and can specific dollar amounts be written down that can be absolutely counted on during a disability? The disabled individual can't even hold a "Will Work for Food" sign at a busy traffic intersection. In trying to formulate a legitimate plan, the idea of borrowing will not stand up to the reality test.

Employer: While borrowing from your employer is a likely non-issue, there may be some salary continuation arrangements that have been made. Prior to an interview, you should encourage your prospect to bring any employee benefit information for your review to see if there are genuine disability benefits among the material. Don't be surprised if the individual confuses health insurance with disability coverage. In an MDRT survey in 2002, 64% of survey respondents believed that major medical plans included disability income insurance.[43] So review the data thoroughly, identify the coverage in place (if any) and compare it to the actual need (necessary expenses that must continue each month) to see if there is a shortfall.

Workers' Compensation: On the job accidents can and do happen. On the job illnesses are far less likely. Still, insurers consider the possible availability of disability benefits under the Workers' Compensation program legitimate, and so should you. Having a private disability insurance plan combined with any coverage accessible through Workers' Compensation gives your client 24-hour coverage against illness and injury. Without DI coverage, there will have to be a valid on the job claim to receive any benefits. Workers' Compensation is *not* a solution to a disability problem. It is potential coverage to be factored in, and you may be able to use an offset rider to help reduce your client's premium, as part of the benefits can integrate formally with any dollars received from Workers' Compensation.

> Production time lost due to off the job injuries totaled about 165,000,000 days, costing the nation at least $184 billion in 2001. In comparison, 85,000,000 days were lost by workers injured on the job.

Social Security: Like Workers' Compensation, Social Security is a valid benefits program that might pay in the event of a serious disability. Remember the Social Security definition? It states that the disability must prevent you from performing any substantial gainful work for at least 12 months or have a condition that will result in death. It's not easy to collect disability benefits on that basis as the numbers below attest.

No wonder the song/movie is called "Things to Do in Denver When You're Dead" and not "Things to Do In Denver When You're Disabled." Now, this data shows the *initial* turndowns. That number improves on appeal, as this book has already demonstrated. But, again, Social Security is not a program upon which to base one's support solely during a disability. Like Workers' Comp., this can be handled by offset rider so that the insured is not paying for duplicate coverage. Social Security benefits also come with a 5-month wait, and decisions often take much longer, eventually paying retroactively but leaving the disabled individual and family out-of-pocket for some time. A private DI

Initial Claim Allowance Rates For Social Security by Region, 10/1/02—4/30/03	
NATIONAL rate:	36.7%
Atlanta	31.0%
Boston	44.6%
Chicago	34.9%
Dallas	36.7%
Denver	27.5%
Kansas City	33.4%
New York	39.0%
Philadelphia	40.4%
San Francisco	45.1%
Seattle	39.2%

Source: Social Security Administration, 2003

policy, including the offset rider, would be furnishing dollars during this interminable wait and helping to maintain the standard of living that they've come to expect.

Other Private DI Coverage: You're a programmer again, sifting through the benefit pages of the existing private insurance to ascertain monthly benefit amount, elimination period, benefit period and any other benefit features. You will then compare what's in the policy to the actual need. If there is a shortage in coverage, it will be obvious to both you and the individual, and you can move on to the application form to apply for additional benefits to replace a higher percentage of income.

Group LTD Coverage: If there is a group plan at work, the one likely to take into consideration is the long-term disability plan. Short-term disability generally runs not longer than 26 weeks (there are some 52 week plans out there) and usually is a 13-week benefit period. You would simply adjust your elimination period so that the private DI coverage would pick up after the short-term group plan has ended. Group LTD offers coverage to age 65 and must be factored in to your final need analysis. Remember that any Social Security benefits will offset the amount payable under Group LTD, so there's no reason to factor this in twice.[44] In fact, DI insurers typically publish a separate limits table that details the amount of coverage that can be issued when a group LTD plan is in place. The benefits of the private plan are not integrated with Social Security payments. The most important point about working existing group LTD into the review of income sources is to not let your prospect be overconfident about the amount of coverage in force. LTD plans are notorious for its offsets, so what looks like a 60% of income benefit is generally far less. Temper the expectation accordingly, and supplement that LTD plan with a small private DI coverage that the individual owns and can take along if and when he or she departs the employer who has the LTD program.

Association Coverage: Individuals that belong to a professional association may have the opportunity to purchase disability coverage through this entity. Review the coverage thoroughly to identify benefits and other plan design features. There is an extra downside to association coverage that is not true with group LTD; that is, coverage may only be available as long as you are a *current dues-paying member* of the association. Failure to continue membership may result in a loss of benefits. Association coverage is also known for its annual whims regarding raising premiums. For example, "the Texas Medical Association Insurance Trust...sent its members a list of...changes. The communication was remarkably candid: During" the most recent five-year period, "the plan, which is underwritten by a major mutual life insurer, lost more than $36 million despite two rate increases and benefit cuts. Disability claims are made more frequently and last longer than originally assumed. Only 300 claims now are being paid, but they require a $90 million loss reserve. Hence rates have been increased significantly. A 52-year-old physician saw his basic coverage increase by 62% for his 90-day elimination period plan."[46] Like some of the other choices listed above, this one also falls short of being the perfect answer to income problems during a disability.

These are the most common sources of money that an individual could draw upon during a disability. None of them are adequate, unless another private DI plan has sufficient coverage to meet necessary expenses. Your rundown of these possibilities will continue to emphasize the need for private DI coverage.

To Your Health

"Be careful about reading health books. You may die of a misprint."

– Mark Twain

Income and occupation are two of the major components of the personal disability income sale. A third key element is health. As noted under the "principles of disability income sales presentations," you are unable to write a policy the day you meet with a prospect even though this individual agrees that private disability insurance is a proper funding vehicle to cover the disability income need.

That's because the insurance company will be scrutinizing your client's medical history in addition to the income and occupation information. This is why it's important to talk to people about this coverage *before* any significant health history arises. For insurers, it's similar to their other risk evaluations. Drivers with a history of auto accidents are going to be in a different rating class—if they can qualify for auto insurance at all—than those who are considered safe drivers, with no such mishaps.

Similarly, people with a history of cancer are going to be viewed differently than individuals with a clean bill of health.

You are the field underwriter, the first line of defense for an insurer. The company is counting on you to bring them reasonably healthy risks. Since you will be the only one to actually see the applicant, your first-hand observations are vital. No one expects you to be Sherlock Holmes, but you can certainly take note of an overweight individual who advises his height and weight are 6 ft., 180 pounds. You can fill out the application with the applicant's answers, but your honesty is greatly appreciated in the section of the application entitled "Agent's Report."

It's a difficult line to walk. You want the policy issued. So does the applicant. But full and accurate disclosure is important up front, otherwise it will come back to haunt all parties at claim time when full medical records reveal information that wasn't on the application. Even if the medical information leads to a counteroffer from the insurer, maybe with an extra premium rating or a reduction in the benefits desired, it is the right thing to do. Many other conditions that could cause disability will be covered, and that's the value of the coverage.[47]

Your personal DI proposal form presented earlier in this section of the book listed some medical conditions that are good to know about as you solicit the proposal from the insurer *before* you even make your sales presentation. These are counseling, diabetes, weight, and high blood pressure.

High blood pressure, controlled by medication, should not present underwriting problems unless there are other risk factors present. Diabetes will be an issue, especially if it was juvenile-onset. Each insurer has a generous height and weight chart, and you should check that if you believe the individual may be overweight. Counseling has become an issue over the last two decades and any type—marital, stress, depression, anxiety—will mean some modifications to the benefits, and sometimes a postponement or even a declination to offer a policy.

If the individual has had some counseling, full details will help pinpoint the risk. Ask about medications—like Xanax or Prozac. Are the counseling visits current, or were they successfully (or unsuccessfully) concluded? Was it a one-time thing? (Some marital or bereavement counseling is.) The more you can disclose, the more accurate a decision can be made.

You will also be compiling good-will points with your underwriter. You may not believe this, but repeat after me: "Your underwriter is your friend." Establishing a trustworthy relationship with your underwriter will help you long-term. There will be borderline decisions that may go your way. There will be a tendency to accept your word rather than repeatedly going to great lengths (in a time-consuming effort) to verify your statements. Being honest with both applicant and carrier will stand you in good stead over the long haul. Believe me, it's worth it.

Take the time to go through the medical questions thoroughly. (See the sample application medical questions below). Don't read them at the same speed as they do the fine print in car dealers' TV advertisements. Try and obtain as much data as you can—name, address, when seen—on the doctor or other provider to speed up the process of collecting medical records to evaluate.

Don't edit the information as to what you think is important. A knee injury and subsequent operation are not much of a concern on a life insurance application, but can be very significant on a disability case, depending on the surgery's success, prognosis and type of occupation. (Is it one that requires physical exertion?)

The insurer may require a medical exam, but often can do with a urine specimen and blood profile. Those readings will tell an underwriter a lot about an individual's present health history. Your DI carrier will advise you of the medical requirements when they furnish the proposal. Make sure you prepare the client for this, and you may even play a role in scheduling the visit by the paramedical examiner to either the individual's home or office.

An underwriting decision that is substandard—an adjustment to what your client applied for—is not necessarily bad. Rather than refusing the risk entirely, the company has altered the benefits to reflect the extra chance it is taking in issuing the coverage. There may be an opportunity to have the decision reviewed in the future, if health changes positively, or there is more distance between the medical condition that inspired the modification and the next review. A rating for being overweight might look better if the individual is now, say, on a low-carb diet. Perhaps in a year, the weight may be within the company's chart for approval without the extra charge and you can furnish updated medical information to make this happen.

Be proactive when your client has a substandard rating. Recently I had a client who seemed to be in good health at age 45 and didn't even have a regular physician—not necessarily a good thing. His blood profile revealed an elevated cholesterol reading that resulted in a rating, subject to review in the future. He took it to heart and adopted a better diet. Within a year, he had lost 30 pounds and his cholesterol was down within normal levels. A new blood profile was done and the insurer removed the rating. Not only was the substandard policy accepted, it helped the insured change his medical habits to his improvement. The removal of the rating on his policy was a bonus for him.

Sample Medical Questions of DI Application[48]

Within the last 5 years, have you had, been treated for, or been diagnosed as having a heart condition, chest pain, stroke, back or neck problem, psychological condition (including, but not limited to, counseling from a mental health or substance abuse provider, and/or psychotherapy), cancer, diabetes, alcohol abuse, or drug dependency? ___ yes ___ no

Current Height _____ Weight _____ Have you lost more than 10 pounds in the last year? ___ yes ___ no

Names and addresses of physicians or hospitals you have visited in the last 10 years:

Names of medications you take or have taken in the past 10 years:

Over time, the role of the insurance agent in taking down medical information has diminished somewhat as insurers rely on the blood profile and an RN calling the applicant directly to ask medical questions as much as the agent's information. However, you can still anticipate areas that an underwriter will want to explore further in full by your prospect's answers and can initiate the process of this medical review faster by getting much of the details up front. It minimizes surprises later if you can prepare the applicant for what to expect based on the medical answers you receive.

Key Benefit Components

"Not all who wander are lost."

– J.R.R. Tolkien

There are two other elements to the personal disability sale that should be discussed at this point. Your DI proposal page contains both—an elimination period and a benefit period—with appropriate definitions. Along with the monthly benefit (established by an individual's earnings) and definition of disability (established by the nature of the occupation and the course a disability might take if it occurred), these are the key parameters used in designing today's disability income program.

Elimination Period: This is the length of time before benefits will be payable. The 90-day elimination period has become the most common sold, primarily because it is the most competitively priced and the one that most carriers prefer to sell. Shorter elimination periods like 30 and 60 days are less attractive and much higher in premium. Most people can self-insure the first 90 days of their disability claim. Like health insurance, it's not the short-term problem (or small bill) that is the issue. It's the catastrophe: the long-term disability.

The cost of the shorter elimination periods like 30 and 60 days are so much higher than 90 day EPs today that it is almost like dollar trading: how much benefit return will you get back for paying higher premiums over time? A disability lasting less than 90 days is financially recoverable: creditors will work with you if they know that a return to work is imminent.

Not so the longer disability. If you own a DI plan with a 90 day EP and a claim occurs that lasts at least 90 days, there is a good chance you will be drawing benefits for a while. The longer the disability lasts, the lower the possibility of a rapid recovery. Thus the need for the DI coverage to handle the long-term income problem becomes more apparent.

> Many employers have experienced significant increases in the incidence of long-term disability. During a two-year period, long-term disability incidence rates increased among 26% of the employers who measured it and decreased among just 9%.
>
> Source: *Mercer Human Resource consulting, Marsh, Inc. 2002 Survey of Employee's Time Off and Disability Programs*

Benefit Period: This is the amount of time that disability policy benefits will be paid. Obviously, the longer the payout period, the better. It will also involve a higher premium. If the prospect can afford the longer benefit period, great! You are, after all, insuring the catastrophic situation: a long-term loss of income. It may not always be the affordable choice, however. There is nothing wrong with having to modify the coverage to a 5-year benefit period instead due to cost concerns.

Average Disability Duration: LTD[49]

CONDITION	# of Months
Nervous System Diseases	49
Circulatory System Diseases	48
Respiratory System Diseases	44
Chronic Fatigue Syndrome	41
Musculoskeletal	35

A 5-year benefit period won't always get it done, but in the majority of situations, it is sufficient. The above-listed conditions and their durations show that 5 years would have worked a large percentage of the time. In some cases, you just have to play the odds.

The other option is to place an unworkable premium amount that may cause a cancellation of the policy at a later date due to a tight budget (and other priorities), and this is not an acceptable situation. The client can always upgrade the policy later (if insurable), when finances are better.

At times, the number of options for a disability income plan can leave both you and the prospect confused. However, if you remember the essentials of these two components—a 90 day EP and the longest BP affordable—you will simplify the individual policy design process considerably.

The Business Prospect

"In the business world, the rearview mirror is always clearer than the windshield."

– Warren Buffett

Working with an individual to solve a disability need is very rewarding. Helping a small business owner fill multiple disability gaps is equally gratifying.

Over the years, I've tended to focus on small business owners primarily because I am one myself. As an independent insurance agent, I run a small business and can easily relate to all of the issues facing the owner: payroll, quarterly taxes, compliance, workers' compensation, etc. I can speak the same language and share stories of woe with the small business prospect.

For those that work this market, there are lucrative advantages. It often leads to multiple sales with the same client, and even some opportunities for worksite marketing sales to employees. For the small business owner is looking at nearly unlimited liability if disability needs are left unexplored.

What's more, it's a large market. Total small business wealth in the United States more than doubled from $3.4 trillion in 1990 to $8.3 trillion in 2000, according to a study by the Small Business Administration, who describes *small business* as those with less than 500 employees.[50]

To work with an individual prospect, you have a Personal Disability Income Fact Finding/Proposal sheet to complete. With a business prospect, it will vary slightly as there are additional needs that you will be looking to fill, if needed. Business owners work with two checkbooks: their personal one that they hate to pull out and the business one, where checks written are most often deductible expenses. Personal disability coverage insures the personal checkbook, but leaves the business one vulnerable should a disability strike.

In the pages below, you will find the Business Disability Coverage form that will serve as your guide to obtain sufficient information to both identify and solve these business needs.

Figure 2.3

Request for Business Disability Income Proposal

Business Disability Coverage

PROPOSED INSURED INFORMATION

Name:_____ Degree_____ DOB___/___/___ Age_____

Male_____ Female_____   Tobacco Use : _____No _____ Yes

Occupation _____ Since_____ Industry_____
(If MD, specify type. If nurse, specify type and workplace.)

New business? _____Yes _____ No Since _____ Home-based? _____Yes _____ No
% of time spent in office? _____% in field? _____% # of employees? _____ State _____

Duties: Breakdown by percentage and add details to a separate sheet with full description.

Sales/Marketing _____% Travel (Local _____% Abroad _____%) Student ____Y ____ N
Administration _____%   Supervisor of _____Manual _____ Administration
Manual _____ (If manual, describe with %) _____

Type of business _____Sole Prop_____Part_____LLC_____S Corp_____C Corp

Government employee? _____Federal (if so, ____FERS or ____SERS)
_____ State _____ County

Income: (include bonus, if regular, and retirement contributions)

$_____ (net income from Sched. C/P&L, last filed tax year)

$ _____ Net unearned income (e.g. alimony, investment interest, passive income)

Expenses: (include all regular expenses except salary and salary of employed professionals doing same work) $_____ Business ownership _____%

Health: Height _____ Weight_____

Problems? HBP ___ Diabetes ____Counseling ____Other. If yes, provide details:
onset age, medication, duration, prognosis, surgery, etc. *A printed cover sheet would help.*

_____
_____

Ever denied coverage? ____Y_____N   Ever had coverage rated? _____Y_____N
Details: (Why? Who?) _____

Figure 2.3 (cont'd)

DESIRED BUSINESS COVERAGE

____Budget (fewer guarantees, options, lower cost)   ____Best (better definitions, more $)

Business Overhead Expense (note: a tax deductible premium):

    Monthly benefit amount (based on qualified expenses): $_____
    Elimination Period _____   Benefit Period _____

Options: _____ Residual _____ FIO? $_____ Other: _____

Disability Buy-Sell (to replace your business interest):

    $_____ lump-sum amount or $_____ monthly benefit amount
    Elimination Period _____   Benefit Period (for monthly only) _____

Options: _____ FIO? $_____ Other _____

Key Person (Whose loss would hurt business the most?):

    Monthly benefit amount (based on key person's salary): $_____
    Elimination Period _____   Benefit Period _____

Options: __ Residual (__FIO $____) __ROP __Step-rate Other: _____

EXISTING COVERAGE

Existing coverage: ____None   or   ____Yes

If yes, specify: Policy type: _____ (BOE, Buy-Sell, etc.) Amount: $_____
    Elimination period: _____   Benefit period: _____

Options? ____ Residual ____ COLA (%)____ ____FIO ____ROP ____Step-rate

    _____ Other

To be replaced? _____ yes   _____ no

Note: The purchase of business disability income coverage involves securing information and specific details that can best determine the type of policy for which the individual is eligible and the cost of this coverage. Be sure to answer all questions on the proposal form. This may also speed up the ultimate underwriting of the application.

Completing this proposal form

PROPOSED INSURED INFORMATION

Note: Some of this information may already have been taken when doing an information gathering analysis.

Degree: PhD, Masters, MD, DDS, etc.

Date of birth: Some companies rate on actual age, so give both for best rate.

Occupation: Be as specific as possible about duties. Break down by percentage what manual duties are if any are performed. This helps place an individual accurately in an occupational classification, an important factor as it affects the rate being charged and the coverage that can be purchased. The term "Business owner" is *not* an occupation, but "electrician" is.

Income: The income information should be taken from the business tax return. It is just as critical in the purchase of business coverage as it is for personal disability coverage, and this return will generally be required to be submitted with the application. For BOE (Business Overhead Expense) coverage, a detailed listing of expenses that can be found in the tax return will determine the amount of monthly benefit one should buy. The individual owner's salary and those salaries of individuals doing the same type of work as the insured will *not* be included in the expense calculation. (Those doing the same work as the individual will likely generate enough revenue to cover their salaries even though the individual owner is out.)

For Key Person coverage, it is important to obtain both the business income and the key person's income. For Buy-Sell coverage, it is important to obtain the total value of the business. The percentage of the business owned by the person applying for coverage is important for both BOE and Buy-Sell.

Health: Good health is a plus when applying for Business DI coverage. This section lets you identify potential health problems early. Early details will help determine if the individual is an insurable risk before you spend your time presenting and writing coverage. If the person has ever been denied or had insurance coverage rated, find out the details and how long ago it occurred. *Any* form of counseling will require full details such as how long ago it commenced, number of visits, current status, any medication, etc.

Desired Coverage

Budget: Check this area if the client/business has a small amount of discretionary funds to spend. The budget proposal can keep the cost down, but might include fewer options and fewer policy guarantees.

Best: Check this area for better coverage that includes better policy definitions and features, more guarantees, but at a higher premium cost.

BOE: Monthly benefits the person can qualify for are based on actual business expenses. This policy is intended to meet the business expense obligations for business owners while personal disability coverage insures the income the individual takes out of the business. For that reason, the individual's salary is not included as part of the regular expenses.

Buy-Sell: This amount is based on the value of the business and the individual's percentage of ownership. For example, if the business is valued at $500,000 and the individual owns half, the benefit amount should be $250,000. It can be written as a lump-sum amount or as a monthly benefit with claim benefits being paid out over a period of time. Instead of $250,000, you might write $10,416/month for 24 months instead. This generally lowers the price, but most businesses (and owners) desire the money on a lump-sum basis.

Key Person: Generally, this amount may be based on the salary of the key person being insured. If the key person becomes disabled, the claim dollars are paid directly to the business to reimburse it for lost revenue.

Elimination period: The number of days before any benefits are payable. The longer the elimination period selected, the lower the premium cost.

    BOE: Usually a shorter EP is used, such as 30 or 60 days.

    Key Person: Usually, an EP of 60 or 90 days is used.

    Buy-Sell: A long EP is selected as a catastrophic type disability is usually indicated before an actual buy-out takes place. The minimum (and most common) EP is 365 days.

Benefit period: The length of time benefits are payable.

> BOE and Key Person: A short benefit period is needed here as the business will either be sold or the owner or key person will have returned to work by then (or the key person may be replaced). 12, 18, and 24 months are common.

Options: Business disability coverage can be tailored to specific individual needs through the use of optional benefits.

> BOE or Key Person: The residual option can be added to a base policy that has a total disability definition to pay a portion of the monthly benefit should the business owner or key person return to work in a reduced capacity. The FIO, or Future Income Option, benefit offers the ability to increase the monthly benefit in the future *without* having to answer any medical underwriting questions. Increased expenses are all that is needed to justify the additional coverage. For a small extra premium, this is a worthwhile benefit as you are guaranteeing your client's future insurability in the purchase of more coverage. The ROP, or Return of Premium, option is a high priced way of getting some of the money paid for the policy back in later years if the policy is either not used for a claim or used very little. It will significantly add to the premium—it is definitely only quoted when indicating a "Best" coverage—but does answer the question about what happens to the premium paid in if little or no claims result.

For Buy-Sell, usually the only option generally available is the FIO.

Premium paid by?:

> BOE: Any type of business can pay for and deduct the premium for a BOE policy. Receipt of benefits is a taxable event when received at claim time, but the benefits are being used to pay business expenses that can be deducted.

Key Person and Buy-Sell premiums are not deductible, nor are benefits taxable when paid.

Existing coverage: There is a limit on the amount of coverage that can be purchased for these plans, governed by the total amount of business expenses or the value of the owner's percentage in the business or the salary of a key person. For this reason, details about existing coverage should be given. Existing coverage may not be a candidate for replacement, especially if the coverage is older. There is always the possibility additional coverage can be written to have adequate benefits when disabled. If the existing coverage is more recent, supply full details as there may be a possibility of improvement.

A Taxing Issue

"There's a fine line between fishing and just standing on the shore like an idiot."

– Stephen Wright

This book has already noted that the market for personal disability insurance sales is still wide open. And personal DI is where the majority of disability need solving has taken place. That makes business DI an even greater opportunity as most agents haven't yet looked past the more obvious personal sale.

There are several ways to break into the small business DI market. Both business overhead expense (BOE) and disability buy-sell (DBS) needs have likely never been discussed with the business owners. Prospecting using these two needs-based ideas is one way to begin the work of business disability analysis. The BOE plan is a relatively small premium and tax deductible to *any* type of business, meaning you are talking to the owner about the business checkbook. With disability buy-sell, most small businesses with two or more owners have probably established a buy-sell agreement. If they haven't, there's your entry right there. If they have, does the buy-sell agreement mention buy-out arrangements in the event of a disability? Generally, these agreements primarily address death, but some have disability clauses in them. If they do, how will the disability liability to the disabled business owner be funded? If not, what would happen to the business if one of the owners was catastrophically disabled? All of these questions can start the business disability review rolling.

The other way to begin conversations with a business owner is to ask the individual about his or her sick-pay program for their employees. Even if the business owner is a sole proprietor with no employees, the question is still relevant. *If someone in your business is out due to illness or injury, do you still pay him?*

Most owners will say that they do. The next question is vital—*have they established a formal sick pay plan to ensure the deductibility of those payments?* The smaller the business, the less the likelihood they have formalized the sick pay plan in effect. Just paying someone that's out is a plan, but the payments are not tax deductible to the business as wages under Sections 105 and 162 of the Internal Revenue Code because the person is not working.[51] Worse, if the payments were made to a disabled corporate owner, this money would be considered a taxable dividend.[52]

This is a fine mess you've put us in Ollie. But it is one that can be easily rectified. Establishing a formal sick pay plan consists of two specific requirements: detailing the plan in writing, and notifying any covered employee who would be a recipient of sick pay. Neither document needs to be filed with the IRS, just kept handy in case of a question during any audit of the business records.

This conversation about how to properly deduct sick pay is an easy one to get into—even with employers who decide not to pay any employee who is out sick to avoid IRS issues. Those same employers will not likely exclude themselves from this decision, meaning their own salary will surely be continued during a disability—they have to have some way to get the money out of the business properly. They will need to set up a sick pay plan.

Of course, that same business owner can say, fine, I'll set it up and self-insure it if it's just for me. That's easily said, but insurance will probably be a better funding choice here because of Financial Accounting Standards Board (FASB) Statement 112. This business owner will be required to carry the net present value of potential payments as a liability on their balance sheets. Since the owner is probably highly paid, that amount could be tough on said balance sheet. A 40-year-old who earns $150,000 per year may require his or her corporation to carry more than a $1.6 million liability for this obligation.[53] Donald Trump would likely fire himself from his television boardroom if he made this kind of decision.

Now you're in the business market. How difficult did that seem? These discussions are easy to get started: you just need a few minutes of the key owner's time. Make the appointment based on any of the above ideas, and you will jump start your DI sales.

The Employer-Employee Disconnect

"The world is filled with willing people; some willing to work, others willing to let them."

– Robert Frost

Working with the business owner can be, as Humphrey Bogart said to Claude Rains in *Casablanca*, "the beginning of a beautiful friendship." Personal disability coverage to fund the sick pay (salary continuation) plan; BOE coverage to insure business expenses during a disability; DBS insurance to provide funds (usually on a lump-sum basis) to buy out a disabled business owner, and even key person disability coverage to reimburse the business for lost revenue due to the loss of an essential employee. These programs will likely be implemented over time, and there will be changes—especially if the business grows.

Disability insurance can also be an important retention tool for an employer. Keeping good workers is a thorny problem these days. Movement in the job market is extremely high, as many key people keep looking for the next best deal. For employers, this is more than just a cost issue—it can be imperative for the survival of the business.

It's a constant battle. Turnover is expected to rise significantly again in the near future once the job market improves, according to a 2003 Job Recovery Survey. Around 83% of managerial employees said it was extremely or somewhat likely that they would actively seek new employment once the job market and economy improved. And 53% of those surveyed indicate that better compensation and *benefits* would be the top reason for leaving their present employment.[54]

Employers today are also battling the (once again) rising trend in health care premiums. Double-digit increases are forcing employers large and small to evaluate their benefit packages with an eye towards eliminating or lessening the benefits offered.[55] This can have an effect on filling disability insurance needs unless you can demonstrate to the employer that your programs can help them save money overall.[56]

According to the Employment Policy Foundation, in March 2002 the average annual total employer cost of health insurance for full-time, year-round employees was $4,202 for family plans and $2,136 for individual policies. At this current rate of growth, the average annual cost for full-time employees is going to rise to $10,946 by 2010.[57] How can a small employer afford that? How can any of us small business owners consistently pay for this expense?

What Worries Small Business Owners[58]

Recession/current economic issues	25%
Retirement or transition	19%
Capital or financing issues	7%
Unexpected growth	6%
Succession	4%

Source: Nationwide Financial 2003 Small Business Survey

This is an opportune time for you to review the new Health Savings Accounts (HSA) legislation as it may be a way of saving money or the employer that can be used to fill in the vulnerable areas of planning not yet addressed, including disability. HSAs focus on the reason health insurance exists in the first place: to cover the large bill, not the small one. So much of the health insurance premium dollar goes to pay a low deductible or co-pay, that immediate savings can be realized on a higher deductible option combined with the ability to contribute on an above-the-line, tax deductible basis to an account that can help pay for the co-pays and low deductibles Americans seem to love. It has the potential to keep premiums affordable again while insuring the main problem: a health condition that can run up thousands of dollars in bills. As mentioned earlier, it is the same idea with a 90-day elimination period: why insure the short duration disabilities when it's the longer ones that wreak the financial havoc? Savings in health insurance premiums help you meet the employer's foremost concern head-on: how to pay for the disability needs.

**Average Direct Costs of Disability[59]
1999-2000 as percentage of payroll**

Workers' Compensation	2.5%
Sick pay	1.7%
Short-term DI	1.5%
Long-term DI	0.6%

**Average Indirect Costs of Disability
1999-2000 as percentage of payroll**

Overtime costs	3.2%
Replacement employees	3.8%
Workstation/job accommodation	1.0%

Source: Nationwide Financial 2003 Small Business Survey

Disability coverage, by contrast, does not carry the same type of high costs that health insurance traditionally has done. This gives the employer more bang for the buck, something that can also help retain a key employee.

Time-off and disability program costs averaged 15% of payroll in 2001, up from 14.6% in 2000, according to Mercer Human Resource Consulting and Marsh, Inc.[60] These numbers continue to force employers to look at their disability needs.

So why is the market so open if these are significant issues to the employer? Remember that today's employer has many concerns on the mind, not just disability. Many benefits marketing experts contend that the insurance industry is letting fate educate too many employers about the importance of short-term and long-term disability benefits to address workplace disability needs. The money that is going towards holiday parties, discount eyewear programs, and even concierge services might be better directed at this arguably more important financial need.[61]

Human resource divisions in companies have their own language. For disability, there are several acronyms to be aware of as your contact in a large employer situation will speak these fluently. Integrated disability management (IDM) is the stuff you know: short and long-term disability, workers' compensation, and family medical leave. Total

Percentage of Employees Covered by Group LTD[62]	
Professional and Technical	48%
Clerical and Sales	26%
Blue Collar and Service	15%
TOTAL	25%

Source: Bureau of Labor Statistics

absence management (TAM) incorporates these with all employee time off from work like military duty, juror service, vacations, and the like. Today's hotter buzz word is Health and Productivity solutions (HPM). The employer goal is to make the workplace as efficient and productive as possible. Disability programs that incorporate rehabilitation and return to work programs will draw the most attention in this environment.[63] Being able to speak in these knowledgeable terms puts you ahead of many agents out there today just trying to make a sale. You want to assimilate your disability solutions into the overall goals of the company.

The threat of SARS (Severe Acute Respiratory Syndrome) may not have threatened the U.S. in any significant way, but it reminds employers how increasingly difficult it is becoming to protect themselves and their employees from communicable diseases in today's workplace. Infections and debilitating illnesses that spread through a workplace can decimate productivity for weeks.[64] Your disability insurance funding vehicles can help recapture some of the lost costs associated with this diminished activity.

Once you have passed the need identification portion of your work, your answers to those issues uncovered will utilize several types of products, depending on the size of the company. Both group LTD and individual disability insurance has its place in the employee benefit world. Group LTD's strength is in its pricing, its simplicity in implementation, and the broad coverage of many lives. You can then build on this by tailoring individual DI plans to those higher earners that need the extra coverage and flexibility these policies provide.[65]

You can be a vital asset to your employer client. Not only do you provide the proper funding vehicles that the employee will have, but you also serve as an important communication line from the employer. The employer often finds that despite the benefits provided to an employee, the appreciation on the part of the worker is not there, especially in relation to the dollars being spent.

This is often the result of something being lost in the employee benefit translation, confusion that you can easily clear up. If the employee truly understands what they have, this is a positive for all. The employer has spent money that the employee appreciates, and is likely to consider that when weighing other job opportunities.

Workers Rank Top 10 Benefits

1. Medical Insurance
2. Paid vacation and holidays
3. Employer-paid pension
4. Retirement savings plan
5. Prescription drug benefit
6. Dental insurance
7. Ability to choose benefits that best meet one's personal needs
8. Sick-leave and short-term disability
9. Long-term disability insurance
10. Preventive/wellness coverage

Source: Aon Consulting, United States @ Work Survey of 1,800 employees, 2002

As you can see from this survey, employees rank disability income fairly low on their priority list. It seems clear that they do not yet understand that their income is the driving force behind all that they and their family do. It helps pay for several of the items that are ranked ahead of DI in these answers. How good is a 401(k) when there is no income to put in it? The employer understands this and you can lock in a long-term client if you can help the employee see the value of the dollar the employer has invested into this employee benefit.

As you know, disability can and does happen. Ignoring the problem doesn't make it go away. In 2002, some 5.5 million Americans were on LTD, a 62 percent surge from 1992 according to the Department of Labor.[66] Your mission is to make this evident to the employee. Employees surely understand that their proclivity for changing jobs or holding out for greater salaries/benefits is driving work outside of this country. White collar jobs are considered the USA's "new money saving export"[67] It's not just factory jobs leaving our shores. Working in conjunction with their employer to accept a reasonable schedule of benefits is one way to help keep these jobs home. Disability income is a centerpiece of this strategy.

Group disability coverage is a sound, practical way to begin the process of funding sick pay. This type of policy provides a base plan of benefits upon which individual DI can be programmed to make up for any shortfall in coverage. Short-term disability starts early (7, 14, 30 day EPs) and ends early (13, 26 weeks), but it is helpful in insuring those frequent sick day misses. Long-term disability starts at 90 days (or longer), and runs through age 65 and beyond, and can be layered with the short-term DI to start when STD ends.

Individual DI coverage works well as a supplement, especially for high earners. Group LTD is flexible in overall design, but individual DI is specifically tailored to the person buying the coverage, who can pick and choose the benefits most important (with your guidance). There are economical ways to funding sick pay and using a combination of vehicles often works best.

Combining programs extends more flexibility to you in working with the employer to create a plan. The individual employer may find that 60% of coverage under LTD to be too high a premium to pay. You can reduce the coverage level to 50%, for example, and save up to 40% in premium costs, while making up for the reduced coverage with individual DI when you meet with the employees.[68]

Benefits Offered by Funding Method

LTD:
Offer the benefit	40%
Employer-paid	49%
Contributory	10%
Voluntary	41%

STD:
Offer the benefit:	42%
Employer-paid	45%
Contributory	17%
Voluntary	38%

Source: LIMRA International, 2003

In designing the disability solution, you will get the opportunity to work one-on-one with the employees and fulfill one of your objectives in bringing the subject of sick pay to the employer's attention in the first place: communicating on the employer's behalf to the employees. Many of these plans involve a combination of product and funding, and you can tell the employees how much the employer is doing in all of their best interest.

The employees will hopefully see it that way as well since the success (to their families) will hinge on how well the group program (if there is one) is supplemented by individual DI. If there is no group LTD, then it is critical that the individual design be meaningful to the fullest extent so as to provide adequate benefits.

There may be a Section 125 plan in place, meaning that employees will be able to pay for their portion of the DI coverage with pre-tax dollars. Cafeteria plans are intended to help employees purposefully create the proper benefit package to cover specific needs. There's far more to compensation than just cash,[69] and the cafeteria plan demonstrates the dollars being paid on behalf of the employees, while allowing individuals to upgrade the benefits in a way that best suits them and is the most economical.

> In 2001, a 15-year-old Wisconsin-based technology firm was searching for a better voluntary benefits package for its 150 employees. The challenge: Enhancing employee voluntary disability income insurance benefits without affecting company budget or administrative capacity. The solution: Supplemental DI coverage via an Internet-based application process. This offered employees a convenient way to apply for increased disability income insurance protection at an affordable cost. The only cost to the employer was the soft cost of time involved introducing the proposal to the employees. The employer invited employees to mandatory initial meetings via e-mail and notices on an Intranet site. There was a prepared presentation, a question and answer session, a review of the Web-based application and the employees were ready to sign up. DI filled an important gap for the employees, the employer enhanced its voluntary package without adding a line item to the expense sheet, and the agent solidified his position with the employer to meet additional needs in the future.[70]

Worksite marketing is a great daytime activity, and the chance to multiply your clients many times over. Often, there is a streamlined approach to enrolling these cases that differs from the typical personal sale. Many of the health questions are reduced to "kickout" questions relating to the most serious medical conditions, where a positive answer results in a decline, rather than any serious underwriting time.[71] The up side is that most employees will be written easily and quickly.

At the start of this section on sick pay, I noted two requirements necessary to formalize the salary continuation arrangements that would satisfy the IRS with regard to deductibility. Samples of these forms that can be tailored to your client are reproduced below for your convenience.

Resolution of the Board of Directors

_____ then discussed the concept of establishing a formal Sick Pay Plan for certain employees of the Corporation. After due discussion and upon motion duly made, seconded and unanimously approved, the following resolution was adopted:

WHEREAS, it is the desire of the Corporation to establish a Sick Pay Plan for certain employees by providing any such employee with an income during total disability and thereby providing any such employee with an added incentive to continue his services to the Corporation, and

WHEREAS, the Internal Revenue Code in Sections 105 and 106 and under the Treasury Regulations pertaining thereto, and Revenue Ruling 58-90, offer an excellent method for accomplishing this purpose,

BE IT RESOLVED, that a Sick Pay Plan for certain employees is hereby adopted in accordance with the aforesaid sections of the Internal Revenue Code, Treasury Regulations, and Revenue Ruling, subject to the terms of the forms exhibited in the meeting, attached to these minutes and incorporated herein:

BE IT FURTHER RESOLVED, that the appropriate officers of the Corporation be, and they hereby are, authorized and directed to execute and deliver any and all endorsements, instruments or power of attorney, and do any other things that they deem necessary in order to establish said Sick Pay Plan.

Dear _____:

In consideration of the valuable services you have performed for the company, the Board of Directors has approved a salary continuation plan for you that will continue your wages during a limited period of absence from work due to personal injuries or sickness.

Your program will continue your wages for up to _____ days in a calendar year if you are unable to work due to injury or sickness.

We thank you for your support and are proud to have you as part of our team!

Sincerely,

Business Overhead Expense

"Beware of little expenses, a small leak will sink a good ship."

– Benjamin Franklin

Personal disability coverage is intended to cover the family expenses of a mortgage or rent, utilities, food, clothing and, in today's age, cable or satellite TV and a broadband connection. If a business owner is disabled and has $5,000/month in coverage and a minimum of $5,000 in monthly expenses to keep the business open, does he opt to take care of his family expenses and close the office down?[72]

This is the financial (and moral) dilemma the business owner will face in this position. To whom does he owe more—the family or the employees of the business? If the office is closed, where does one return if there is a recovery from the disability—more likely in today's medical technology world?

The more important question for financial advisors is: *why should the business owner have to make this Sophie's choice?* If the owner holds both a personal DI and a BOE policy, both the family and the business will be taken care of until recovery is complete.

Under a BOE policy, business expenses such as payroll, employee benefits, rent or mortgage, utilities, maintenance, equipment leases and professional fees can be reimbursed to the owner over a short period of time: 12, 18, or 24 months.[73] Keeping the business as a going concern can psychologically help the owner, knowing that the practice he or she built up will be there, relatively debt-free, when he or she is ready to get back in the business saddle.

If the individual understands the reason for personal DI, it's not a giant leap for mankind to comprehend the role a BOE policy can play. It's a matter of insuring the "other" checkbook that is near and dear to the business owner's heart. Put simply, if the owner's gross monthly revenue is $12,000 and $7,000 is put towards expenses and $5,000 represents take-home income, personal DI will only insure the $5,000, not the $12,000. The other $7,000 can largely be covered with the BOE plan.

Business Overhead Expense insurance is designed primarily for owner-employees of small partnerships, closely-held companies, and professional businesses.[74] It is a relatively smaller premium than personal DI because the benefit periods are short in length. That's because the policy is intended to keep the business open as long as necessary before a decision has to be reached—that the owner is either coming back to the practice or not. If not, that should be known in at least a few months after the disability commences. This gives the owner and family a chance to sell the business and obtain a decent price for it. The BOE policy helps make this happen because the owner is not forced to sell quickly for monetary reasons.

Shorter elimination periods may be more practical here—to meet payroll and other expenses. Both 30 and 60 day elimination periods are available in addition to the more popular 90-day EP. If there is more than one owner with expense responsibility, each can buy a BOE policy covering his or her liability. If there are several owners sharing expenses, then there may be less of a need as the business may not miss one owner from a cash flow standpoint.

Reed and Wright, Inc.

Reed and Wright, Inc. is a successful literary agency, representing a number of authors. The principals, equal business partners, have spent their time cultivating these relationships, each with their own set of writers they've developed. They understand that if one of the owners was disabled, it could seriously imperil the rapport with that agent's group of authors, causing a significant loss of income. They employ two administrative people, two manuscript readers and a copy editor. Their monthly expenses break down as follows:

Owners' salaries:	$15,000
Employees' salaries:	10,000
Office Rent:	1,500
Telephone:	750
Electric:	250
Employee Benefits:	2,500
Office Supplies	300
Computer Service	150
Meals & Entertainment	1,000
TOTAL EXPENSES:	$31,450

The expenses not covered by BOE: Principals' salaries of $15,000. Amount remaining to be insured is $16,450, or $8,225 apiece. They also assume some of the entertaining expenses (author/publisher meals) would be reduced by the disability of one of the principals, so they decide to buy $8,000/month each in BOE coverage.

One of the key motivating factors in the purchase of BOE coverage is its tax-deductible premium. Any type of business entity can take the full deduction for the amount of the policy premium. Benefits are taxable, but the money is being used to pay expenses that can still be deducted.

Most business owners do not have this product in their financial portfolio simply because they are unaware of its existence. It's time to go out and change that!

Disability Buy-Sell

> *"It is our responsibilities, not ourselves, that we should take seriously."*
>
> – Peter Ustinov

It's safe to say that if a business owner(s) does not have a BOE policy, then there is almost no chance that the disability buy-sell (DBS) has been addressed. This is bad news for the business, but good news for insurance agents: it's a large market.

Business owners have probably been approached about a buy-sell arrangement, but may or may not have acted on it. According to a 2000 American Business Family Survey, 75% of small businesses do not have a succession plan.[75]

As noted earlier in this section, asking an owner about the buy-sell agreement gives you two paths to potentially follow. The first is if no buy-sell agreement is in force. Obviously, the importance of this document must be stressed and both life and disability needs addressed. There are several reasons to establish a buy-sell agreement: retirement, a guaranteed market, surviving owners' future, reassurance for creditors and other partners, succession planning in the event of life and/or disability, and establishing a business valuation method.[76]

The second route for you is if there is an agreement in place. Does it have a provision for disability? If so, it is funded? How is the business going to come up with the money to buy the disabled owner out, especially if that owner was a strong contributor to the company's bottom line? If not, why not? Why address only the potential death of the business owner when disability presents a greater need before retirement? Studies show that a 42-year-old business owner is three and a half times more likely to suffer a disability than death before age 65.[77]

Consider the scenarios of a disabled business owner. A disabled business owner can continue to collect salary and profits while not actively contributing to the firm. A replacement might be found that is costing money. The disabled individual becomes more conservative about business practices to protect his or her investment. A disabled majority-shareholder-owner might decide to sell out to someone who would become the new controlling partner. Creditors and suppliers may become nervous, especially if the disabled owner was a key element to the business enterprise.[78] Add in that the disabled owner's family may want to become more involved in the business to protect that interest, and you have several untenable situations for the healthy owners.

The problem here is that most business owners don't realize their interest in the firm is insurable. They are vulnerable, yet the issue is easily solved. Many business owners who own life insurance to fund a buy-sell arrangement in the event of death won't need much explaining to realize that they face the same (and arguably greater) problems should a catastrophic disability strike one of the owners.

In a partnership situation, with two owners, each can own the policy on the other. With three or more owners, the business entity is more often the owner of the policies, purchasing one on each, thereby avoiding the multiple policies involved when each owner buys several policies on the other owners.

This latter arrangement, the entity purchase, now may be subject to new Financial Accounting Standards Board (FASB) rules: Statement 150 to be exact. Here, the mandatory redeemable ownership share that is obligated to be bought back in the event of death, disability, or other reason in exchange for cash or other assets, may no longer be carried as equity on the company balance sheet.[79] This may be a good reason to involve the firms' attorney and/or CPA. The cross-purchase agreement, with its multiple policies, may be back by default for larger firms.

Insuring the owners' interest under a DBS policy can be done on either a lump-sum or installment basis. Most prefer the lump-sum, meaning the entire amount insured is payable on the previously elected trigger date, the end of the elimination period. No benefit period need be selected in this case. The elimination periods run from a minimum of 12 months (to likely assure that the disabled owner will not be returning to the business) to 18 and 24 months. Selecting the elimination period is similar to choosing the *benefit* period under BOE: at what point does it seem unlikely that the insured would ever return to work?

To keep policy premiums down, some owners may opt for the installment method, where the insurer spreads the payments out over a specified period, 12, 24, 36, or 60 months. The elimination period choices remain the same. Thus, at the conclusion of the elimination period, the buy-sell is triggered. The insurance company simply pays the money out over time. The payments continue regardless of a change in the insured's health.

The DBS policy, like its BOE business counterpart, is another way of breaking into the business market.

Key Person DI

The final disability business need that should be reviewed is Key Person DI. It is rarer than the previous two coverages, but could be important to a firm.

Key people that have no ownership in the business are more difficult to find these days, which explains the relative obscurity of this product. Yet, identification and insuring of a key person is often done for life insurance. Why not as a protection against the threat of disability?

A key person to any firm is one whose absence would affect bottom line revenue. Insuring a key employee for personal DI may not directly help the business. It could satisfy sick pay plan funding, and it will certainly pay necessary personal expenses for the individual and family, but the business will still be out the aforementioned revenue.

This is where Key Person DI comes in. It indemnifies the business, not the individual insured, during that person's disability. This at least gives the *business* money to either find a substitute, pay overtime to healthy employees pinch-hitting in the star's absence, or to help pay bills that needed those lost profits.

This is another short-term coverage, like BOE, where the elimination period is early—30 or 60 days—and the benefit period is not lengthy—12, 18, or 24 months. The amount insured is generally a multiple of the insured's salary: 1 or 2 x income.

You'd probably rank this last in order of need fulfillment behind sick pay, BOE, and DBS essentials. That doesn't mean the need isn't there, and you will find it out when you complete the business fact finder/proposal sheet.

Closing The Sale

"Winning is a habit. Unfortunately, so is losing."

– Vince Lombardi

At this point, you've done all you can to motivate a previously uninterested and uninformed prospect to take action to protect income—be it personal or business. You've identified the need and proposed the most suitable answer. If the solution involves insurance, you have the further challenge of overcoming the usual objections that essentially all come down to the same thing—affordability.

In response to this, you've even altered some of the design components of your proposal as suggested in the previous pages, to come within the client's budget. While cost will always be an issue, think about this: if the client is struggling a bit to come up with money to pay a reasonable premium for DI coverage, how bad will the situation be financially when *no* money is coming in during a disability?

Altering coverage is OK to do, but remember the priority order: choosing between total and residual disability definitions based on the type of work a person does and how that individual is paid; elimination period to 90 days; benefit period (5 years vs. age 65); and, lastly, the amount of the monthly benefit (coming down to only the absolutely critical expenses that have to be paid). I've always quoted the maximum coverage available, since it is based on current income and is still less than the person takes home today. As one veteran agent put it recently, "When I hear someone question the validity of buying the maximum amount of disability coverage available, I remember that I have never spoken with a disability claimant who thought that he had more than he needed."[80]

One of the best final motivators for an individual is a third-party testimonial. It's always good to have that extra aid in your briefcase as these stories help the prospect to hear about what happened to others who became disabled and have had to battle through it.[81] You may have some of your own examples and your client may have heard about someone that has been disabled. You are always welcome to use the stories printed in this book to assist, including the one reprinted below:

> "The headline read, 'Man Critically Hurt in Hunting Accident.' As I read on I discovered that 'the man' was my client. He had climbed a tree to get a better view, slipped and fallen to the ground. The tragic result was paralysis from the waist down. His vocation was farming. Several days later I visited my friend and client. We both knew he would never be able to farm again. He asked about his insurance and I explained that all of his life insurance had a waiver of premium. In the event he could no longer earn a living, no further premiums would be required and the policies would continue to accumulate cash values. 'That's good,' he said, 'but what about replacing my income.' I had to tell him he had no coverage. He asked why I had never suggested it. There was no appropriate answer. All I could say was sorry for failing to do so. My friend passed away recently. He had, however, lived many years after the accident, restricted to a wheelchair. His wife is a terrific person who drove a school bus to keep the family together and provide the basic necessities. This event was a career-changing experience. Never again would I fail to point out the need for disability income insurance."[82]

You will not convince every prospect to whom you make these sales presentations. Even Serena Williams loses a tennis match every once in a while. You've still uncovered a need and planning ahead is crucial, so you can take the next step with the form reproduced below. It is both an excellent financial reference tool should disability strike this prospect and also another attempt at having the individual reconsider the self-insured route.

Figure 2.4

FINANCIAL FUNDING ALTERNATIVES IN THE EVENT OF DISABILITY[83]

Client's Name: _____ Date-of-Birth: _____

Types of savings/investment plans you now own: _____
_____

Of these, do any have fulfillment provisions in the event of a total or residual disability?
_____

How much are you currently contributing to your savings and investment programs on a regular basis?
_____

How do you feel about managing your investments in the event of a disability?
_____
_____

If you were to manage your own investments, how important would it be to provide a hedge against inflation now and in the event of a disability? _____

What percentage of your invested assets would you wish to deplete in the case of a disability?
_____

What percentage of your assets would you like to maintain as liquid in the event of your disability?
_____

In the event of a disability, how would you rank these financial priorities?

Savings and investment for education	Amt: $_____	Rank _____
Savings and investment for retirement	_____	_____
Savings and investment for parents' long term care/income needs	_____	_____
Estate creation or family security in the event of death	_____	_____
Overhead expenses of your business	_____	_____
Overhead expenses of your household	_____	_____

_____   _____
Signature of individual   Signature of agent/advisor

    _____   _____
    Date   Date

The answers to these questions further underscore the need to address these questions up front, not after a disability occurs, when there is managed chaos, at best. It may demonstrate to the prospect that the savings and investment programs are not nearly where they should be to provide a steady income for a number of years. It will also expose some of the financial sacred cows—education, retirement—that most people refuse to touch.

Disability is not an easy item for which to budget. No one knows when disability will occur—tomorrow, the day after, next week, next month, next year, or several years from now. Time may be very much of the essence in putting aside enough dollars to self-insure this risk. If only we had a crystal ball, or at least a working Ouija Board.

Will this form increase your closing sales ratio? Sure, and so might this form, the final sign-off by the prospect that, while the need is understood, there will be no action taken today. This is the Disability Income Waiver Form and it may help to dissuade those litigious individuals who become disabled, have no income and are looking for someone to blame. It can also help close a sale as some people are going to be reluctant to waive liability here.

Figure 2.5

I, _____, acknowledge that _____ (hereinafter, "the agent") has alerted me to the potential loss of income in the event of a disability. The agent has urged me to purchase a disability income policy to insure myself against the potential economic loss as a result of said disability as it is the most suitable solution available to fulfill this need.

Regardless of the above, I choose not to apply for a plan of disability income protection at this time. Therefore, I release my agent from any liability in the event that I do become disabled from a sickness or an accident.

I do not expect the agent to contact me in the future regarding the purchase of a disability income policy. I hereby agree to contact the agent and/or another insurance professional if I decide to consider the purchase of disability income coverage in the future.

_____   _____
Signature   Witness

Date: _____   Date: _____

These forms reprinted above are not "tricks of the trade." The first form is a legitimate way of identifying an income strategy following a disability when no insurance funding vehicle is present. The latter document is for the agent's protection. There have been countless lawsuits for the last three decades filed against agents and other financial advisors who do not make disability insurance a part of the person's financial portfolio. Do not make the mistake of overlooking these forms. If they serve to help close a sale, terrific!

If you've convinced your prospect to make an offer to the insurance company, then it's time to review the insurer underwriting process and what it entails for you and your client.

Underwriting

> "Virus is a Latin word used by doctors to mean your guess is as good as mine."
>
> – Bob Hope

Underwriting. The necessary evil of insurance. At least that's one of the more re-printable things agents say about the policy approval process. But you can't have it both ways. You have told the prospect (that you hope to make a client) that you couldn't sell a policy the day you presented your DI proposal. You could, however, complete an application to make an offer to the insurer to see if their consent could be obtained.

In truth, you wouldn't want the carrier's underwriting department to use a rubber stamp on your applications, a system that could easily be automated. Insurers are supposed to take risks, but not foolish ones. Adding a large number of unhealthy insureds to the company's block of business does no one any good in the long run. We've already proven that as an industry—let's learn from this bit of history. Agreed?

Disability is a chance. It might happen; it might not. The underwriter has to decide if the applicant's conditions add up to odds that are tipped heavily in favor of the individual. If they don't, the policy will be issued on some basis. If the risk is too great, then another strategy must be adopted to provide funds in the event of an injury or illness.

You have asked some medical questions to the applicant already. If there is some history present, then *at that time* you should advise the person that this health information may adversely affect the benefits that may be issued. It's not the time to be the complete optimist. Your prospect is making an offer to the insurer, and the insurer will likely be coming back with a counteroffer. When it arrives, you and the applicant can then discuss it at length and decide what the course of action should be.

These are challenging days for underwriters. America's love for the television has outdone the fitness craze. Forego the balanced diet in favor of the latest food fad that promises quick, sizable weight loss in less than three weeks. The average American would drive his car to the bathroom if the door was wide enough. Heart, circulatory, and joint problems abound, and these factors all contribute mightily to a potential disability.

Companies are also aware that there is a trade-off from underwriting too conservatively. Sure, profit margins can improve in going by the book, but if sales are flat or diminishing (as was the case during much of the 1990s), the long-range prognosis for profitability may not be that rosy. There is a balance, and the underwriter often has the key task of finding it.

Overall, DI business is issued under much closer medical and financial scrutiny than ever before. Some companies require blood testing of some form on all business, and some seek financial documentation on all applicants.[84] The underwriting departments today employ RNs and CPAs to help sort through the intricacies of health and money to better assess the risk.

Tools of the Trade

Medical Underwriting: Bodily fluids. Most carriers require a blood profile and a urine specimen for all ages, policies, and benefit levels. For an underwriter, this generally beats an Attending Physician's Statement (APS) since the numbers will tell a lot about a person's current state of health. Hence, it's a must. For the very high benefit levels, the insurer will go to the trouble of doing a full paramedical exam and, in some cases, an electrocardiogram. All of these tests can be done at the applicant's convenience: at home, the office, or even the ballpark. The APS is not an antiquated instrument, either. The more recent the visit, the more extensive the medical history, the more likely the order. The underwriter will assemble all of this information, consult with the RN and the MD on staff, and decide on the best issue (or not) possible. Check with your individual DI insurers for their specific rules.

Build chart: Most insurers use a height and weight chart. This section has already noted the difficulty in assessing weight from a field underwriter's perspective. We often simply take the applicant at their word. That's because DI insurer height and weight charts are relatively generous. Here's an example of how one insurer sets out their chart, giving you the range of weight for each height at which a standard issue can be expected (if there is no other history), and the points at which ratings will be assessed on issue.[85]

	Build		Percentage Rating		
Height	Standard Rating	25%	50%	75%	100%
5'0"	107-171	180	194	204	209
5'1"	109-176	185	199	209	214
5'2"	112-179	189	203	214	219
5'3"	115-184	194	208	219	225
5'4"	118-189	199	214	226	231
5'5"	121-195	205	220	232	237
5'6"	124-200	210	226	238	244
5'7"	128-206	216	233	245	251
5'8"	131-211	222	238	251	257
5'9"	134-216	227	244	257	263
5'10"	138-222	234	252	265	271
5'11"	141-228	239	257	271	278
6'0"	146-234	246	265	279	286
6'1"	149-239	252	271	285	292
6'2"	153-246	258	278	293	300
6'3"	157-252	265	285	300	308
6'4"	162-260	273	294	310	317
6'5"	166-267	281	302	318	326
6'6"	171-276	290	312	328	336

For those whose weight is over the 100% rating, there is little chance that the policy will be issued. Ratings may also go up (or, in rarer circumstances, down) depending on other medical history involved. There may also be some modification of the elimination and benefit periods.

It's important to know that the days of you hearing about reasons for coverage adjustments due to medical history are over. In the new HIPAA (Health Insurance Portability and Accountability Act of 1996) world of privacy protection, information about a counteroffer or decline to issue a policy can be sent to the individual directly or, more likely, to the individual's personal physician. Unless the client tells you what's up, you will only know the case is rated, contains an exclusion rider or has been altered or declined.

Financial Underwriting: Can you say "tax return"? At some point in the 1980s, a few claims examiners began pointing out to the underwriters that there were some inaccuracies in statements of income on the application and that far more coverage was issued than was justified. Some of this was normal confusion: writing down gross income instead of gross income *after* business expenses but before taxes. Others were mistakes of delusion—the hope that the income would be at the level signed off on by the end of that particular year. Still more was the result of a phenomenal earnings year coinciding with the application, while times before and since were not nearly as flush. And, finally, there were the pushes toward the highest limit that could be written before anyone actually checked. So, federal tax returns are now used to verify all income. These documents are the usual suspects, depending on whether you are an employee or a type of business owner:

Form 1040: Individual Income Tax Return (that could include):

> Schedule C—Profit or Loss from Business
> Schedule E—Supplemental Income and Loss

Form 1065 Partnership Return (with supplemental schedules)

Form 1120: U.S. Corporation Income Tax Return

Form 1120S: U.S. Income Tax Return for an S-Corporation

Form W-2: Wage and Tax Statement

Balance Sheet: Required for DBS sales (along with Profit & Loss statement)

You simply turn these forms over to the CPAs in the underwriting department and they review to determine if you have the income (and the benefit it can buy) correct on the application.

Using tax returns has helped to eliminate the guesswork that was long part of the DI sale. Income was simply a number you used to determine the monthly benefit available. Now, you can legitimately ask for the tax returns as part of your personal or business fact finder. That will give you the sense that you are more accurately quoting what the individual will qualify for in terms of monthly benefit amounts.

There will be some applicants that won't want to give you their tax returns. Some people don't even like to share that information with other family members. This is fine. You can still ask them how much benefit they would like to have so that you can generate a proposal and, ultimately, an application. I carry an extra large mailing envelope with me that has the underwriter's name and address on it for the times that people are shy about their income information. I let them put a copy in the envelope and seal it and I never see it. Don't let it stall the sale. The underwriter will correct the benefit amount if it is not appropriate—and you've already informed the individual that this may happen.

Multi-life underwriting: There are some occasions where typical underwriting guidelines will be streamlined to enroll a large group. It might be an employer-employee situation or a sizable association. Here, individual underwriting is brought closer to group LTD, where there is very little done. The recognition here is that volume works into the theory of the "law of large numbers" and that the insurer will be receiving an appropriately balanced amount of good and bad risks reflective of the general population. Substantial costs are saved in this effort, also adding to the bottom line result. There might be one or two medical questions, an "actively at work" verification, and a set amount of benefits that can be issued on this basis.

Avocations: Unusual hobbies will catch an underwriter's attention if it presents additional risk. Stock car racing with Paul Newman or dancing with Janet Jackson during halftime of the Super Bowl are extreme examples. But there are those that love their parachute jumping, hang gliding, scuba diving, rock climbing, and weekend flights in their plane, and it could mean some changes to the benefits applied for depending on the extent these are practiced. These activities may simply be excluded from coverage. Watching your favorite sports team at the local pub is generally OK.

Types of counteroffers: Not all cases can be issued as applied for, although nearly 75% of the applications are typically not changed. For the others, here are some methods of issuing the policy in some manner:

Exclusion rider: This is language intended to eliminate the risk for the carrier for a certain medical condition. Backs are the primary culprit here: that pesky part of the anatomy where recurrence is a strong likelihood. The words associated with the rider are very specific, and there will be no disability coverage for it. This does not alter the rest of the contract and any perceptive insurance agent will truthfully advise the client that there are hundreds of other disabling conditions that are covered.[85]

Rating: There are medical conditions for which exclusionary language simply won't work, such as diabetes or (as seen above) build. It doesn't mean the insurer can't cover the risk, but it can't be at the same charge as a standard risk would pay. There is no exclusion here, only more premium to cover this particular individual. Ratings usually start at 20% and can range as high as 150% in exceptional cases, but usually the extra premium is limited to 100%.

Limited condition rider: This is a form of the exclusion rider and instead of eliminating the coverage entirely for a condition, the underwriter specifies under what circumstances there will be coverage for the medical problem. For example, an individual applies for coverage with a 90-day elimination period and an age 65 benefit period. The individual has had some flare-ups with a peptic ulcer that never seems to last that long, but could still present some extra risk. Rather than completely remove peptic ulcers from coverage, the underwriter offers the following: "coverage beginning on the 181st day and continuing for 2 years." This avoids the short-term claims that have been the issue so far, and also evades any long-term claim brought on by the ulcerative condition. This way, there is some coverage for the medical problem and, of course, standard coverage for all those other unhealthy possibilities that loom out there.

Benefit modifications: When there are a number of risks present and some of the other tools are not suitable for use, the underwriter has the option of changing the benefit design components. Increasing the elimination period, decreasing the benefit period, lowering the monthly benefit amount are all ways of addressing a risk while still being able to offer some kind of coverage. Sometimes, a rating can be used in conjunction with these changes. In any event, it is a counteroffer that you can review with your applicant.

Modified policy: Some insurers have a specific policy form they could use to offer to an individual who has multiple health conditions. The policy definitions are more conservative, the policy renewability is more restrictive, the policy benefits may be graded, going up gradually each year to an ultimate amount.[86] It is another way of offering coverage rather than simply not accepting the risk.

Again, underwriters are, to a certain extent, playing the averages here. They look at each specific individual, but often have to go by what the average person's medical condition prognosis is likely to be. This separates "insurance" medicine from your doctor's opinion. Your physician is treating you personally and may like your chances better than someone else with your similar symptoms. Underwriters can't really view it the same way. They have to stay within the pricing theory that certain conditions will have, on average, the same measurable results.

The insurance carrier considers individuals, for whom they have had to make such a counteroffer, "impaired" or "substandard" risks. I don't think I have to tell you not to use those words with your clients. They are not going to view themselves in those terms, and neither should you. Someone with a history of health challenges is obviously a greater risk to an insurer than a healthy person but, from the perspective of that individual, they see their risks in life as the same as everyone else. Cancer, stress, arthritis, diabetes, back trouble, or any other ailment does not define who a person is, so be sensitive to that feeling.[87] These individuals are aware of their problem and are coping with it, paying closer attention to their health, perhaps, than you. They understand the chances of disability quite well as they have already experienced it in some fashion. They may be pleased to be able to acquire DI coverage in any form.

The underwriter may send the modified policy with an offer to review the decision in a year or two. This means that the risk has a chance of improving, or that more time between the last occurrence and the next review will reassure the underwriter about the person's condition. This offer will not be made if the health history has little or no chance for positive medical progress. But if it is extended as part of the counteroffer, it is another positive note on which placing the case may turn.

Not every case will be issued as you and your client wish. But modification of the plan you sent in does not mean the coverage is any less valid. These are the individuals who, perhaps, need the coverage the most. Nothing has changed from when you identified the need. Placing of the policy is paramount in importance for this individual and family.

Claims

"Wisdom is what's left after we've run out of personal opinions."

– **Cullen Hightower**

In an earlier discussion of the definition of residual disability, you learned that it is important to understand what types of financial statements will be needed at claim time to determine income loss. This knowledge can speed up the handling and issuance of a check in the proper amount when your insured client needs it most—at claim time.

Your entire sales presentation—from identification of the need to the benefit design and taking of the application—has a purpose: to have a source of funds for an individual should they become disabled. You are anticipating a claim—even if it never happens. A claim is what the policy is about; it's why it was purchased. People don't buy this insurance hoping they will use it, but if something happens, they want to be able to count on it.

Today's good news is that many of your disabled clients have an outstanding chance to return to work. This is everyone's goal. The significant majority of disabled insureds can't wait to get back to work. The job somehow validates many people and not being able to work creates a sense of frustration that can seem much worse than the gripes they had about work before they became disabled. There's just so much *General Hospital* you can watch.

All this is to say that you sold the policy to have it be a source of dollars should a lengthy injury or illness occur. Now that it has, it's not a time to sit by on the sidelines; it's more appropriate for you to say, "Put me in, coach!"

> A Louisiana agent went the extra mile when he handled the DI claim of a manager for an oil field service company in the town of Lafayette, the unofficial capitol of Cajun country, and a city where oil is big business. In March 2001, the agent was referred by one of his client law firms to one of the city's oil field services firms with 50 employees, many of whom had been with this company for many years. The company wanted to design some group benefits for their key people. They didn't mind spending money on their managers, but didn't have as much to allocate for the rank and file. The oil business is cyclical and they wanted to keep their expenses to a minimum. A review of the firm's employee benefit program demonstrated a glaring need for LTD coverage. After completing a fact-finder and doing some research, the agent proposed a group LTD plan that paid disabled employees 50% of their salaries after a 90-day elimination period. The company's executives and managers received an additional 25% of salary in the event of disability. The company bought the plan in June 2001.
>
> During the installation of the plan, the agent met the firm's manager of wire line operations, a 45-year-old married with three teenagers. About three months after the program was in place, this same manager was diagnosed with esophageal cancer. He had treatments and appeared to have recovered, not going on disability. After being in remission for a year, the cancer reoccurred; this time, much worse. The manager went on disability leave and the agent began the process of establishing the claim even though the elimination period started after the 90th day of disability. The agent helped the family deal with the man's deteriorating condition and reassured them that the claims paperwork was well underway. He obtained statements from the claimant, employer, and physician. He packaged those documents together with a cover letter and made sure it went to the proper claims examiner. In March 2003, the insurer started paying the disabled manager's monthly benefit of $4,500 and continued to do so up until the man passed away three months later. The claim process went smoothly because the agent took the extra steps to be sure the paperwork was both complete and directed to the proper source.[89]

At the same time, these claims can be very complex. Do you know the pre-existing and fraudulent misstatement language in the policy and in your state's statutes? What do you say to a disabled client who tells you the insurer wants him examined by an independent medical doctor? Does the insured *and* the doctor need to complete a progress report every month?[90] Are you up on the policy language about the length of time the insurer has in evaluating a claim?

A claim is not a slam dunk. It's where you really earn your commission, if it happens. Do you know what a transferable skills analysis is? Would you know if it is appropriate based on the definitions of disability in the contract you sold? This type of review identifies the key abilities the disabled insured has and searches for other work that the insured might be able to do that will allow the person to return to a job and may effectively end the claim.

For example, a pulmonary technician at a hospital was unable to perform her job duties because of a degenerative spinal condition, the vocational rehabilitation consultant handling her case conducted a vocational review and assessment and was successful in helping the individual obtain employment as an asthma health educator.[91] When your total disability language is "unable to work at any gainful occupation" this is the type of job switching work that an insurer could do on behalf of the claimant. It's your job to be sure the insurer's resources that are available to the claimant are properly and adequately utilized.

Communication with the physician is essential. One question commonly misunderstood by physicians is, "When is the patient expected to return to work?", accompanied by a list of terms: "your occupation," "any occupation," "part-time," and "full-time." Many doctors, with limited time to complete the forms and little knowledge of policy language, often shoot from the hip and wind up submitting inaccurate information. For example, when asked to provide a date that the claimant will be back to work, the physician may, in error, insert the date that he or she will reassess your client.[92] This is why it's important to understand not only the contract language, but also the insurer's claims practices and its procedures. I've been to many seminars where I've had a full room listen to me about selling disability income, but many clear out when the person representing a disability insurer's claim department comes up to speak. Why? You are probably going to hear tips for assisting both client and carrier during a claim and it is information you should want to hear.

> For 2001, participating carriers reported that the average decision timeframe for new claims (business days from submission to decision) was 34.5 days for LTD and 5.9 days for STD.
>
> *Source: JHA, Inc. 2002 Disability Rate Study and Risk Management Survey*

There will be times when the details are too intricate—perhaps a policy buy-out offer, or a request for photocopies of income and activity statements—when the need for an attorney and possibly a CPA will be necessary for your disabled client. You may be asked to help find these resource people, so knowing who handles such matters in your area is part of the homework you can do, well before any claims occur.

There has long been a difference between group and individual claims practices, but the two are drawing closer together than ever before.

It only makes sense. Group carriers put much of their focus into returning the disabled employee to work with the same employer. Because of highly successful medical advances, and changes in the definition language of total disability, this will be the goal of individual DI insurers, too. A recent study shows that early intervention (proactive claims management) can return employees to work 20% sooner and save all parties—employer, employee and insurer—a significant amount of money.[93] So why not do it? As long as it is medically feasible, complies with policy language, and the employee and employer are willing, this type of claims practice will become more routine.

It is not news that disability insurers have taken some substantial hits in the last 15 years. Business written that was long considered hallowed—high earners with large amounts of coverage and correspondingly high premiums—started going on claim in unanticipated multiples. The tables reproduced below[94] give you an indication of problem areas that have necessitated more micro-management of claims, something you should be sensitive to as an agent. You have to believe that insurers want to pay legitimate claims, and also be aware that you will need to do some legwork at claim time to be sure your client's claim is properly and timely handled.

TABLE ONE

Actual to Expected Ratios by Elimination Period and Benefit Period 1990—1999

Elimination Period	ALL	Benefit Periods LIFETIME	TO AGE X	OTHER
Less than 30 days	87%	94%	73%	88%
30 days	86%	109%	97%	81%
60 days	70%	88%	71%	68%
90 days	125%	174%	118%	128%
More than 90 days	94%	140%	94%	92%

Note: "To Age X" is typically to age 65; "Other" is usually 2-year or 5-years.

TABLE TWO

Actual to Expected Ratios by State from 1990 to 1999

California	123%
Florida	123%
Other States	87%

As you can see, there is a legitimate financial reason that "lifetime" benefit periods do not exist any longer. It is also easier to see why California and Florida premium rates are higher than other parts of the country. Surprisingly, the 90-day EP experienced the worse results, yet remains the more popular EP choice by insurers. The 60-day EP performed the best.

Long before the events of September 11th, disability insurers were shoring up their claims departments to handle mental and nervous disorder and substance abuse claims. These types of claims began to emerge in the 1980s and while not nearly as frequent as musculoskeletal claims (back, etc.), their durations meant as much if not more claim money was being spent on conditions like severe depression, bi-polar disorder, and other psych-related claims. Disability insurers staffed accordingly, hiring clinical psychologists, psychiatric nurses, and social workers to assist in the evaluation of these claims.[95]

Terrorism on our own soil accentuated a newer disease: post-traumatic stress disorder (PTSD). Despite assurances from our political leaders that we can go about our normal lives, many people continue to shun flying, or travel of any kind. To experience disquiet or fear after a terrorist attack and anticipate future assaults is normal. But when do a disability carrier and the claims examiner draw a line between fear and true PTSD? Studies have shown that deliberate violence creates longer lasting mental health effects than natural disasters or accidents.[96] These considerations today have added more specialists to the claims team to try and assess the situation accurately. You, too, are a specialist: in helping your client furnish the proper information on a speedy basis to the insurer's claims handling area.

Communication—just as it is in conducting a sales presentation—is the key to success here. Comprehending the claims process will help to ensure that your disabled client's claim will be handled as accurately and judiciously as it can.

Placing the Policy

"The future will be better tomorrow."

– Dan Quayle

There are three scenarios after the underwriters are through reviewing your client's application offer for DI coverage:

1. A policy is mailed, issued as applied for.

2. A policy is mailed, with a counteroffer.

3. A letter explaining why no policy is being mailed arrives.

Let's look at each situation separately.

#1 – Issued as applied for: Break out the champagne, the policy is here. If you did your job properly, it's likely that this was a relatively quick process and the client has not had any memory loss about purchasing this coverage to fill a specific economic need. What you need to do now is to collect any outstanding requirements (money, papers to be signed) and review the key policy features with the insured.

Disability policies are lengthy and wordy and your client is not likely to plow through these pages unless there is an insomnia problem. But it is no less important to do so, and that's part of the policy placement process. Circle every benefit feature in the policy schedule page and policy itself where dollars would be paid. That includes total disability, residual disability, presumptive total disability, rehabilitation, waiver of premium and more. If possible—and in most cases it should be—write in the dollar amounts next to these provisions. For example, a $5,000/month policy would mean that you write $5,000/month next to the total disability definition; and % of $5,000/month in the residual feature. Calculate each dollar amount for the corresponding contract language.

These are your money provisions. You won't be delivering policy language should a claim arise; you will be bringing a check. Spending this time will help clarify for your clients what it is exactly that they have bought. You should also indicate here, as mentioned in your sales presentation, the total amount of possible dollars involved on a claim. Simply take the monthly benefit amount and multiply it by the number of months (or years) in the benefit period. It's not difficult to determine the number of years from your client's present age to age 65 if that is the benefit period selected and issued.

Claim forms are always enclosed with the policy. Review those with your client and make sure they see these documents are included with the contract. Point out any initial instructions on the form. More important, take your business card and clip it to the claim form with a note to call you should something happen.

Ask for referrals. Inquire as to who they might know who could benefit from the same type of analysis you have done for them. See if they can contact the person to let them know you will be calling them, or obtain a signed letter from the client to bring with you on your first appointment.

You may also be able to pivot from DI to long-term care during your policy placement review. Does your client have parents? Is the client someone who should also consider LTC? The two products are very similar in benefit parameters that it's often best to discuss it while the terms (elimination period, benefit period, definition of disability) are still fresh in their minds.

#2 – *Policy is mailed with a counteroffer*: As noted earlier in this section, these are individuals who already have health issues, but who should realize it and know how important a disability income contract can be. Note that there are many other medical conditions that are covered. If there is an offer to review the decision at a later time, make a copy for you and put it in your file for follow-up purposes. Believe it when I say the underwriting department is *not* going to contact you or your client in the future about the reconsideration. Stay in touch with your client to see if all is progressing well, health-wise.

You may also offer to "shop" the decision around a bit with other carriers to see if a better offer might be forthcoming. You will need to have a copy of the medical information if your client will give it to you, even in a sealed envelope. Some insurers look more favorably on certain medical conditions than others. Who is in a position to most likely know this? Your local DI brokerage agency is usually up to date on this type of information. High volumes of DI run through these offices, so they are aware of who is doing what in the medical and occupational arenas. Your client should put this coverage in force first, though, to be sure some coverage is in place in the event a disability occurs before your additional search is completed. The underwriting decision in hand may be the best offer your client receives, so it's best to pay for it and see what happens later.

This means you should conduct your "money provisions" review as outlined in the #1 scenario above. Ditto for referrals and the LTC sales transition.

#3 – *Declination*: These are never easy to take because it is probably unexpected. If you understood your medical underwriting guide correctly, you did not submit a case that was liable to be declined. Therefore, some more information has cropped up that you didn't know about, or underwriting guidelines suddenly changed for the worse for your client's medical condition. This means you will be delivering a letter—a copy of which will also be mailed to the client directly along, with any monetary refund of deposit made—instead of a contract.

There are two primary tasks to do now. First, you should refer back to the *Financial Funding Alternatives* form reprinted in this section for you as this will now identify the initial sources of money that the individual and family will have to look to in the event of a disability. This form is useful in organizing the financial information and asking the difficult questions that will have to be answered. Better to do this now before any disability strikes. It is not going to replace the value of a DI policy, and you may not feel up to doing it, but it is the right thing to attempt.

That being in place, you can move to your second activity—to contact the local DI brokerage house to see if they have placement suggestions. One company's decline may be a modified issue somewhere else. You don't know until you've tried. You may end up with referrals from these individuals simply because you made the extra effort and didn't simply disappear from the bad news.

Always treat the client the way you would like people to behave towards you under similar circumstances. You never know when this client may be in a position to help your career farther down the road.

That's how you work with a client. Part 3 of this book will focus on how you distinguish between the various product designs today.

FOOTNOTES

1. Richard Weikart, CLU, ChFC, "Speak No DI, Hear No DI, See No DI," *Advisor Today*, May 2002, p. 42.
2. "Shifting Priorities," *Advisor Today*, March 2002, p. 33.
3. "Disability Insurance," *Consumer Reports*, July 1999, p. 65.
4. Issue and participation limit chart courtesy of Standard Insurance Company.
5. Mark Amleigh, "Do a DI Needs Analysis to Uncover Need for Life or LTC Insurance," *National Underwriter*, Life & Health/Financial Services Edition, Cincinnati, OH, February 25, 2002, p. 8.
6. Source: Union Central Life Insurance Company Issue/Participation Limit Table, June 2002.
7. Ron Keller, "Tailoring a Disability Income Plan to Your Client," *Life Insurance Selling*, December 2002, p. 46.
8. Richard Weikart, CLU, ChFC, "Speak No DI, Hear No DI, See No DI," *Advisor Today*, May 2002, p. 40.
9. Richard A. Magro, FSA, CPA and Joel Kastin, CSA, "Individual Income Protection: A Growing Market, An Evolving Product," *Life Insurance Selling*, December 2002, p. 30.
10. Student limits courtesy of Standard Insurance Company.
11. This form was prepared collaboratively with Larry Schneider of Disability Income Resources, Inc., as was the Business Disability sheet reprinted later in this section.
12. Lawrence Ian Geller, "Why Not Allow Your Clients to Choose?" *HIU Magazine*, July/August 2003, p. 23.
13. Source: John Hewitt Associates, Inc. 2002 Disability Insurance Survey, as noted in *Employee Benefit Adviser*, June 2003, p. 12.
14. Source: Lord Bissell Brook, "State Temporary Disability Insurance: Non-Occupational Disability Laws," October 2002, and VPA, Inc. (www.VPAinc.com).
15. Paul Chavez, "Calif. Enacts Paid Family Leave," *Associated Press*, September 24, 2002.
16. Craig Gunsauley, "Workers' comp costs surge as claims drop," *Employee Benefit News*, September 15, 2003, p. 13.
17. Source: Lord Bissell Brook, "Workers' Comp," April 2000.
18. Donald T. DeCarlo, "The Courts Expand the Scope of Workers' Compensation AIDS Claims," *Lord Bissell Brook Newsstand*, April 2000.
19. Vincent Armentano, Esq., "Reinventing Return-to-Work," *Florida's Workers' Compensation Institute*, p. S-53, special issue of *Florida Underwriter*, published by The National Underwriter Company, Cincinnati, OH, August 2003.
20. Jesse A. Lipnick, M.D., "The Aging Work Force—More Problems for Workers' Comp," *Florida Workers' Compensation Institute*, p. S-69, special issue of *Florida Underwriter*, published by The National Underwriter Company, Cincinnati, OH, August 2002.
21. Cyrille Cartier, "Study: Most Plan to Work Into Their 70s," *Reuters News Service*, Sept. 23, 2003.

22. Source: U.S. Department of Labor.
23. Source: Railroad Retirement Board.
24. Marcy Gordon, "Study Finds Worker Coverage Lacking," *Associated Press*, April 23, 2001.
25. From the Social Security website: www.ssa.gov.
26. Source: *2005 Social Security Manual*, published by The National Underwriter Co, Cincinnati, OH.
27. "Supreme Court Upholds SSA's Right to Determine Benefits Eligibility," *Employee Benefit Plan Review*, May 2002, p. 13.
28. Allison Bell, "Claims Assistance Firms Get Social Security to Pay Its Fair Share of the Disability Benefits Bill," *National Underwriter*, Employee Benefits Report, Life & Health/Financial Services Edition, Cincinnati, OH, April 15, 2002, p. S-28.
29. "Social Security Solvency Gains; Medicare Ebbs," *AARP Bulletin*, April 2003, p. 2.
30. "Expect Longer Life for Social Security, Medicare Funds," *Employee Benefit Plan Review*, May 2002, p. 47.
31. Allison Bell, "Filling Disability Benefit Gaps," *National Underwriter*, Life & Health/Financial Services Edition, Cincinnati, OH, December 22/29, 2003, p. 14.
32. W. Harold Peterson, "DI Important for Cash Flow Replacement," *National Underwriter*, Life & Health/Financial Services Edition, Cincinnati, OH, April 4, 2000, p. 23.
33. "Do You Have Enough Disability Coverage?" *Kiplinger.com*, October, 2002.
34. "Smart Decisions Provide for a Family," www.life-line.org, 2003.
35. Allison Bell, "Boomers and Disability Insurance: An Uphill Education," *National Underwriter*, Life & Health/Financial Services Edition, Cincinnati, OH, January 26, 2004, p. 19.
36. Source: Principal Financial Group.
37. Mike E. Evans, CLU, ChFC, "Everything Rests on Income," *HIU Magazine*, May 2000, p. 65.
38. "Older Americans Month: MetLife Analysis Reveals Most Common Disabilities Among Older Employees," *Business Wire*, May 14, 2003.
39. Darius N. Lakdawalla et al., "Are the Young Becoming More Disabled?" *Health Affairs*, January/February 2004, p. 168.
40. This idea courtesy of W. Adam Clatsoff, CLU, ChFC, CFP, RHU, *Adam's World radio show*, Coral Springs, Florida.
41. Donald Jay Korn, "Disability Disinterest," *Financial Planning*, February 2001, p. 71.
42. Allison Bell, "Even Affluent Boomers Need Adequate DI," *National Underwriter*, Life & Health/Financial Services Edition, Cincinnati, OH, November 24, 2003, p. 17.
43. "Debunking Misconceptions About the Need for Income Protection," *HIU Magazine*, May 2003, p. 17.
44. Douglas I. Friedman, "Agents Need to Make Disability Planning A Priority With Clients," *National Underwriter*, Life & Health/Financial Services Edition, Cincinnati, OH, March 5, 2001, p. 17.
45. Patricia Metzner, "Agents Need to Instill Realistic Expectations," *National Underwriter*, Life & Health/Financial Services Edition, Cincinnati, OH, March 5, 2001, p. 8.
46. W. Patrick Cunningham, CLU, ChFC, MSFS, "Lessons From Association Disability Coverage," *Life Insurance Selling*, January 1999, p. 76.
47. Brad Parks, "In DI, It's Full and Accurate Disclosure of Ailments That Counts," *National Underwriter*, Life & Health/Financial Services Edition, Cincinnati, OH, November 12, 2001, p. 11.
48. Application questions example courtesy of Principal Financial Group, 2004..
49. Source: JHA, Inc. *2002 Disability Rate Study and Risk Management Survey*.
50. Donald Jay Korn, "Taking Care of Business," *Financial Planning*, April 2003, p. 52.
51. Michael F. Greco, "In Sickness and Health," *Financial Planning*, October 2003, p. 111.
52. Richard A. Dulisse, CLU, ChFC, MSFS, LUTCF, "Insured Salary Continuation Plans," *AdvisorToday*, November 2002, p. 20.

53. Michael F. Greco, "In Sickness and Health," *Financial Planning*, October 2003, p. 111.
54. "Retention seen tougher in '04," *Employee Benefit News*, October 2003, p. 11.
55. Gary E. Meyers, "Live to Work, Work to Live," *Benefits Selling*, June/July 2003, p. 21.
56. Allison Bell, "Health Costs Could Shrink DI's Piece of Pie," *National Underwriter*, Life & Health/Financial Services Edition, Cincinnati, OH, April 3, 2000, p. 6.
57. Elizabeth Sniegocki, "Bottom Line on Business Insurance," *Florida Underwriter*, published by The National Underwriter Company, Cincinnati, OH, August 2003, p. 24.
58. Source: *USA Today*, September 4, 2003, p. 1B.
59. Source: Watson Wyatt, as reprinted in *Employee Benefit Plan Review*, March 2000, p. 17.
60. Kevin Sweeney, "Time Off, Disability Become Greater Cost Concern for Employers," *Employee Benefit News*, April 15, 2003, p. 11.
61. Allison Bell, "Employers Not Getting DI Pitch from Brokers," *National Underwriter*, Life & Health/Financial Services Edition, Cincinnati, OH, March 20, 2000, p. 1.
62. Source: *Disability Newsletter*, November 2002, Milliman USA publication, page 1.
63. Karen Trumbull English, "Where Does Disability Insurance Fit on the Health Productivity Continuum?" *National Underwriter*, Life & Health/Financial Services Edition, Cincinnati, OH, June 23, 2000, p. 58.
64. Sharon K. Moorhead, "Planning Ahead Can Help," *Florida Underwriter*, published by The National Underwriter Company, Cincinnati, OH, August 2003, p. 6.
65. Mark Ameigh, "What DI Producers Need To Succeed in Multi-Life," *National Underwriter*, Life & Health/Financial Services Edition, Cincinnati, OH, March 1, 2004, p. 26.
66. Kevin Sweeney, "Study Finds LTD Claimants Vulnerable to Job Loss," *Employee Benefit News*, September 15, 2003, p. 30.
67. Stephanie Armour, Michelle Kessler, "USA's New Money-Saving Export: White-Collar Jobs," *USA Today*, August 5, 2003, p. 1B.
68. Don Schamay, "Cross-Sell Opportunity: Add DI to the Long Term Disability Sale," *National Underwriter*, Life & Health/Financial Services Edition, Cincinnati, OH, February 25, 2002, p. 5.
69. Michael Schrage, "Cafeteria Benefits? Ha! You Deserve a Richer Banquet," *Fortune*, April 3, 2000, p. 274.
70. Source: *Life Insurance Selling*, April 2003, p. 56.
71. Daniel D. Skwire, FSA, "Worksite Marketing of Disability Insurance," *Disability Newsletter*, November 2002, p. 1.
72. Barry Higgins, "Don't Forget Disability in Small Business Plans," *National Underwriter*, Life & Health/Financial Services Edition, Cincinnati, OH, September 15, 2003, p. 4.
73. Pauline Lucas,CLU, ChFC, RHU, "Protecting Small Businesses from Disability," *AdvisorToday*, web exclusive, April 2004.
74. Laura Martin, "Protecting Business Interests with Disability Insurance," *HIU Magazine*, December 2002, p. 50.
75. Bob Dehais, CLU, ChFC, LUTCF, "The Benefits of Using Disability Insurance in a Buy-Sell Agreement," *National Underwriter*, Life & Health/Financial Services Edition, Cincinnati, OH, January 5, 2004, p.14.
76. Patrick Lang, JD, "Six Key Reasons For a Buy-Sell Agreement," *National Underwriter*, Life & Health/Financial Services Edition, Cincinnati, OH, September 23, 2002, p. 8.
77. Bob Dehais, CLU, ChFC, LUTCF, "The Benefits of Using Disability Insurance in a Buy-Sell Agreement," *National Underwriter*, Life & Health/Financial Services Edition, Cincinnati, OH, January 5, 2004, p. 14.
78. Mark Ameigh, CLU, "Consider Disability Scenarios in Buy-Sell Planning," *National Underwriter*, Life & Health/Financial Services Edition, Cincinnati, OH, February 24, 2003, p. 14.
79. Ted Kirchner, JD, CLU, "Will FASB 150 Have a Chilling Effect on Entity Buy-Sell Plans?" *National Underwriter*, Life & Health/Financial Services Edition, Cincinnati, OH, September 15, 2003, p. 42.

80. Lawrence Ian Geller, "Why Not Allow Your Clients to Choose?" *HIU Magazine*, July/August 2003, p. 23.
81. Larry Schneider, "8 Steps To Selling Disability Insurance," *National Underwriter*, Life & Health/Financial Services Edition, Cincinnati, OH, September 23, 2002, p. 60.
82. Thomas J. Wolff, CLU, ChFC, "Disability Income Must be a Part of Every Plan," *AdvisorToday*, April 2004, The Back Page column.
83. A version of this form was first developed by John Hancock Life Insurance Company in the 1980s and is still quite useful today.
84. Daniel D. Skwire, FSA, "New Underwriting Solutions for Individual Disability Income Insurance," *Disability Newsletter*, March 2001, p. 3.
85. Build chart is courtesy of Standard Insurance Company.
86. John G. Micheli, CLU, "Understanding Underwriting Concerns is Key to the Disability Sale," *National Underwriter*, Life & Health/Financial Services Edition, Cincinnati, OH, March 31, 2003, p. 12.
87. Mark Ameigh, CLU, "If a DI Prospect has a Health History, Consider Impaired Risk DI," *National Underwriter*, Life & Health/Financial Services Edition, Cincinnati, OH, November 18, 2002, p. 14.
88. Brad Parks, "Guidelines to Follow When You Have an Impaired Risk DI Client," *National Underwriter*, Life & Health/Financial Services Edition, Cincinnati, OH, November 18, 2002, p. 17.
89. Chuck Jones, "Anatomy of a DI Claim," *AdvisorToday*, Web exclusive, October 2003.
90. Arthur L. Fries, RHU, "25 Questions to Ask Before and After Your Client Files a Disability Claim," *HIU Magazine*, July/August 2002, p. 15.
91. John O'Hara, Craig Seminara, "Selling the Back End of Income Insurance: Resources At Claim Time," *Life Insurance Selling*, p. 46.
92. Arthur L.Fries, RHU, "How Agents Can Help Their Clients Get Disability Claims Paid," *National Underwriter*, Life & Health/Financial Services Edition, Cincinnati, OH, November 18, 2002, p. 27.
93. Ken Arruda, "Early Intervention = Substantial Savings," *National Underwriter*, Life & Health/Financial Services Edition, Cincinnati, OH, March 5, 2001, p. 29.
94. Robert W. Beal, FSA, "IDI Claim Incidence Update," *Disability Newsletter*, November 2003, p. 1.
95. Hal Stucker, "Disability Insurers Tighten Up on Psych Claims Management," *National Underwriter*, Life & Health/Financial Services Edition, Cincinnati, OH, March 15, 2000, p. 7.
96. Linda Beckman, "Handling Disability Claims in Uncertain Times," *HIU Magazine*, May 2002, p. 55.

PART THREE:
WHICH PRODUCT SHOULD I CHOOSE?

"Choice has always been a privilege of those who could afford to pay for it."

– Ellen Frankfort

Key Concepts

1. DI products are being unbundled to offer more options, increase flexibility, and lower premium costs.

2. In disability sales presentations, focus on the "money provisions" of the contract; those features for which you can indicate the benefit potential.

3. Total disability definitions range in degree of restriction by the number of eligibility tests applied during a claim.

4. Residual disability or income replacement may have more widespread applicability and may make more economic sense to the client.

5. A Guarantee of Insurability rider is a must for any disability sales presentation.

6. A Business Overhead Expense plan is a reimbursable, not an indemnity, policy.

7. Disability Buy-Out coverage is typically purchased in a lump-sum amount.

8. Key person DI is not easy to find, but is the only DI policy that pays benefits directly to a business.

9. Payroll deduction products are often streamlined for simplicity purposes in a voluntary worksite marketing sale.

10. Group STD and LTD sales are on the rise as employers attempt to upgrade their employee benefit portfolios.

11. Critical illness insurance directly addresses people's greatest fears: catastrophic disability.

The concept of income protection is, I believe, easy to understand. There are always mental hurdles to clear, be it affordability, insurability, or the willingness of many to simple gamble that it will never be an issue for them.

But these are all manageable, and are not usually the reasons why agents, planners and advisors shy away from the disability income sale. It is what they view as the complexity of the product that is often the obstruction that leaves many consumers unaware of this coverage and vulnerable to an injury or illness.

Is the product really so complex, or is it simply too vague? Former President Clinton taught us that even the word "is" can be misconstrued, so the language in a DI policy is a veritable wilderness of verbal traps. Varying definitions are jam-packed into a dozen or so pages, an array of qualifiers that leave many wondering about the "what if's" of a disability.

Life insurance, by contrast, is not as intricate. Death, and the resulting certificate attesting to it, is straightforward. Experience has taught that the nature of disability is anything but.

Two people. Same disability. One is a salesperson, the other an electrician. Both are in car accidents, fracturing several bones, and are hospitalized. Each is in rehabilitation, with physical therapy prescribed. The salesperson returns to work within a month, sore, with two separate casts on, but able to drive. The electrician, though at the same point of recovery as the salesperson, cannot wield the tools of the trade, and the inability to work continues. This will be true for another three months.

Disability can be so dramatically different for two people with the same condition or two individuals in the same line of work with different health problems. This is why the language of a disability policy is often intentionally vague. The open-endedness of some of the definitions makes it impossible to answer some of the more specific questions a prospect might ask. This lack of clarity, while frustrating, is well intended. Language that is too precise may not leave any wiggle room for allowing a claim to continue if it takes some unexpected path.

And it will. You can be sure of that. No disability is ever the same, and each case is individually treated.

But this is not a reason to avoid discussing this risk with any working consumer. While there is some policy language to avoid, it is important to approach DI sales with the idea that if a disability is legitimate and causes an economic loss, trust in the insurer to do the right thing.

Carriers pay out millions in claim benefits each year. This money only goes to prospects that had the opportunity to buy the coverage. There are product and definition choices to make and this section of the book will attempt to sort those out simply for you. Don't let the mass of words and phrases put you off the vital task of providing income protection.

DI Unbundled

Over the past few years, disability income insurers have taken to unbundling the disability income product to allow more choice and flexibility for the consumer. While this complicates an already multifaceted product, it has arguably resulted in further opening DI sales opportunities for you.

Unbundling gives you the ability to market to a wider range of income levels. It also gives you a tool to do a more thorough job by identifying the client's needs and then building a DI policy to meet those needs.[1] This unbundling can result in finding more ways to sell a product to fill the need, both from the agent's and underwriter's perspectives.

It also means that in comparing any disability income product, you will have to look at both the price and the features. Looking at premium alone won't help you unless all the features of both plans are identical. Each provision has a cost and it will be important (and not necessarily difficult) to sort out the various parameters and definitions of a plan before reviewing the price.

> Total new DI sales premium, including guaranteed-renewable, non-cancelable, and Buy-Sell, totaled almost $321 million from 19 insurers writing the bulk of DI premium in the United States. 2003 in-force premium grew 3.8% over 2002, and in-force policies and benefit amounts also showed positive growth rates of 1.1% and 6.3% respectively.[2]

You will also be able to change these assorted features to stay within the prospect's budget. This section of the book will review the essential provisions of a disability plan and their variations that can be tailored to a specific client. These key elements will be a part of most DI sales, so once learned you will recognize the familiarity of the language and you will more easily see the patterns of their usage.

The Money Provisions

It has always been easier for me to explain disability income products to people when highlighting the "money provisions" of the contract. By this I mean the policy features that actually have a potential quantifiable claim amount to them.

This way the prospect can see the total potential dollars at stake. There's much more to a DI policy than the monthly benefit amount, and focusing on these money provisions illuminates this for the individual.

These include

- Total disability definition,
- Residual disability definition,
- Presumptive total disability provision,
- Waiver of Premium,
- Rehabilitation provision,
- Automatic Indexing, and
- Optional features.

The Money Provisions

Total disability: $1,800,000 potential (5,000 x 12 months x 30 years)

Residual disability: percentage of $1,800,000 potential based on loss of earnings

Presumptive total disability: $15,000 (due to waiver of elimination period)

Waiver of premium: annual premium cost x 30 years potential

Rehabilitation: Cost of rehab program in addition to benefits listed above

Automatic indexing: 3% of $5,000/month for 5 annual increases = $750/month x 12 x 25 years or $225,000 potential on simple basis; $796/month x 12 x 25 years or $238,800 potential on compounded basis

---

For example, if a 35-year-old person is considering buying a $5,000/month disability benefit, with a 90-day elimination period and an age 65 benefit period, the various policy definitions and provisions can now be illustrated with dollar signs, as follows:

Your policies may have more money provisions in them than those expressed above. What you have done is replace the language with dollars. This is, in essence, the point of the need you are filling. You are providing a funding vehicle to replace income. The two-dozen or so bound pieces of paper you deliver in the form of a policy will be transformed into cash at the time of claim. You are merely projecting the dollar potential of this protection.

Unbundling the product means that some of the provisions detailed above may be elected separately. This can help to keep the premium in accordance with the budgetary guidelines of the prospect. Whatever provisions remain after this work, the exercise remains the same, and helps someone see what they have bought so much easier than leaving them only with policy language that may not be clear.

It also makes the premium amount seem more reasonable in light of the benefit potential each policy represents. It's easy to see a $500,000 life insurance face amount and compare it to the premium. It's quite another to see the prospective value of $1,800,000 from a $5,000 policy, but that's the potential dollar amount that could be paid if the insured is disabled in the first year of owning the policy.

Keep the dollar transformation in mind as you read the policy language detailed in the next few pages. This portion of the book will explain how the definitions work, but it is the bottom line of monetary value that must be properly communicated to the prospect. Your sales interview up to the point of product selection has been focused on the dollars needed during a disability. By continuing in this vein throughout the process of choosing the right product, you will find the person's comprehension of the policy to be much higher.

THE MAJOR PRODUCT FEATURES

"When you make the finding yourself – even if you are the last person on Earth to see the light – you'll never forget it."

– Carl Sagan

Renewability

On the face page of the policy you bring back to your client is the contract's renewal provision. This indicates the terms under which the policy will be continued and what strings are attached to both the insured and the insurer. It's important enough to have on the front of the policy, so let's deal with it first.

There are two primary renewal provisions in individual disability income contracts. If your policy doesn't contain one of these two renewal definitions, then the odds are stacked in favor of the insurer, an unnecessary concession.

Guaranteed Renewable (GR): Under this policy provision, the insurer is required to continue the policy and its benefits in force as long as the insured pays premiums on time. This provision generally lasts until age 65.

The insurance company does have one option with this provision. It can increase premiums in the future, if it can (a) justify the rate hike to the state insurance department, and (2) rates are raised for all policies within a particular class. Because of this ability to increase premiums, the cost of this renewal provision is less than the non-cancelable version discussed below.

> New Guaranteed Renewable DI sales declined 2.9% in 2003, a minor change when compared to the 11.4% decline in 2002. Within the GR product line, personal DI premium sales decreased 3%, while Overhead Expense plans improved by 6.9%.
>
> – Source: JHA Individual Market Survey 2003

This type of renewal language has enjoyed a renaissance of sorts in the past five years as some insurers, burned by non-can claims results, sought to staunch the bleeding by reintroducing policy terms that gave them the opportunity to adjust premiums if claims experience went south on them. Many welcomed the return of this provision, part of the unbundling effect, where an individual could choose between this lower-cost (at least initially) feature and the more expensive, guaranteed premium non-cancelable parameter.

A word about the rate increases possible under a GR policy: they aren't scheduled nor are they likely to happen frequently. Actuaries still price the GR plans to last the full renewal period (to age 65) and will only adjust the premiums if experience turns out to be worse than expected.

Over the last couple of years, the new premium for Guaranteed Renewable-type DI policies has dropped, as consumers opted more for the non-can plan, and the rate guarantee that comes with it. Still, GR policies have their place, and in the world of voluntary payroll deduction sales, the worker earning $25,000 might find the price of the GR policy more affordable.

Non-cancelable (Non-can): This is the most liberal of the renewal choices. Non-can means, as it does with GR policies, that the carrier must continue to renew the policy for a stated length of time (usually age 65) as long as the premiums are paid by the insured on time. What sets it apart is that the premium *cannot* be changed throughout this guaranteed renewal period. Once purchased, the price will stay the same, a guarantee not found in other health insurance-type products.

Because of this guarantee, non-cancelable policies are the most expensive type of continuance provision.[3] But, if one can afford the premium, why not lock in the rate? That the premium you quote in your DI proposal cannot change for many years regardless of the insured's health, or, more importantly, the experience the insurer has for this policy series, is certain to appeal to many consumers.

Non-cancelable policies dominated (and for the most part still do) the individual disability market. Many are attracted to the rate guarantee, especially if it's affordable. While insurers brought out the guaranteed renewable provision as a "new" choice a few years ago, they were also making adjustments to the definitions and features of their DI policies as a reaction to poorer claims results. A higher comfort level with the policy language has led to a re-emphasis on the singularity of the non-can renewability, a buying consideration not available with other forms of disability-related coverage, be it long-term care, major medical, Medicare Supplement, or other health insurance-type plans.

> New Non-Can sales premium fell 0.8% in 2003, after a sharp increase in 2002. Within Non-Can, both personal DI and Overhead Expense premium declined less than 1%, 0.8 and 0.3% respectively.
>
> – *Source: JHA Individual Disability Survey 2003*

What happens with renewability after age 65? People are working longer than ever today, and even Social Security has raised their retirement age for full benefits to age 67 for many consumers. There are conditions in most policies to continue the coverage. Generally, the individual insured must still be working, must accept a new benefit period (usually 2 year maximum), pay a new, recalculated premium, and may even have to furnish evidence of both work continuance and income level. There is even some consideration being given to increasing issue ages to recognize the delayed retirement habits of today's older workers, so simply because the renewal provision terminates at age 65, it doesn't mean the coverage must cease.

Other Renewal Provisions: While the aforementioned two renewal provisions dominate the DI marketplace, you might find some other renewal language in group or association-type DI plans. Often called *conditionally renewable* plans, the insurer places additional caveats on the automatic continuation of coverage. These range from employment requirements (group) to membership status (association) in order to continue to have coverage under the plans. Group disability plans often have a rate guarantee period, such as 5 years. Association plans could be non-can as far as premiums are concerned, but may still require the insured to be a member on good standing to continue to be eligible to hold the contract. When reviewing one of these types of plans, be sure to read the renewal provision carefully to see what the conditions are to keep this policy on force.

Definitions of Injury or Sickness

To be eligible for any monetary benefits under the DI contract, there must be a disability. It seems obvious but, in any event, the insurer must define what constitutes this disability requirement. In DI plans, there are definitions for injury (or accident) and sickness (illness) to satisfy this need. If a person is injured or sick in some way, the disability clock is triggered under the policy and then it remains only to judge the depth of the disability in accordance with other definitions (more on this shortly).

Injury (or Accident): This is usually defined as "accidental bodily injury that occurs while the policy is in force." This covers the wide range of accidents that could occur. Even though this is the least likely disability (versus sickness), many prospects have a higher belief in this possible occurrence when considering buying DI because it can be an unexpected event that one can't anticipate. This is easier to justify the purchase of the coverage then considering the possibility of a future sickness.

Sickness (or Illness): A sickness is any illness or disease first manifested (makes itself known) while the policy is in force. It includes complications due to pregnancy or childbirth. It also includes normal pregnancy or childbirth after a disability period of 90 days. This definition covers both physical and mental conditions, although the mental portion of this definition could be modified, either in the policy or by a rider, limiting coverage to 24 months, and lowering the price of the policy as a result. (More on this in policy features/optional benefits.)

> Timing is everything. A client or prospect can insist on postponing a decision to buy DI insurance, only to regret it a week later. Or, timing could truly save someone's dignity and future. An insurance agent visited a store one day to discuss the benefits available to the employees under their elective benefits program. A 23-year-old stocker who had just finished his shift stayed late to talk to the agent. The agent explained that all depends on the ability to earn an income. The 23-year-old saw the wisdom in this and was surprised at the affordability of the premium. He completed an application that day, paid a deposit and went home. That journey home changed the young man's life, as he was involved in a serious auto accident that resulted in damage to his spinal cord and paralysis in his lower extremities. The insurer reviewed the application thoroughly, but there was no medical history that would otherwise prevent the issuance of the policy. Because the application had a deposit, the insurer was bound to issue coverage from that date and cover the accident. The 23-year-old is making solid rehabilitative progress, and is going back to school to be retrained. With the DI coverage, he knows his personal expenses will be covered and he can focus on the rest of his life.[4]

Definitions of Disability

Arguably the most important words in the contract are the definitions of disability that qualify an insured for claim benefits. An injury or illness triggers the examination of these definitions to see if eligibility can be established and payments made after satisfaction of the elimination period.

Oh, what a tangled web we weave! This is where the policy language causes migraines and people's eyes to glaze over. Each of the two primary definitions has a variety of possible forms, although their essential notion is easy to grasp.

This is the key to understanding these concepts. If you know the overall essential intent of the definition, the variations shouldn't throw you. These distinctions are a refinement of the original concept, in many cases narrowing down the qualification possibilities even further. This will become more apparent as you view each provision choice.

The two primary definitions are total and residual disability. These are often separate choices that one can select over the other based on the type of work and income earned and the likely course of one's disability when it happens.

These definitions may also be written together, a more expensive proposition but an opportunity to cover all possible disability contingencies that might arise and often in the most liberal way possible.

TOTAL DISABILITY

This benefit eligibility provision measures an individual's **physical** ability to perform work subsequent to an injury or illness. The key word here is "physical" as the insurance claims examiner will be measuring the claimant's capacity for work, to perform the duties of his own or, in some cases, another occupation.

Who should consider this type of disability definition? Remember that during your sales interviews, you asked your prospects to envision the probable course their own disability might take given their working circumstances. Highly specialized professionals, employees and manual workers are the people most likely to have situations where the measurement of physical ability is likely to be a more accurate analysis of the nature of their disability.

This would include employees whose income would not be cut back if they were able to return to work in any capacity following a disability; any working individual whose income would not be affected unless they were fully unable to work; any specialist for whom a disability that impairs their ability to work in their field would mean a substantial income setback; individuals whose jobs comprise physical labor that ordinarily requires a completely healthy demeanor in order to perform their tasks.

This type of policy is used in many group disability situations. To cover the rank-and-file employees of a large company, a "one size fits all" definition of the total disability variety usually works best for the majority of workers.

Generally, most total disability definitions have **two** tests that an insured would have to satisfy to become eligible for disability insurance benefits.

The first test measures your ability to work in your field. This definition language is generally phrased as "the inability to perform the duties of your occupation." Some policies might say the "substantial and material" duties, or the "important" duties, but it essentially all means the same for claims adjudication purposes.

Purchasing a policy where this is the **only** test of total disability is possible for certain professions. While expensive, there are certain high-earning, specialized individuals (CPAs, pharmacists, architects, executives, some MDs, and attorneys) who should consider buying the one-test definition. These highly trained people are earning an income that is likely not going to be replaced as adequately as they would like with a total disability income policy. If they are unable to work in their occupation, these motivated folks are more likely to go seek out another profession and try to work their way up to a reasonable earnings level as a supplement to their total disability claim payments that, when combined together, bring the disabled claimant back up to acceptable (to them and their family) income levels again.

This one-test definition is more commonly referred to as "own occupation" total disability, since it only measures your ability to perform in your job. It is popular with the professionals who can buy it because if they can't perform the activities of a demanding career due to a disability, they don't want to be denied benefits because they can work in another field.[5]

The second test can vary considerably. This alternative assessment might only be applied *after* a certain amount of time during which only the first test is used to measure disability eligibility. The most common periods of first-test-only definitions are 2 or 5 years, or maybe to a specific age like 50 or 55, with the second requirement then becoming a part of the claims analysis.

The second test has two primary wordings:

1. You are not engaged in any gainful occupation. This language does not measure your physical ability to work in another occupation, only whether you are actually doing so. If not, and you are still unable to work in your own occupation, you are eligible for total disability benefits. This gives the insured the option of personally electing *not* to work in another field if unable to return to his or her own profession without an effect on benefits.

2. You are unable to perform the duties of any gainful occupation by which you are suited based on education, training, experience, and with due regard to prior earnings. This is an ability test based on your projected physical recovery, not a choice as in #1. The claims examiners have more control here than the claimant as they would judge, based on medical records, whether the individual could return to a similarly lucrative although different field. If so, total disability benefit payments would cease. This language, however, does not allow an insurer to force you into "any work that exists in the national economy" as the Social Security definition of disability does. It must be reasonably based on past training and income. Reasonable is often purposely vague, but some insurers define it as paying at least 60% of former earnings. In the words of one agent, "insurers won't take a highly paid machinist and make him flip hamburgers."[6]

Prices for this type of coverage will vary depending on how restrictive the qualification language is in determining claim eligibility. Here's a quick summary, from highest to lowest cost:[7]

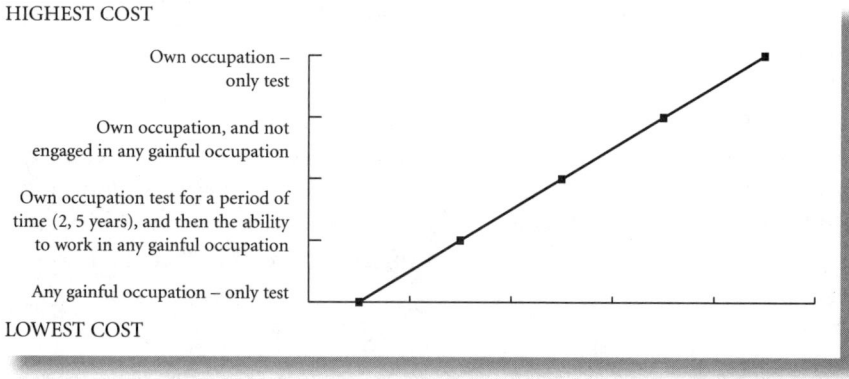

Most DI insurers give you several of these choices in helping a client design their DI coverage. Obviously, own occupation remains the definition most would like to have. Over the years, carriers have restricted who can buy it, and how much coverage can be purchased.

But the other definitions serve a purpose, too, and can keep the price of the policy down for the middle to lower income worker who needs the protection as much as the professional but has less discretionary money to play with in paying the premium. Few elect the any occupation definition, the least expensive language. Some occupations, due to their volatile and hazardous nature, may only be able to purchase that total disability choice.

Familiarize yourself with the definitions of the carrier(s) you represent. You will see some consistency and develop a comfort level with the various terms and their pricing.

Residual Disability

With the definition of total disability, you have a medical claim; with residual, it becomes a financial one.[8] This is a provision that mainly measures your loss of earnings after a disability, emphasizing your **economic** recovery rather than just your physical improvement. It may also be called *partial* or *proportionate* disability.

Residual disability was introduced to the individual disability market in the early 1970s and was developed as a response to a growing claim concern. The "own occupation" definition of total disability had dominated sales of the DI product for a number of years. But, in a claims analysis, its weakness was revealed. Claimants were experiencing periods of total disability and then returning to their own jobs. After all, this is where years of training had placed them and the first thought following a disability was how soon they could return to their familiar surroundings.

The own occupation definition made no allowances for this claims route. Total disability benefits were paid if the person couldn't work at all, or if they couldn't perform their own occupation, regardless of what else they did. But a limited return to that own occupation was not covered in this language.

At the time, there were short-term arrangements for this return, with half of the total disability benefit payable for up to six months. But this was proving insufficient and product designers went to work to solve this problem.

The result was residual disability – a longer term period of disability payments based on the individual's partial ability to work and earn an income. Most disabilities then and today are generally resolved by a successful return to work, and this definition both encourages this claims path and provides policy benefits that can make that return financially feasible.

This residual definition also addresses the individual who does not have a one-test own occupation definition of total disability. If they cannot perform their job ever again, but can pursue another career, they may no longer be able to meet the "inability to work in a gainful occupation" test. In this case, if residual disability was part of their policy, they could work in another job and the residual definition would then be applied.

Who should consider this type of definition? It is applicable for any worker who will suffer an income loss upon a return to work, and for whom it will take some time to achieve the earnings level that had been attained prior to disability. Self-employed, small business people especially fit this description.

Generally, residual disability policies will be of two kinds. Like the total disability definition, there may be either one or two tests to measure eligibility for disability benefits. The *income replacement* approach is based purely on one test – the calculation of income lost after an injury or illness has affected the person's ability to work. This one test determines income loss, typically requiring a minimum 20% loss of earnings following an injury or illness. An individual may be able to eventually return to work in a full capacity, but if earnings are still reduced, benefits are payable.

The other policy type is usually called *residual disability* and there are two tests to be eligible for benefits here. The first is income loss, as above. The second test is a physical one; that is, in addition to the minimum income loss, the disabled policyholder must also be unable to perform one or more of the important duties of one's occupation, **or** be able to perform all of the duties but on a less than full-time basis. Either one will satisfy the second test. This second requirement ensures that there is a correlation between a reduced ability to work and a loss of income.

There are a lot of variables to this residual or income replacement definition, and these are spelled out within the policy language. This is where some agents and advisors get bogged down and abandon ship. But these additional definitions are necessary in order to compute lost earnings. Otherwise, how would it be established? An example will help see the importance of this before we define the variables.

Month	Prior Earnings	Current Earnings	Loss of Earnings	X	Total Disability Benefit	=	Residual Disability Benefit
1	$5,000	$ 500	90%		$3,000		$3,000*
2	5,000	1,000	80%		3,000		3,000*
3	5,000	1,500	70%		3,000		2,100
4	5,000	2,000	60%		3,000		1,800
5	5,000	2,000	60%		3,000		1,800
6	5,000	2,500	50%		3,000		1,500
7	5,000	2,750	45%		3,000		1,350
8	5,000	3,000	40%		3,000		1,200
9	5,000	3,250	35%		3,000		1,050

*full total disability monthly benefit paid if earnings loss is at 5% - 80% of prior earnings.

What are the variables in the above calculation? There are: prior earnings, current earnings, loss of earnings, total disability benefit and residual disability benefit. We know what the total disability benefit is – in this example, $3,000 – and it would be paid if the individual was totally disabled. The residual disability benefit is a calculated amount, and it has already been defined above. What remains are three of the key pieces of the residual benefit determination.

Sure, it's more definitions, but they are critical to the formula. Let's define them.

Other residual definition considerations:

Prior earnings: Insurers will look back prior to your disability for a certain period of time (up to 60 months) to accurately measure your prior earnings. This is a key figure in the income loss calculation. This is a key number and the insured will want this figure established as high as possible. For most people, the most recent earnings history is likely to be the highest. So insurers check back over the 12 or 24 month consecutive period immediately before disability started. But this doesn't always accurately reflect earnings. What if last year's earnings were an aberration and didn't reflect the typical income year? Many insurers will give the insured a choice in selecting a longer look-back period if that will compute a higher figure and more accurately reflect the complete earnings history. Look-backs for 36 and 60 months are common. This means the insurer will use the best 24 consecutive month average out of the previous 36 or 60 months. The longer the look-back period, the better the chances are of having the highest prior earnings possible, although many will be satisfied with the recent 12 months income results.

In our example above, the prior earnings number established was $5,000/month.

Most DI insurers include an indexing feature for this prior earnings figure. Over time, that initially calculated number will less accurately reflect today's economic climate, so to help it keep pace, the amount is adjusted annually by the change to the Consumer Price Index. Thus, in the 13th month of a claim, prior earnings will be adjusted to allow for inflation. In some policies, this index is fixed at 3, 4 or 5%.

Current earnings: This is how new income after a return to work is measured. These earnings are all wages, fees, salaries, bonuses, commissions, pension and profit-sharing contributions, and deferred compensation payments less any normal business expenses.

When considering this definition, be sure and find out from the insurer how they measure income. Is it cash basis (income when received) or accrual (income when earned, but not necessarily in hand)? Many insurers offer you a choice of these accounting methods, and you can elect it at claim time. Both prior and current earnings will be determined using the same mode.

What type of records would you have to furnish to validate the income loss? This is an important question, because income loss determination will require earnings records. It is better to understand up front what your clients will be asked for, so that their accounting will be set up as the insurer may ultimately require during a claim.

Whereas prior earnings is a static figure (at least for the first year), current earnings will vary up and down. In our example above, earnings rose steadily. This is not always the case, but for the purpose of seeing how the residual benefit is derived, it will suffice.

Loss of earnings: This is the calculation made by subtracting current earnings from prior earnings. This will yield a percentage loss of earnings. In the seventh claim month in our example, the current earnings of $2,750 are deducted from prior earnings of $5,000 for a $2,250 result. This $2,250 represents a 45% income loss. That percentage is then multiplied by the total disability benefit ($3,000/month in our example) to determine the month's residual disability benefit. The result is a $1,350 monthly benefit.

You will notice the incentive built into this policy feature to encourage as early a return to work as feasible. If the insured was totally disabled and not working anywhere, the benefit payable would be $3,000/month. If the individual returns, as most desire, to their own occupation, the money coming in is now the current earnings plus the residual disability benefit that is computed. In month four of our example above, that equals $3,800 ($2,000 current earnings plus $1,800 benefit), or $800 more than the total disability benefit is paying. There is no penalty for going back to the job. In actuality, the established formula ensures that the individual will always end up with more money that way.

There are a couple of other variables that affect the calculation.

Substantial loss of earnings: If the insured loses 75-80% of prior earnings after a disability, usually the *full* total disability monthly benefit will be paid. The earnings loss calculation in this situation is not applied to the total disability benefit. In the example above, for the first two months of the residual claim, earnings loss was at least 80% or more and thus the residual benefit equaled the total disability benefit of $3,000 during that period.

Minimum benefit: There is a floor of benefits for an initial period. Usually, 50% of the total disability monthly benefit is the minimum amount that will be paid for the first six months of the claim. Thus, if the residual calculation indicates an income loss of less than 50% during that time, this minimum benefit provision will kick in. In our example, that means the residual benefit would never be less than

$1,500/month ($3,000 total disability benefit x 50%) for the first six months of the residual claim.

Return to work: The insurer may choose to make some other concessions to the disabled insured in the initial stages of a residual claim. After all, the carrier would like to see the person go back to work as it will ultimately reduce the amount of benefit payment the company will distribute. Some insurers with a two-test definition of residual will allow use of only the first test (income loss of at least 20%) for an initial period of time (6-12 months) before then requiring the partial loss of time and/or duties in addition to the earnings reduction.

Other policy language variations stipulate that the insured can work full-time (no loss of time or duties) for a period of time (6-12 months) and still be eligible for benefits based on earnings loss only. This acknowledges that, in some cases, even though the individual has returned to work full-time, it will still take a little time for income to catch up.

Yes, there are many variables to the residual disability benefit. But they are necessary to properly assess income loss and fairly pay disabled insureds the money they are due.

Other Policy Provisions

Naturally, there is much more to a disability income policy than total or residual disability definitions. There are several other important parts to a policy, some that have already been labeled as "money provisions."

Definition Summary

TOTAL: physical loss of ability to work, either in one's own occupation or another gainful occupation

RESIDUAL: economic loss sustained due to an injury or illness, with a reduced ability to work in one's own or another occupation.

REGULAR CARE AND ATTENDANCE OF A PHYSICIAN

This is a secondary part of the requirements for meeting the definitions of total and residual disability. To be eligible for policy benefits, the insured must be under the regular care and treatment of a physician appropriate for the condition causing disability.

If the insurance company's claims examiners believe that continued medical treatment would not improve the condition, then this prerequisite will be waived. Certainly there are medical conditions that no longer need the constant attention of a doctor, but still impair the ability of an individual to work. In this case, the insurer will not strictly enforce this provision.

In 2003, the U.S. Supreme Court became involved in a disability claim case (The Black and Decker Disability Plan, Petitioner *v.* Kenneth L. Nord) where the disabled insured's treating orthopedist certified him unable to work due to degenerative disk disease causing chronic back pain. The insurer, Met Life, asked a third party neurologist for an independent evaluation, a right that DI insurers maintain by contract.

The neurologist concluded that, aided by pain medication, Nord could perform some sedentary work. The insurer denied the claim, and the employer, Black and Decker agreed. The claimant appealed this decision under ERISA, and eventually the Ninth Circuit Court of Appeals overturned the insurer's decision, citing a "treating physician's rule" that requires the insurer who rejects the treating physician's opinion to come forward with specific reasons for the decision, based on substantial evidence in the record. The neurologist's report was not enough.

The "treating physician" rule was originally developed by the Court of Appeals as a means to control disability determinations by *administrative law judges* under the Social Security Act. In those cases, legal bureaucrats were making claim decisions and in some cases giving little weight to the medical evidence presented. To extend this rule to all ERISA-based plans was a stretch, and the insurer had relied on medical advice from their appointed third party examiner, not an administrator.

The case made it to the Supreme Court and Judge Ruth Bader Ginsburg wrote the opinion for a unanimous Court who upheld MetLife's and Black & Decker's original claim denial based on the medical evidence they found. The Court, Judge Ginsburg said, found no reason to expand the Social Security "treating physician" rule to all ERISA-based plans.[9]

Thus, while the opinion of the treating physician is required here, the insurer is not necessarily bound by it. In the majority of claims circumstances, these medical findings are sufficient. There may be times when the insurer utilizes its right to seek another medical opinion. A claims examiner won't overrule a doctor, but another physician might see it all differently.

Elimination Period

This is, as you already know, the number of days that an insured must meet the definition of total (or, when present, residual) disability before benefits will commence. In some DI plans, it is referred to as the *waiting period*.

You should read your DI policy carefully to see what days of disability count towards the elimination period. Generally, if the insured purchases both total and residual disability as definitions in the contract, either of those types of disability days will count.

In some plans, total disability may be required *before* residual disability days can be used. This sacrifices some flexibility (remember that the nature of disability makes it fairly unpredictable) in satisfying this requirement, but will also save some premium dollars in return.

There may also be the opportunity in the contract to accumulate days towards fulfilling the elimination period. With many plans having 90-day elimination periods now, this could be more important. For example, if an individual is disabled under the policy for 50 days and then recovers, that person is still 40 days short of qualifying for benefit payments. Let's say following the return to work that, within two months, the insured is disabled again from the same medical condition. The accumulation provision (usually found under the paragraph entitled *recurrent disability*) allows the claim to resume at day 51 rather than start over, a distinct advantage to the claimant.

Presumptive Total Disability

Disability of a catastrophic nature will create problems for an insured and family. In some cases, the DI insurer will loosen the reins a bit in its requirements to prove total disability. These concessions, and what initiates them, can be found in the presumptive total disability definition in the contract.

In general, if the insured has experienced the total, permanent and irrecoverable loss of hearing, sight, or speech, or the use of two limbs, then the insurer requires no other proof of disability. No inability to work in your own or gainful occupation, nor the care and attendance of a physician, will be necessary.

What makes this a money provision in the policy is that the elimination period is usually waived as well. This means, with a 90-day elimination period, an extra three months of benefits. Since you know the amount of the total disability monthly benefit, this number is easily quantifiable as an additional benefit.

This provision is being expanded to include a broader list of conditions, such as those found in a long-term care insurance product. This includes the loss of ability to perform 2 or more activities of daily living (a more rigid disability test than performing the duties of an occupation), or a cognitive impairment like Alzheimer's or senile dementia.[10]

Some insurers have made this clause a detached benefit in the policy paying a *separate* monthly benefit or lump sum *in addition* to the total disability monthly benefit. In any event, this money provision recognizes that such disabilities as included in this contractual language are serious and will result in substantial financial hardship for the disabled insured and family. It is almost a given that disability will be permanent in nature and thus the willingness on the part of the insurer to make things smoother at claim time.

Automatic Indexing

Many DI insurers include an inflation adjustment in their policies to help the monthly benefit keep pace, at least initially, with inflation. The increase to the monthly benefit occurs annually and is usually valid for the first five years. The insured need do nothing other than pay the additional premium (benefit increases are calculated at attained age rates) for the extra coverage.

Here is an example of how this provision works:

Year	Index Used	New Monthly Benefit
1	–	$5,000
2	5%	5,250
3	5%	5,513
4	5%	5,789
5	5%	6,078
6	5%	6,382
7		evidence of financial insurability needed

In this example, the indexing factor used was the change in the CPI index with a minimum guarantee of 5% annually. Some carriers use only the CPI increase, with no guaranteed rate, while others have lower or higher guarantees.

This feature was instituted to help policyholders keep their benefit levels within reasonable distance of their incomes. Many people receive raises each year, but don't equate that with a need to increase their income protection under DI coverage. This makes it easy – the insured doesn't have to think about it – only pay the premium for the additional coverage.

As you can see from this example, this provision can increase the benefit amount considerably over time. If no one paid attention to the upward changes in an insured's income, the policyholder in the 5th year would still have a $5,000/month policy rather than the 20% higher level ($6,078) that the automatic increases facilitated.

This is still no substitute for the guarantee of insurability benefit (see Optional Riders later in this section of the book), but it helps stay up with the smaller changes in one's income from year to year.

The insured has the right to refuse an increase and not pay the additional premium for it. Usually there is a limit to the refusals (two is most common) before the provision is suspended and no more automatic increases are made.

At the end of five such increases, the insured must furnish the insurer with financial evidence that justifies the increases that have been made to date. In our example, the individual would have to show tax returns that substantiated the new benefit level of $6,382. If the evidence was sufficient, the index feature would renew for another five years (depending on age). If not, the $6,382 would stay at that level but there would be no new increases. No medical evidence of insurability is ever required.

REHABILITATION

In the late 1970s, following the widespread introduction of the residual disability benefit in the individual disability market, a new policy provision was added to many contracts: rehabilitation. This feature was in the same vein as residual, emphasizing a return to work and signaling a willingness on the part of the insurer to help with this process if it made sense for all concerned.

An insured who is totally disabled generally wants to return to work. The residual disability benefit encourages this financially as already illustrated. The rehabilitation clause further advances this cause by helping to retrain a disabled person to effect that return.

The policy language is typically vague, stating that if all parties agree, the insurer will pay for the reasonable expenses of a program of occupational rehabilitation. These expenses can include assessments, examinations, vocational testing, training programs, books, tuition, and even living expenses, *in addition to* the total disability monthly benefit. Thus it is another of our money provisions.

Generally, the carrier will not place a dollar limit on this offer, but will make the overall decision about funding the costs of the program based on their opinion that it might change a total disability claim into a residual one or, even better, a full financial recovery, thus ending the claim.

An example illustrates the types of costs and savings involved. If a disabled insured has a $5,000/month total disability benefit, payable to age 65 and is disabled from performing his occupation at age 40, the benefit payout, if nothing changes, is $1.5 million (and there are no Cost of Living benefits attached). If the claimant is willing to undergo rehab with the opportunity to work at a new job where residual disability calculations will take over, the expenses to be reimbursed under the contract are relatively minor in comparison.

If the program costs $30,000, and the insured is back to work within two years and earning income, the ultimate savings to the insurer could be a million dollars or more. That's worth every cent of rehab coverage to them. For the claimant, it is a cost-free opportunity to be a productive member of the working world again. Don't underestimate what this means to people psychologically. The majority of people are going to jump at this opportunity.

This feature has seen a growing utilization over the years. Claim departments today are now fully staffed with rehabilitation specialists coordinating just such endeavors on behalf of both insurer and insured. Emphasis on this provision is not without merit.

BENEFIT LIMITATION FOR MENTAL/NERVOUS DISORDERS

The 1980s saw a disturbing claims trend: a growing number of mental and nervous disorder claims, including substance abuse. This is a delicate claims area where proving—or, in the insurer's case, disproving—the validity of the claim is challenging. It wasn't so much the frequency of claim that was the concern, but the significantly high cost of each one. These types of claims were large dollar ones, and needed case management to help rein in the numbers. It was certainly adding to the loss ratio woes many DI carriers were then experiencing.

Disability insurers have long been proud of their track record for having a minimum number of exclusions in their policies. Mental and nervous disorders have been treated the same as any other illness for many years. This claims trend caused a rethinking of this strategy.

Many insurers today have an option for individuals to elect, reducing the maximum benefit period for mental and nervous disorders, including substance abuse, to 24 months. In exchange for this, policy premium is discounted as much as 10%.

In some states, this rider (and its discount) is required, with states like Florida and California leading the jurisdictions where this benefit limitation is mandated.

Many prospects for DI coverage are more than willing to reduce their benefit periods for these conditions and take the discount. It is not an area of illness that concerns them, whereas the amount of premium grips their attention.

WAIVER OF PREMIUM

This provision is built into the contract, unlike life insurance where it is an optional benefit. It addresses the situation where an individual is disabled and unable to earn an income but is still required to pay a premium for this disability income policy.

Obviously, that doesn't make much sense, so insurers built in a premium waiver after a stipulated period of time, usually 90 days or the elimination period, if longer. At that point, future premiums coming due are waived as long as the individual remains disabled under the terms of the contract. In addition, any premium paid during the initial 90 days (or elimination period, if longer) is refunded to the claimant.

If a policy includes both total and residual disability definitions, either or both of these types of disability days can satisfy the time period before waiver is triggered. It is another money provision that you can quantify by determining the potential refundable premium.

RECURRENT DISABILITY

Mentioned briefly in this section under "elimination period," this policy feature addresses how the insurer views brief recoveries from disability and subsequent relapses. This provision has a couple of purposes.

First, for an individual that is disabled for a time and then attempts to return to work too soon or is hit by a recurrence of the same condition within a short period of time, it would be somewhat unfair to require satisfaction of the elimination period all over again. This part of the contract ensures a direct continuation —of either finishing the days in the elimination period or picking up where benefit payments leave off—as if the brief recovery never took place.

Second, if an individual had a short benefit period such as 2 years, and used the entire amount, then returned to work for a brief time and the same condition recurred, the insurer would not be obligated to pay the same benefits all over again.[11] If enough time passes—and the insured has resumed paying the policy premium—then the benefit period would be restored.

The recurrent period is typically set at six months. In the first case above, this means the insured could suffer a recurrence within 180 days, and it would be considered a continuance. In the second case, the insured would need six disability-free months before the policy benefits would be considered restored should a new disability occur.

This provision can be especially important in a residual claim when there could be wild fluctuations in income. An individual could earn more than 80% of prior income (meaning the 20% loss of income requirement is not met) in one month, and 40% the next. The recurrent provision is in effect, meaning the insured would have to earn more than 80% of prior earnings for six consecutive months before the claim would have to start over again if earnings dropped again due to disability.

Treatment of Injuries

This policy benefit pays if the insured does *not* qualify for any disability payments under the policy. It does so in the form of expense reimbursement for an injury that requires treatment by a physician within 90 days of the occurrence. This includes injury repair to one's natural teeth.

There is a maximum limit to the expenses that will be paid that varies and generally won't exceed one total disability monthly benefit. But it is another money provision, assisting with costs when an injury occurs that otherwise would go un-reimbursed by the DI policy.

LTC Conversion

Long-term care insurance is also a disability-based product. It provides income and asset protection in the form of reimbursement for medical expenses not often covered by other forms of insurance. Since it occurs with more frequency at the advanced ages, it is often considered the disability policy you need after you stop working.

Due to this seemingly natural transition, insurers who offer both types of coverage have offered a conversion privilege to move from your DI policy to a LTC one. Generally, no medical evidence of insurability is required and the premium to exchange one plan for another is not unreasonable.[12] This feature helps to ensure continued important income protection as people move into another phase of their lives.

Still other carriers are experimenting with all-in-one type plans that include both disability and long-term care benefits. Here, rather than a formal conversion to another policy, the insured can simply trigger the transformation of the type of benefits one is eligible for.[13] The same policy stays in effect, but the definitions and benefit amounts adjust accordingly.

Protection of this sort is a task that the agent, planner or advisor should be looking after on behalf of the client anyway. These provisions simply help make that job easier for everyone.

EXCLUSIONS

There was a time during the go-go '80s when some insurers removed virtually all their exclusions, with at least one insurer proclaiming that it had no exclusions in its policies. A few retained one: disability caused by war or act of war. Normal pregnancy (covered by the policy if it lasts 90 days or longer) was also eliminated as an exclusion, even though at the time male and female rates were generally equal.

What were the DI insurers thinking? Some exclusions have always made sense, but product development and enhancements during that specific era had the same discipline as a 16-year-old teenager with the car keys for the first time.

Cooler heads have long since prevailed and these are the more common exclusions that can be found in today's DI policies:

Pre-existing: There is a 24-month period from the issue date of the DI policy during which a disease or a physical condition that existed prior to that time would not be covered—unless the condition had been disclosed on the application and not specifically excluded by the insurer at issue time of the policy. These conditions are defined as those that have symptoms for which a normally prudent person would seek medical treatment.

War, or act of war: Benefits are not payable for an injury or sickness caused or contributed by war, declared or not, or any act or incident of war, or as a result of active military service (usually lasting longer than three months). The terrorist attacks in New York and Washington, D.C. on September 11, 2001 were, technically, undeclared acts of war, but there is no DI insurer that denied claim benefits as a result of these tragic events. There are some circumstances that warrant extra consideration and where insurer carriers simply, in the words of Spike Lee, do the right thing.

Self-inflicted injury: Intentional, self-inflicted injuries are not covered.

Commission of a crime: If the insured is involved in committing a criminal act, or is involved in an illegal occupation or activity, any injuries or illnesses sustained in these pursuits will not be covered. It's safe to assume this would include most of the Sopranos.

Loss of license: Unless you lost your professional or occupational license or certification because of a disability, the loss of these credentials that prevents you from performing your occupation is not covered. Medical personnel who are diagnosed as HIV-positive, and could no longer practice would have coverage. A lawyer disbarred for embezzlement would not.

Normal pregnancy: A sickness resulting from pregnancy will be covered if it lasts longer than 90 days. Complications from pregnancy, including a Caesarian section would be covered.

These are the most common provisions of a disability income contract. As you can see, there are a number of ways to collect under a disability income plan. Detailing these for the client, with any amounts that you can calculate indicated, is an excellent way of presenting the disability income policy as an income protection solution.

Optional Benefits

"Have no fear of perfection. You'll never reach it."

– Salvador Dali

With insurers unbundling their products more enabling an almost infinite number of designs—think Dell Computers—there are some provisions noted above that might appear as optional choices with an insurer. The idea of options is to tailor a plan specifically to the interests and needs of one individual. It also leaves an opportunity to balance benefits with cost to stay within reach of a client's budget.

Optional Benefit elections vary from DI carrier to carrier, but the selections noted here appear most often in insurer DI portfolios.

Own Occupation/Residual

The definitions of total and residual disability are often broken out today as optional benefits.[14] Generally, the basic DI contract will contain either a restrictive definition of total disability (that can then be upgraded to own occupation or similar language by option) with residual disability as an option, or an income replacement/residual definition with the chance to add a total disability benefit for comprehensive coverage.

These are broken out this way due to the high price tag that came with having both definitions built into the basic contract. This created an affordability issue for the many occupations who could effectively choose one or the other definition, depending on the best fit for their work and probable claim circumstances.

Therefore, even though both total disability (and its various definitions) and residual disability have been discussed as part of a contract earlier in this section of the book, know that there is a strong chance that one of the two will be offered through a rider by your DI carrier.

Guarantee of Insurability

As one ages, the likelihood of qualifying medically for DI coverage, at standard rates, decreases. Unfortunately, when one is in peak earnings years and needs the additional protection, it is the most difficult time from a health standpoint to acquire more benefits.[15]

Not everyone will buy young. Nor will every policyholder buy as much as they need in their youthful years. A guarantee of one's medical ability to purchase future coverage is a must for nearly every client.

This can be accomplished through the addition to the basic contract of a guarantee of insurability (GOI) rider.

The GOI rider is different than the Automatic Increase Benefit discussed earlier. That feature, usually built into the base contract, increased benefits by a small amount like 5%, or the CPI yearly change that Social Security uses, and though it cost nothing extra to have, the insured paid for the increased coverage each time it occurred.

With the GOI option, there are scheduled increase dates, generally annually or bi-annually, and the monthly benefit amount that can be added is far more substantial. These options can be exercised until the insured reaches age 50-55 or so. The individual does not have to increase coverage on the option date, but could lose the privilege if more than a couple of opportunities are skipped.

The reason this benefit is so important is that it does not require medical evidence of insurability to qualify for the increase—only financial. I can't stress enough how important this is in keeping the coverage up to date with income. Health qualifications to obtain DI coverage are stringent, and as the years advance there are many more likely medical issues that could endanger a standard DI purchase.

There is no reason for an individual once insured to have a problem buying additional coverage. The GOI rider might add 10% to the premium cost, but it is worth every penny. I have seen several occasions over the years where additional coverage was purchased through this option even though the individual would have difficulty qualifying medically if this type of evidence was considered.

For this reason, I include it with every DI proposal I make. I rarely have a prospect tell me they don't want this feature after my explanation of it.

So, while the Automatic Increase Benefit can be a convenient way to make minor adjustments to the benefit level, the GOI rider is more useful for larger increases in income. When exercised, the new benefit is usually just added to the older policy and a new policy schedule page reflecting the new benefit and the increase in premium is sent out. There may be some insurers that issue an additional policy, especially if the older policy is part of a discontinued series.

The GOI rider is also tailor-made for client reviews. It is easy to lose touch with your insureds, but if you are faithful about scheduling annual reviews, the GOI rider is a good reason to give the client a call.

Social Insurance Offset Rider

In Part 2 of this book, there was a section that analyzed the existing public programs that could monetarily assist a disabled individual, and a summary page of the public programs that could be left behind was included in this discussion. As noted, these potential benefits have to be considered by the insurer to avoid an over-insurance situation.

Yet we all know that qualification for these programs is far from a sure thing: just the opposite. In the late 1970s, issue limit tables (what the consumer could buy in DI benefits based on income) reflected the possibility of qualification, but there was no remedy for the person if their public program application was denied, as the majority were. Insureds were left with a DI policy that may not have done an effective job of helping the individual and family maintain the standard of living to which they had become accustomed.

The answer to this problem was to develop a benefit rider that could be activated if the insured *did not* qualify for this public assistance. This way, the insured had a higher portion of his or her gross income covered, and the insurer avoided the problem of an insured collecting too much in the way of benefits. This option, in effect, guaranteed that this extra money would be there at claim time, whether it was from the insurance company or the government program.

This rider was called the Social Insurance Rider and the amounts of the option that could be purchased were added to the issue limit tables as a separate entry. The chart below illustrates the difference in what could be purchased before and after the introduction of this rider.

Income Level	Basic Coverage	Social Ins. Option	Total Benefit
$40,000	$1,400	n/a	$1,400
$40,000	$1,400	$950	$2,350

As you can see, there is a significant difference in these two entries. The first line illustrates the issue limit before the Social Insurance rider. Insurers couldn't afford to take the chance that an individual might qualify for public DI money, so their numbers simply reflected this concern. By adding the rider, insureds now had a higher percentage of income guaranteed for coverage. The Social Insurance option added, in this case, 60% more potential benefit for the DI buyer. The insurer's concerns were relaxed as this extra benefit was only payable if the public plans denied the individual any benefits.

How did this work?

Public Programs: The rider coordinated primarily with Social Security, Workers' Compensation, and Railroad Retirement benefits, hence the term "social insurance." Some of these riders only interacted with Social Security and are called Social Security offset riders rather than Social Insurance offset options.

Integration: There are three principal ways benefits are paid under this rider: dollar-for dollar, all or nothing, or a percentage based on the number of social insurance qualifications.

> *Dollar-for-dollar*: This is the most common and the most logical (not always an insurance company preference). Here, the rider amount is reduced by whatever the individual receives in social insurance DI benefits. Using the $950 rider example above, if the individual qualified for $720 in social insurance, the rider payout would be $230, thus ensuring the full $950 would be paid from some source.
>
> *All or nothing*: This was the early version of integration in this option, where the benefit rider was only payable if the insured did not qualify for any social insurance assistance. But this still leaves a potential shortfall as in the above example the insured would not be eligible for any rider benefits even though the $720 the individual qualified for was less than the $950 rider purchased.
>
> *Percentage option*: The rider is payable based on the number of social insurance programs paying. Usually, if the insured qualifies for any one of the Primary Insurance Amount under Social Security, Workers' Compensation, or the Railroad Retirement Act, one-third (33%) of the rider is payable. In our example, this would amount to $317. The rider will either pay the full benefit ($950 here) if no social insurance is awarded to the insured; one-third ($317) if only one award is made; or nothing (-0-) if eligible for the Maximum Family Benefit under Social Security or two or more social insurance awards.*Dollar-for-dollar*: This is the most common and the most logical (not always an insurance company preference). Here, the rider amount is reduced by whatever the individual receives in social insurance DI benefits. Using the $950 rider example above, if the individual qualified for $720 in social insurance, the rider payout would be $230, thus ensuring the full $950 would be paid from some source.

There are five additional points to make about this rider.

1. It is a way of writing the full amount of coverage your client can buy in the least expensive way. The rider amount is less costly a benefit than the base coverage because the basic benefits are guaranteed whereas the social insurance offset rider is not. Insurers have restructured their issue limit tables over time and give some occupations the opportunity to buy the entire amount (base + social insurance rider) on a *guaranteed* basis. When watching the premium budget though, writing the combination may be more feasible.

2. There is a five month elimination period for Social Security benefits. Often, the review process is a lengthy one and benefit awards could be several months farther along. What does the insured do in the meantime? This rider provides an answer. While the Social Security Administration is operating on "island time," this offset benefit option will be paying along with the base benefit. If Social Security eventually awards the applicant DI benefits, the amount initially paid will include retroactive coverage back to the end of the fifth month of disability. But the insured will not have to pay back the rider benefits that provided needed dollars during the long wait.

3. This rider works well on policies that contain a residual disability benefit. Because the disability definitions of public programs are very restrictive, there is likely no way the insured would ever qualify for this financial help if back to work in any capacity. Thus, the rider is virtually certain to be used in the calculation of the residual benefit. In our example the combined benefit amount ($2,350) would be used to multiply the percentage earnings loss by, not just the base $1,400. This is an attractive part of this option, considering the lower cost for it.

4. Many DI insurers have dedicated a staff person to assist with the application process for Social Security. The maze of paperwork is often befuddling to the disabled worker and family, and the insurer is more than willing to take the lead on this front. And why not? It's in the insurer's best interest if the individual does

qualify because it reduces its liability. This could include the use of an attorney if necessary. It is a benefit to both parties.[16]

5. Once the individual insured has qualified for Social Security, it doesn't mean this is, as Eric Clapton might say, a forever thing. Social Security has a system of Continuing Disability Reviews (CDRs) where there is an ongoing check (every two to three years or so) to ensure the person still meets the disability guidelines. When the late Ronald Reagan was President, he ordered a "full-court press" back in the early 1980s to review thousands of existing claims in the hopes of reducing Social Security disability payouts. If the disabled insured is approved for Social Security and later booted off the rolls, the rider benefit can be activated immediately providing the individual still meets the less stringent policy definition of disability.

Considering the versatility of this benefit option, it is a highly recommended choice to consider. There is a premium savings and many likely uses for the benefit, and you would do well to consider using this feature even when there is a choice between buying all basic coverage and this combination approach.

Cost of Living Rider

Inflation is an economic issue addressed in three ways by DI policies. The Automatic Benefit Increase is typically part of the policy and applies a CPI-like addition to the monthly benefit on an annual basis. The Guarantee of Insurability rider, for an extra premium, locks in one's medical insurability to effect larger benefit increases at stipulated times over the succeeding years after issue.

Finally, there is the optional Cost of Living (COL) rider that becomes operational during a disability claim. Without this inflation protection, the monthly benefit in effect at the time of disability will remain level, creating potential financial difficulties for the insured and family if the disability is long-lasting.

It is only effective during a claim, whereas the other inflation-fighting features work primarily during the time before a claim is filed. It adds a significant cost (up to 25% or so) on to the basic disability coverage, so it should be carefully considered if the premium budget is tight. But it does provide a measure of financial security for a disabled insured.

Here's how it works. With a total disability claim, this option directly increases the monthly benefit payable. It does so one year after the claim starts, and annually thereafter. The amount of the increase may be tied to the CPI (usually with a minimum guarantee of 3-5%), or have a stipulated rate (from 3-8%) that is not dependent on any index. The increases are usually compounded.

The example below illustrates a $3,000/month policy with a COL rider tied to the CPI with a minimum increase of 3%.

Year	Total Disability Benefit	CPI	Rate Used	Total Disability Benefit
1	$3,000	-	-	$3,000
2	3,000	3.3%	3.3%	3,099
3	3,000	1.7%	3.0%	3,192
4	3,000	1.6%	3.0%	3,288
5	3,000	2.7%	3.0%	3,387
6	3,000	3.4%	3.4%	3,502
7	3,000	2.4%	3.0%	3,607

CPI Data Source: Bureau of Labor Statistics

At the end of seven years of disability and six increases, the monthly benefit has increased by over $600/month even though most years were adjusted only by the minimum guaranteed percentage of 3. That's an extra $7,284 in benefit payments annually that is sure to assist the insured and family with increasing costs. The CPI numbers were taken from the most recent history of its adjustments.

During a residual disability claim, the increase index would be applied *twice*. It will adjust the prior earnings figure of the formula in addition to increasing the basic total disability benefit to calculate the ultimate residual dollar amount.

Year of Disability	COL Rate	Prior Earnings	Current Earnings	Total Dis. Benefit	Percentage Loss	Residual Benefit
1	-	$5,000	$1,500	$3,000	70%	$2,100
2	3.0%	5,150	1,650	3,090	67%	2,070
3	3.0%	5,305	1,760	3,183	67%	2,132
4	3.0%	5,464	1,900	3,278	65%	2,131
5	3.4%	5,650	2,015	3,389	64%	2,169
6	3.0%	5,820	2,100	3,491	64%	2,234
7	3.0%	5,995	2,350	3,596	61%	2,194

COL Rate is based on CPI indexes as provided by Bureau of Labor Statistics, with a minimum guarantee of 3% annually

In this example, the prior earnings are being indexed by a minimum of 3%, as is the total disability monthly benefit. The first factor influences the income loss percentage while the other is used to directly calculate the residual benefit. If the COL rider was not present, in the seventh year, the percentage income loss would have been 47% ($5,000 level prior earnings less $2,350 current income) instead of 61%, a more accurate reflection of the dollar buying value. In addition, the ultimate residual benefit would have been $1,410 ($3,000 x 47% loss) instead of the COL enhanced benefit of $2,194.

The Cost of Living option can be a powerful tool against the effects of inflation. While the CPI has been extremely low the last few years, there is still a dramatic difference in claim benefit calculations, enough so to consider adding the feature if affordability is not an issue.

RETIREMENT BENEFIT PROTECTION

What happens to your client's retirement plan contributions during a disability? These contributions stop and the worker stands to lose substantial retirement plan value as a result.[17] A disability threatens both an individual's present *and* future situation.

As a result, some DI insurers have created an optional benefit to replace those retirement plan contributions. It is a separate benefit apart from the total disability monthly benefit and pays benefits into an account or trust established for the individual's retirement. The benefits are not paid directly to the insured, unlike regular total disability monthly benefits.[18]

What's at stake for the disabled insured and family is a significant potential nest egg. One example illustrates this potential bonanza. A 35-year-old who contributed $9,400 to a 401(k) plan every year (below today's maximum but you'll get the idea) for 30 years, with an employer contribution of $3,400 annual contribution would, at an 8% return, boost the account value to $1.5 million by age 65.[19] This would be lost if the contributions could not be made, and that would likely be the case for a disabled individual.

Why risk it? Some DI carriers today offer a Retirement Protection Benefit to prevent this from happening. Ongoing personal expenses are only part of the disabled person's financial story. The loss of retirement money earmarked for the future is yet another devastating loss a disabled person and family faces.

If the individual has this benefit option and passes away after a few years of disability, the assets paid into the trust through this rider will be distributed to the designated beneficiary of the insured. For taxation and trust information surrounding this benefit option, your clients should consult their CPAs and attorneys. Insurers publish some of their own guidelines regarding this option, and you can distribute that without actually giving any advice.

These are the essential optional benefits. There are others, from shorter-term residual disability benefits to longer benefit periods past age 65 to waiver of premium during periods of unemployment. Every DI carrier has some different choices. Any of these may appeal to the client looking for some specific coverage option. Utilize these benefit choices to design a plan particular to your client's needs.

While personal DI coverage is the most often sold of all DI policies, there are many important business needs filled by other DI plans.

BUSINESS OVERHEAD EXPENSE

"In the business world, the rearview mirror is always clearer than the windshield."

– Warren Buffett

The personal disability income market is the area in which most agents who work with DI spend their time. But, as noted in Part 2 of this book, that is a good way to miss some wide-open opportunities in this insurance field.

Employers have two checkbooks: two sets of expenses for which they are responsible. While personal DI can help with one checkbook during a disability, unless further steps are taken, the second checkbook representing business expenses is at great risk.

The Business Overhead Expense (BOE) policy is sold by most DI insurers and its premium is a tax-deductible expense to any business owner.

With millions of small businesses to prospect, the BOE plan is a natural door-opener to begin conversations with any business owner. It fills a real need, and can allow the business to stay open (or at least not go into debt) while the disabled owner is recovering. In many small firms, the business expenses may represent a much higher amount of gross revenue than the net paycheck an owner takes home. To write personal DI, and ignore the BOE risk is to only do half the job for the owner.

2003 BOE Sales Results – Non Can[20]

New sales premium: -0.3%
New policies: -0.7%

Average BOE monthly benefit = $10,251 (+0.6%)

Average BOE premium = $2,017 (+0.4%)

The problem is the owner won't recognize the need for BOE coverage until after a disability has commenced. By that time, if it is a serious disability, the business may well be preparing to close its doors. Since the majority of disabled individuals recover in the first year, many businesses could be saved if only there was a source of income to pay business expenses until the owner returns to the job.

There is a resource: the BOE plan.

Reimbursable Contract

The first noticeable difference in a BOE contract from a personal DI plan is that it is not an indemnity policy, but a reimbursement one. It is intended to specifically replace actual expenses incurred during a claim.

A personal DI plan will pay, in the cases of total disability, a level monthly benefit. If the policy is for $3,000/month, that's what the policy will pay during a claim if there is no Cost of Living rider attached.

However, in a BOE policy, the payment each month is predicated on the amount of reimbursable expenses that the business must pay. Thus the benefit amounts may vary widely from month to month. Like a residual disability contract whose unknown variable is an individual's current earnings, BOE payouts are dependent on what expenses need to be paid in a given month.

During a claim, the disabled insured submits that month's reimbursable expenses, and the insurer calculates the claim. This continues until the individual recovers, or benefits are depleted, or the disabled owner no longer has responsibility for expenses.

Maximum Total Benefit

Here is difference #2. Because the monthly payout is variable, there is an overall maximum benefit calculated that represents the total value in the policy. The amount of the monthly claim check is then subtracted from this total amount each month.

The maximum total benefit is calculated by multiplying the monthly benefit purchased by the number of months in the selected benefit period. Let's look at an example.

Monthly Benefit	X	BOE Benefit Period	=	Total Maximum Benefit
$10,000	X	18	=	$180,000

This means the insured business owner has $180,000 of total benefits in the policy. If the expenses incurred run less than $10,000/month, the policy would run longer than the 18 month benefit period as long as the individual still meets the disability qualifications in the policy. Benefits would not exceed an average of $10,000/month, although payments can be more or less than that level in any given month.

Carryover Account

Difference #3 is the possibility of paying out more or less than the specific monthly benefit amount. This is due to the nature of varying expenses. There are always bills that are consistent each month like the rent or mortgage payment on the business space. But there are other costs that may come in less frequently like a malpractice premium or real estate taxes. This means bills could (and should if the BOE coverage was written properly and kept up to date) average close to the monthly benefit level, but there will be ups and downs each month.

To allow for this and to attempt to track business expenses as closely as possible for the insured, the BOE contract has a carryover feature. There are two types of carryover numbers.

1. Unused benefits: If the monthly claim payment is less than the purchased monthly benefit level, the unused portion of that amount will be carried forward to be paid out in a later month where expenses are greater than the monthly benefit amount. For example, if the BOE monthly benefit is $10,000, and expenses are only $8,000 in the first month, the additional $2,000 in benefits that could have been paid will be placed in a *carryover account* and used later. If, in the next month, expenses are as much as $12,000, the carried forward $2,000 can be added to the regular $10,000 monthly benefit to be paid out at that time.

2. Unreimbursed expenses: If the business expenses in a month exceed the monthly benefit level and any carried forward amount available, the unreimbursed portion of expenses will be placed in a *carryover account* to be reimbursed at a later date if possible. For example, if the BOE monthly benefit is $10,000/month, and expenses are $12,000 in the first month, the policy benefit paid will be $10,000 (since it is the first claim

month, there are no unused benefits in the carryover account yet). The $2,000 of expense not yet reimbursed by the contract is carried forward to be paid out in another month where expenses are less than the monthly benefit. If, in the next month, expenses are only $8,000, the full $10,000 monthly benefit can be paid, the $2,000 unreimbursed expenses added to the $8,000 of regular expenses for that month.

This is really not as complicated as it sounds. The DI insurer's claims department will track the expenses and the balances due. The primary responsibility on the part of the disabled business owner will be to make sure the DI carrier receives the actual bills, invoices or records of the ongoing expenses each month for fast and accurate service.

Summary of Differences

The major differences between the BOE and personal DI policies can be summarized, as follows:

1. Monthly benefit: This is calculated based on business expenses, and not income.

2. Maximum benefit: The BOE plan uses the benefit period to calculate the total policy value by multiplying the monthly benefit times the number of months in the benefit period.

3. Type of payment: The BOE policy is a reimbursement contract based on actual expenses, while the personal DI plan is an indemnity plan paying a specified amount each month.

4. Carryover: Due to the potential erratic nature of business expenses, the BOE plan contains a carryover feature to account for unreimbursed business expenses and unused policy benefits not yet reimbursed. This helps to track the monthly expenses more closely and means that the monthly claim check could be the same or more or less than the actual purchased monthly benefit amount.

The following example is based on these policy parameters: $10,000/monthly benefit, 30 day elimination period, 18 month benefit period.

Month of Disability	Monthly Policy Benefit	Actual Expenses	Account Balance	Monthly Benefit Payable	Unpaid Benefit Amount	Expenses Carried Forward
1	30-day EP	non-reimbursable		-0-	-0-	-0-
2	$10,000	$ 8,900	$10,000	$ 8,900	$1,100	-0-
3	10,000	9,550	11,100	9,550	1,550	-0-
4	10,000	9,245	11,550	9,245	2,305	-0-
5	10,000	13,600	12,305	12,305	-0-	$1,295
6	10,000	9,500	10,000	10,000	-0-	795
7	10,000	8,650	10,000	9,445	555	-0-
8	10,000	9,150	10,555	9,150	1,405	-0-
9	10,000	10,780	11,405	10,780	625	-0-
10	10,000	12,650	10,625	10,625	-0-	2,025

In this ten-month claims example, all the policy differences between the BOE plan and the personal DI contract are evident. The first month is the elimination period, and there are no benefits payable as the insured is responsible for those costs. The claim begins after 30 days.

The policy benefit is $10,000/month and this is the amount available to the insured in the first month of claim to reimburse expenses. This amount available each month is shown in the account balance column. It will consist of the monthly policy benefit (in this case, always $10,000) and any unpaid benefit amount from the previous month. In the first month, there is no unpaid benefit, so $10,000 is the amount in the account balance.

The second month's expenses are less than $10,000 and come in at $8,900. The policy benefit payable is $8,900, leaving an unpaid benefit amount in the account balance of $1,100. This will be carried forward to the next month and added to the account balance.

The third month's expenses are also less than the policy monthly benefit at $9,550. The policy could have paid out as much as $11,100 that month (new $10,000 plus unpaid benefit balance of $1,100), but the policy reimburses only, so the benefit paid is $9,550, and the new unpaid benefit amount now totals $1,550, for a new account balance in the fourth month of $11,550.

In the fifth month, reimbursable expenses are higher than usual at $13,600. The account balance has only $12,305 in it and claim payments cannot exceed that number. So, the policy reimburses $12,305, and carries over the unreimbursed expense amount of $1,295 ($13,600 - $12,305) to be paid out in a later month when expenses are again under $10,000.

This happens in the next month when expenses are only $9,500. The account balance has $10,000 in it, so an additional $500 can be paid, bringing the unreimbursed expenses down to $795 ($1,295 - $500).

As you can see, this type of payment method does track expenses closely and does not leave the insured out of pocket for much or for long in this example. Understanding how BOE claims are paid will help you see the differences between this business policy and the personal DI plan that is designed to help pay personal expenses.

Renewal Provision

Like the personal DI plan, there are two renewal provision choices: guaranteed renewable and non-cancelable. In a guaranteed renewable policy, the insurer cannot cancel the policy until the end of a specified period—usually insured's age 65. The insurer can, however, raise the premiums in the policy on any policy anniversary date, as long as the rates are raised for the entire policy class and approved by the state insurance department.

With a non-cancelable provision, no rate increases can be made in addition to the inability on the part of the insurer to cancel the coverage prior to age 65. This is the most popular form of renewal elected by business owners for their BOE policy for obvious reasons. It's nice to have a tax-deductible premium. It's even better to have one that stays level to age 65.

Definition of Total Disability

Because the benefit period choices in a BOE policy are short-term (12, 18, or 24 months are the most common), the definition of disability tends to be an "own occupation" one. That is, the business owner is considered disabled if unable to perform the duties of his or her own occupation. This is the "one test" definition, and the most liberal of policy language.

Some insurers add another test: that the insured be also not working in another occupation. Here, they are not measuring ability to work, but whether the disabled insured has actually entered another profession when unable to perform the old job.

Thus, the BOE definitions of total disability are typically the best two policy language provisions available in the market.

Residual Disability

What if the owner returned to work on a part-time basis? Or, returned to work at or near full capacity, but whose income lagged well behind in the first few months back?

These are the ways a BOE policy addresses this situation.

1. No benefit is payable: Some BOE policies cover only a total disability, so if the individual returns to his or her own occupation, no further claims expenses are reimbursable.

2. Percentage payable: If the individual returns to work in a reduced capacity, either an inability to work as much time or perform the same duties as prior to disability, or there is a loss of net income, the policy will pay a benefit. This benefit is equal to either a stipulated percentage (50% is most common) of the regular monthly benefit for up to a specific period (such as 3 months). Here, the insurer may not even require any submission of expense receipts. Or, the policy will continue to track expenses, but the maximum payable in any one month is limited to a percentage of the full monthly benefit, with 50% again being the most likely cap.

3. True residual calculation: In this circumstance, the BOE plan pays a percentage of the incurred monthly expenses that is in direct relation to the percentage of earnings loss that month. Thus, the insurer would calculate a true residual disability payment based on income loss. (See the discussion of residual disability under the personal DI section covered earlier in this Part 3.) If the insured also has a personal DI policy with the insurer that contains residual disability benefits, the income information is already being sent in, so applying that to the BOE payment is easy.

The idea of the residual benefit is to not penalize a disabled business owner from returning to work, and to offer some financial assistance commensurate with the person's economic loss. This policy feature may be offered as an optional benefit or be built into the contract.

Covered Expenses

Policy difference #4. Where a personal individual DI plan's monthly benefit amount is calculated based on income, the BOE plan's monthly benefit is based on actual covered expenses that would be reimbursable during a disability. These expenses can be found on the business tax return, and it will likely be an underwriting requirement to submit this form anyway along with the application.

EXAMPLES OF COVERED EXPENSES

- Rent or mortgage payments for space occupied for business purposes

- Utilities

- Telephone

- Employees' wages, including payroll taxes and contributions for benefits

- Premiums for malpractice, property, or liability insurance

- Laundry, janitorial, security, and maintenance services

- Postage

- Lease payments or Scheduled Depreciation for furniture and equipment used in business

- Real estate taxes

- Office supplies

- Accounting, billing, and collection service fees

- Interest payments on business debts

This list of expenses includes the more obvious ones that are incurred during the routine course of business. If the expense item is generally accepted by the IRS as a deductible item, there's a good chance the insurer will consider it when calculating the eligible monthly benefit amount that can be issued.

There are, of course, expenses that are not covered. This is a shorter list.

Expenses Not Covered

- Salaries, wages, or other forms of remuneration of the owner (personal DI will take care of that), any other owner or person sharing business expenses and performing similar duties to owner, or a family member not already employed on a paid, full-time basis 60 days prior to application date

- Any expense that does not require a cash payment

- Any expense for which the owner is not liable

- Cost of goods, inventory, and merchandise

- Cost of any expenses that are passed directly on to a client

- Any expense covered under another BOE policy

Each insurers' BOE contract will have a list contained in the policy itself. Within those lists, it is probably more important to read what's not covered as this is far more specific. Those expenses that can be used should be added up to determine the amount of monthly benefit the owner should have in protection. The more accurate this number is (and stays), the more likely a future claim will closely track the actual business debt situation of the owner to provide real financial assistance. A BOE plan that is not close in amount to actual expenses will be of lesser help during a claim.

Conversion Privilege

Policy difference #5. This is also a different wrinkle to the BOE plan. This policy is put in place to offer economic help with business expenses. If, over the course of time, the person sells their business ownership stake and no longer has responsibility for these types of expenses, the policy will no longer have any validity.

Not all is lost, however. The BOE plan gives the insured the opportunity to convert this BOE plan to a personal DI policy if so desired, without evidence of medical insurability required. The personal DI plan will be based on the individual's attained age and current occupation. The policy benefit period will be no more than 24 months, and the elimination period will be no shorter than the one contained in the BOE plan. The amount of the benefit will be limited to the amount in the BOE policy (some carriers have specific caps on the conversion amount). The amount of coverage to be determined will also factor in other personal DI coverage owned by the insured, and will take into account the issue and participation limits the company has in force at that time, based on the insured's current income level.

In any event, it is a chance to add some extra personal coverage easily when the insured's business ownership changes.

Death Benefit

Policy difference #6. If the disabled insured dies while benefits are being paid under the BOE policy, up to three more months of expense reimbursement may be made for the (now) deceased insured's portion of these expenses. This will give more time for the family to settle personal and financial affairs and then sell the business if they choose, rather than simply cut benefits off because the individual insured has passed away.

Legal/Accounting Fee Benefit

Policy difference #7. In the event the insured decides, due to a disability, to sell the business, this feature reimburses the insured up to a stipulated amount for the legal and accounting fees that will be incurred in the divestiture of the firm.

As noted earlier, the BOE policy's purpose is to buy the insured some time during a disability. At some point, there will be a decision reached that the individual will either return to work or not. If not, the business will likely be sold. In addition to assisting with paying the ordinary expenses, this policy provision helps with costs sustained in selling the company. The idea of not letting the owner fall into debt due to the disability is carried out even through the sale of the business.

Other Policy Provisions

There are several other policy provisions that are similar to their counterparts in the personal DI policy.

The *regular care and attendance of a physician* that is part of the definition of disability to determine claim eligibility is in the BOE contract as well. Like the personal DI plan, this provision is waived if no further treatment would be of any value to the insured.

The *presumptive total disability* clause waives the normal qualifying procedures and the elimination period for certain catastrophic disability situations like loss of sight, speech, hearing, or use of two limbs.

The *rehabilitation* provision permits the insured to participate in a vocational training program (and be reimbursed the costs of it) in addition to continuing to pay the BOE claim. Agreement between all parties to this retraining is necessary and will likely happen if insured and insurer feel it is in both of their best interests.

The *recurrent disability* language of the policy is intended to allow for a seamless continuation of a claim if it recurs within a six month period for purposes of either satisfying the elimination period or picking up from the point in the benefit period where the insured recovered. It also provides a dividing time frame between recovery and the recurrence of the same disability where both the elimination and benefit periods would start again.

The *waiver of premium* feature kicks in when the insured has been disabled for 90 days (or, with some insurers, the elimination period if less). Satisfaction of the disability definition for this period means the carrier will refund any premium paid during that initial 90-day period, and will continue to waive premium payments in the future until a recovery is made where the insured no longer satisfies the claims eligibility requirements.

There are also *exclusions*, including a *pre-existing condition* definition that is similar to personal DI coverage. War, self-inflicted injury, involvement in an illegal activity or non-disability reason for losing an occupational license or certificate that prevents practicing one's profession are the usual exclusions.

Optional Benefits

There are also a couple of optional riders that can be added to basic coverage under a BOE policy. The BOE policy comes with a total disability definition, usually "own occupation," as the standard contractual feature. To this, one can add a Residual Disability benefit rider, the substance of which has been discussed earlier in this section.

In addition, there are two other optional benefits most commonly found in BOE plans.

The *Guarantee of Insurability* option is as important here as it is in the personal DI sale. This allows the insured to add more coverage at future specified option dates without evidence of medical insurability. The insurer will only ask to see proof of current expenses to issue additional benefits. This is vital protection because it allows for an easy increase to existing coverage when financial responsibility for expenses increases. To not add this (about 10% of total premium) is to risk not being able to add to this policy in the future, a situation that could leave the insured well short of necessary funding during a disability.

The *Substitute Salary Expense* rider is a benefit that helps the insured business owner hire a temporary replacement to take over his or her duties until recovery can be made. The salary and wage expenses of this substitute must be incurred after the disability commences.

Normally, the salary of someone doing the same duties as the owner is an exclusion under the BOE policy. This option suspends that exclusion when it comes to having to hire someone to fill in to keep the practice thriving. The substitute cannot be a family member. There are limits on the amount of this benefit that varies by insurer. This benefit is paid in addition to the regular BOE expense calculation. This benefit will be paid following the elimination period, or the date of hire of the substitute, if later.

It is another instance where this disability policy is trying to keep things, financially, status-quo, until the individual business owner is able to return to work and begin earning again.

These optional benefits are intended to supplement the purpose of the basic BOE plan. With a tax-deductible premium as a carrot, there seems no logical reason why a business owner wouldn't carefully consider filling this business need with a BOE disability policy.

Hopefully, all you have to do is ask.

DISABILITY BUY-SELL

"Every great mistake has a halfway moment, a split second when it can be recalled and remedied."

– Pearl S. Buck

If BOE plans play second fiddle to personal DI policies, Disability Buy-Sell or Disability Buy-Out (DBO) contracts are even farther down the sales ladder. DBO sales accounted, in 2003, for only 3% of all DI sales amongst those DI insurers that even offer the DBO product.[21] If you utilize the Employer PowerPoint sales presentation in the *DI Sales Power Kit*, this should not happen. Both the BOE and DBO plans feature prominently in your interview with a business owner and, thus, can scarcely be overlooked.

> In 2003, Buy-Sell new sales premium decreased 4.5% from 2002. Sales of new policies fell by 9%.
>
> Source: JHA 2003 Individual Disability Market Survey

To assist with protecting a business owner's personal disability needs and also provide coverage for business expenses, but overlook the individual's ownership stake in the business, is to leave an important need uncovered. If a disability is serious enough, an owner is going to want his or her share from the business, and the healthy owners are going to want this interest back within the company.

The question becomes how does the business, possibly reeling from the loss of a key owner, come up with the financial scratch to buy back this ownership interest? Using a DBO policy supplies the firm with the dollars necessary to make this buy-out happen.

Ownership Interest

Personal DI insures personal income. BOE plans insure business expenses. DBO policies insure ownership interests.

Calculating the amount of this ownership interest is the first step after convincing the owner that an insurance policy is the best solution for this need. There are two key financial documents that will assist the DI underwriters in determining the amount of coverage that can be issued. These are (1) the balance sheet and (2) the income (profit & loss) statement.

1. Balance sheet: The balance sheet is a current picture of the firm's finances. It lists business assets, liabilities, and the equity that owners hold in the company. Two types of assets are generally listed: current and fixed. Current assets are liquid, like cash or other holdings that can be converted quickly to cash. Fixed assets are longer term and less likely to be liquid. These items are carried on the books from year to year, like furniture and office equipment. This type of asset does depreciate, and the balance sheet will reflect this annual adjustment. Liabilities are also categorized as short-term and long-term. The difference being how fast these debts are planned to be paid off. The owners' equity is the amount the owners have personally invested in the business since it began. Liabilities plus owners' equity equals assets on a balance sheet.

2. Income statement: Also referred to as a profit & loss (P&L) statement, the numbers on this statement give a financial picture over a period of time, such as 12 months. It shows revenue generated and expenses paid for the business. The difference between the two is the profit or, of course, the loss depending on how the firm is doing. Revenue sources depend on the type of business entity. A personal service corporation will generate client fees, while a commercial business will earn its money through the sales of goods. Expenses are the costs incurred during the course of the business, and you may have already reviewed the most recent income statement in your work done for the BOE sale.

Submission of these two forms along with one or two years' tax returns of the business will be the financial data the insurer will need to determine the amount of DBO coverage that may be written. The firm may have had a recent valuation done, and that information can also be included when sending in the other documentation.

Elimination Period

Where a personal DI plan will likely have a 90-day elimination period and a BOE plan have an even shorter time frame before benefits start, a DBO elimination period will be substantially longer. The buy back of an owner's interest is essentially the last resort in a disability situation. This is the point where it's clear the individual is not coming back to work—that the disability is serious enough to warrant a need for the money that the ownership interest in the firm represents.

This type of transaction is not done casually. Often, a BOE policy and a DBO elimination period will often be coordinated together as part of the business disability planning. The owner needs assistance with business expenses right away and for a short period of time. At the point of a buy out, expense responsibility will cease. Thus, the end of a benefit period for a BOE plan is often the elimination period elected for a DBO policy.

BOE benefit periods are commonly either 12, 18, and 24 months. DBO elimination periods are long-term, starting either 12, 18, or 24 months after a disability commences. The EP is long because the disability must be catastrophic enough to trigger a buy-out. Thus, the elimination period selected for the DBO contract can be based on the benefit period taken for the BOE plan.

The elimination period should also coordinate with the trigger date of the buy out specified in the buy-out agreement, so that the source of primary funding is available when the interest is scheduled to be purchased. The agreement will also need to be sent in to the insurance underwriting department.

Payment of the Policy Proceeds

There are three payment method options in most DBO policies.

1. Lump sum

2. Monthly installments

3. Combination of (1) and (2)

Unlike personal and BOE disability policies, the DBO plan can be paid out in one lump sum. After calculation of the owner's current business interest value, the total amount that can be insured will be known. Many insurers have a minimum amount, like $100,000 as well as a maximum cap, such as $2,000,000. There might be a limit to what the insurer will offer on a lump sum, and the balance of the interest would then be written on an installment basis.

For example, if the business is valued at $1,000,000 and there are two 50% owners, each would be eligible for $500,000. Once identified, the decision can be made as to how best to have the policy proceeds paid out during a claim.

Lump-sum: $500,000 each is the benefit amount purchasable by the two owners. After satisfaction of the elimination period, this lump-sum amount is payable. The policy premium is not deductible to the business, so the lump-sum payment will not generate any income tax liability for the insured. However, there may be capital gains taxes depending on the value of the business interest at buy-out versus what the owner has paid in personally.

Installment: If there is a large capital gains tax liability, or if the owner and family prefer the payments to be spread out, there are choices in how this $500,000 can be paid. The installment period options are usually 24, 36, or 60 months. The buy-out would be triggered at the end of the elimination period, but the $500,000 would then be divided by the number of months in the installment choice to determine the monthly payment.

Combination: There may be owners who wish to have part of their ownership interest up front and the rest spread out over time. This could also be to mitigate the capital gains tax liability, or to use some fiscal restraint by not having the money be paid all at once. In our example, the owners may choose to have a percentage, say half of the amount, $250,000, paid in a lump sum after satisfaction of the elimination period, and the balance of $250,000 spread out over 24, 36 or 60 months.

Once the elimination period has been satisfied, the buy-out is triggered. The disabled insured will no longer be required to satisfy the definition of total disability under the contract even if all or a portion of the payments are being made under an installment plan.

Minimum Ownership

DI insurers selling the DBO policies will have some requirements for a business owner to be eligible to apply for coverage. Obviously, there must be two owners. Some DI insurers will allow up to 10 owners, depending on the occupation class of the prospects. The owners must have at least 10% ownership in the business and be actively working in the firm. There may also be a guideline for how long the business should have been in existence, typically three years, although some professional firms may be in business for a shorter time than that and still be eligible.

It is always best for you to research this basic information before proceeding to your initial sales presentation featuring this product.

Valuation

As noted earlier, the underwriter will be looking at the two key financial forms: the balance sheet and income statement. The valuations will often be a function of the owners' salaries and business profit plus the book value and, in some cases, a goodwill factor. Book value is total assets less total liabilities and can be found on the balance sheet. The owners' incomes will be on the income statement. Goodwill is not a tangible asset, but the reputation of the firm, its length in the business, and its size may contribute to an overall stability factor that is not quantified by either financial document. Insurers will assign a multiple to this goodwill factor and it may be used for coming to a final valuation amount.

Renewability

The DBO policy is *conditionally renewable*. This isn't as severe as noted in the discussion of renewal options under personal DI plans. Here, the rate is guaranteed until age 65 and the company cannot change the provisions of the policy, similar to a non-cancelable renewal provision.

But there are some events that could end the term of coverage earlier than age 65:

- lack of premium payment,
- the insured ends active full-time employment with the firm for a reason other than total disability, or
- the buy-sell agreement is terminated.

These conditional exceptions all make sense in terms of non-continuation of coverage. Because the coverage could end prior to age 65, the DBO plan, like the BOE plan, has a conversion privilege.

Conversion

The DBO policy, if no longer necessary to the insured due to a change in business ownership status, can be exchanged for an individual DI plan if done prior to a certain age, typically age 60. Like BOE, the benefit period is limited to 2 years, and the elimination period must be at least 90 days or longer. The monthly benefit allowed will vary—$2,000 to $2,500—and will be coordinated with all other personal DI coverage in accordance with the insured's current income status.

Most important, no medical evidence of insurability is required. Ownership of the DBO policy gets you a free pass on the health portion of the underwriting process. Policy rates for the new personal coverage will be based on attained age.

Definition of Disability

No need for residual disability benefits here. The DBO plan is an all-or-nothing deal. Since it involves a catastrophic disability that must last for at least 12 months (the minimum elimination period), it must be serious in nature. That would only involve *total disability*, the only definition available for this type of DI contract.

It's primarily an own occupation definition—unable to perform the duties of your occupation—with one caveat. The insured must also not be working in another capacity in his or her company. A requirement that there be regular care and attendance of a physician is also part of this definition, but as in the other contracts, it will be unnecessary if future treatment would be of no benefit to the insured.

Transfer Privilege

In this economic age, it is not inconceivable that a business owner could sell his or her share of the interest in one business and buy into another firm. Under this DBO policy feature, the insured could continue the existing policy and transfer it to the new buy-out situation. The policy must be in force for a minimum amount of time (2-3 years), and the insured must be actively at work full-time in the new company, and not totally disabled.

In this case, the medical evidence of insurability is waived, and the insured preserves original age by not exchanging the policy for a new one, saving a (potentially) substantial amount of money. The policy benefits will have to be recalculated based on the new interest value in the current business. The policy benefits cannot be increased above the previous maximum limit, and may be reduced based on the results of the valuation.

But the lower premium and the good health that allowed the original DBO policy purchase is preserved.

Professional Fee Reimbursement

There will be a cost to enact a buy-sell agreement, probably generating both legal and accounting fees. This policy feature of the DBO contract will reimburse the owner for the costs of these services up to a stipulated maximum. These fees are paid in addition to the policy benefit. This feature may be available as an optional rider rather than included in the contractual language.[22]

Waiver of Premium

This standard provision will waive policy premium following 90 days of disability, even though the elimination period is much farther out. The basic principle of having financial trouble due to a disability, including the payment of DI premiums, still applies here.

Exclusions

The usual exclusions of war, self-inflicted injury, illegal activity, and loss of license apply here as with both personal and BOE plans.

Optional Benefits

The principal optional benefit offered by insurers selling a DBO product is the *Guarantee of Insurability* benefit. This carries the same weight and importance as it did under the two previous policy lines discussed.

There will likely be an updated valuation done from time to time—annually is common—and the owner's stake in the business may rise. In some cases, it may rise dramatically, as the owners/creators of a small board game named "Trivial Pursuit" found out when it took off on a grand cultural scale in rapid fashion.

These valuations may not see that large a rise in your client's business share, but it is important to keep it updated to ensure the accurate amount of funds will be there for the owner and firm if necessary. Once again, the key to this option is the waiving of medical evidence of insurability in order to acquire the additional coverage.

There will be specified option dates, an age cut-off (50-55), and the right of refusal limitation to keep the benefit alive. It is a simple way to prompt an annual review with your client to see if anything has changed that would require alterations in the coverage already bought.

Remember, so many firms address their <u>life</u> buy-out needs and forget about the higher risk during the working years—disability. Don't let that happen to your business client!

KEY PERSON DI

"We are always anxious to be distinguished for a talent that we do not possess, than to be praised for the fifteen we do have."

– Mark Twain

Corporate insurance buyers understand risk. They instinctively know that managing all phases of risk is critical to protecting shareholder value. In today's economy, human intellectual capital reigns supreme. Intellectually rich companies tend to be highly dependent on one or two key leaders who drive shareholder value. To not protect this important person from the risks of disability, where the vision and plan of one individual might not be executed because of an unexpected illness or injury, is not in the best interest of the business.[23]

Key person disability insurance, while rare, can still be found through some specialty disability brokerage outlets. Like the buy-sell need, there are many arrangements where life insurance is purchased to cover the risk of loss of a key contributor to the business bottom line.

But, once again, the disability risk is ignored, leaving the firm vulnerable to the loss of this vital individual.

In handling the business needs to date, the help has primarily been given to the business owner. Money is there to help pay business expenses, dollars are available when a buy-out is enacted, and even the owner's take home pay from the firm can be insured through personal DI, more financial assistance directly to the individual.

What about the business? The loss of a key person is certain to also trigger a loss of revenue to the firm. BOE and DBO prevent a substantial backslide, but lost income to the firm is rarely replaced. This is the purpose of key person DI.

Who is a Key Person?

Identifying the person most responsible for revenue generation in a business may be the trickiest part of the entire sale. What is the nature of the business? How large is the firm? What are the duties of the main players? Is there a key talent that, without it, the firm would never be on the positive track it is? If such an individual exists, can a business quantify what the loss of this individual would mean in financial terms?

Who can substitute for the person if he or she is out? Is another person readily available within the business to fill in? If so, this diminishes the likelihood of that person being truly key and difficult to replace.

Older employees, closer to retirement, are not likely to be considered key people. The firm should have long since groomed a replacement for the day when that individual is no longer with the business. Is the person also an owner in the firm? Generally, the greater the percentage of ownership interest, the less necessary the coverage. The business will receive assistance from BOE and DBO plans in the case of an owner.

But a person with less than a 50% ownership stake, who helps the company bring income in, and who performs duties that, in the absence of this person, would create an economic hardship for the firm, is a probable candidate for key person DI coverage.

Maybe it's a salesperson bringing in 75% of the company's gross receipts. Or perhaps it's the creator of a specific system who alone understands its processes and can explain it the best to potential customers.

DI insurers who offer this coverage may have a questionnaire to be completed that will help to identify who the insurer believes to be a key person. Utilize this form, if there is one, to help you through this process.

More often than not, it will be evident if one person is vital to the operation of the business. If you recognize that scenario, know that there is an insurance product to reimburse the business for the loss of revenue sustained during this individual's absence.

Key Person Benefits

The value of a key person usually goes well beyond the individual's salary. This is one of the measurements of a key individual, whether loss of this worker would have a major impact on the firm.

The business can often buy up to 100% of the salary of a key person as coverage here. For a $50,000 employee, this is a possible $50,000 coverage paid out in monthly benefit checks.

Now, the key employee can also obtain personal DI coverage for that $50,000 as well, giving the business in effect twice the salary coverage on the employee. The salary of the key person is covered through personal DI and an amount up to the salary can be reimbursed directly to the business through the key person DI plan.

Each insurer of this type of DI plan will publish their issue limits for this coverage. Study this information before your appointment to understand what your benefit guidelines are for this product.

Elimination Period

The business will be looking for revenue assistance right away, similar to the BOE need. Like BOE, the revenue can be covered while buying time to see if the key person will recover enough to return to work. If not, the hiring and training process of a replacement will have to begin.

Therefore, the elimination periods available are shorter than personal DI with 30 and 60 days being common and 90 days also available.

Benefit Period

This also tracks the BOE parameters. With shorter elimination periods, the benefit periods will also be limited. Generally, 12, 18, or 24 months will be benefit periods in play here. This should allow time for a key person's recovery or, failing that, to find, employ and train a new employee to fill the shoes of the key individual.

Renewability

This provision will be similar to the language of a DBO contract. It's non-can, sort of, with premiums guaranteed and the insurer unable to change policy language. There are a couple of provisions that could cause an end to the plan prior to age 65, however.

1. The insured must continue to be employed full-time (defined as 30 hours per week) with the firm unless, naturally, the person is totally disabled. Part-timers are not considered key employees.

2. The key employee's ownership interest must remain below a certain level, typically 50%. There will be times when a key employee is made an owner, like Rico at the funeral parlor in "Six Feet Under." The insurer reserves the right to re-evaluate at that point, depending on the amount of ownership interest the person now controls.

Definition of Disability

Like DBO, only total disability is a consideration here. The partial loss of a key employee will probably not have the same revenue ramifications as the complete loss of this person. This will be an "own occupation" definition of total disability since that's all that concerns anyone—the key individual's ability to perform the duties in that firm. The benefit period is short, so it's not a large concession from the insurer to use this most liberal of total disability definitions.

Regular care and attendance of a physician will still hold true here unless further treatment would be of no value to the insured.

Conversion

As is true with both BOE and DBO plans, there might come a time during this policy's lifetime when the key person no longer is, well, key. If the key employee's role within the company changes, or he or she decide to leave the firm, the key person policy is no longer necessary.

This conversion privilege benefits the insured, not the business, even though it is to the business that key person policy proceeds are paid. Here, the insured can convert the plan to personal DI coverage with the same or longer elimination period, the same or shorter benefit period, and up to a specified monthly benefit limit, like $2,000. Premiums will be based on whatever policy series is available at time of conversion.

Some plans offer an original age conversion feature, meaning that while the policy issued will be that being sold at time of conversion, the rate will be based on the age when the key person policy was originally issued, thus saving some premium dollars.

Waiver of Premium

The key person DI policy also includes a waiver of premium provision, usually after 90 days of disability where future premiums coming due (paid for by the business) are waived and any money paid during the initial 90-day period is refunded.

Optional Benefits

There is usually only one optional benefit written with the key person DI policy. It's called the *Personnel Replacement* benefit, and it would reimburse the costs of searching for and training a replacement for the key employee. Expenses like classified advertising, employment agency placement fees, relocation expenses, and even the initial months of salary to the replacement can be included in this benefit. The key employee should have been disabled for at least 90 days before these expenses will be considered. The amount of the rider can be up to $5,000.

Taxation

The cost of the premium, paid for by the business, is not deductible to the company. Benefits, when paid during a claim, are not subject to income tax.

Key person DI is important coverage in that it actually reimburses the business itself for lost revenue during the disability of a vital employee. All other plans benefit the insured directly, so your employer clients may be very interested in filling this type of need.

WORKSITE DISABILITY PROGRAMS

"A human being must have occupation if he or she is not to become a nuisance to the world."

– Dorothy L. Sayers

What's a human resources director to do these days? In addition to trying to fully comprehend HIPAA privacy compliance and final regulations to COBRA, there is the ever-present health insurance rate increases eating away at the employee benefit budget. Moreover, employers seem increasingly intent on trying to do more work with less people. Take two Advil and call me in the morning.

The smaller the firm, the more likely it is that only one or two people are in charge of these employment issues. The details of salary continuation were discussed in Part Two of this book, and put you in the vital place of being the disability consultant for these smaller firms. Salary continuation created a large potential audience for a disability income product.

With so many bureaucratic considerations, human resource managers rarely focus on disability and, thus, have no working knowledge of the DI product itself.[24] There are a variety of product solutions for a salary continuation plan: group short and/or long-term disability plans, voluntary individual personal DI products, specialty products like critical illness, or a combination of these programs.

Voluntary DI Plans

With smaller firms who have a limited budget for employee benefits, you will likely be able to establish a short sick leave program and then work on getting appointments, on company time, to talk to each employee. During this chat, you can explain their new sick leave plan, and then sequence into a disability income presentation to fund the need after the employer's benefits have expired.

Employees understand the need to keep income coming in even if they are unable to work. They may have even seen magazines like *Consumer Reports* advising that "insurance should be for catastrophic" events and that primary needs can be filled with a "term-life policy to cover one's contribution to family expenses; a comprehensive health policy; disability coverage to provide income when you can't work, and homeowners and auto insurance to replace lost property."[25] The disability coverage, you can explain is of vital importance to the prospect and family, to ensure that money will continue to flow to pay bills and stay out of debt.

> Voluntary LTD sales grew significantly in 2003, increasing by 29%. In contrast, growth in voluntary STD sales slowed, decreasing by 1%.
>
> Voluntary disability sales premium per life grew at 7% for LTD and 8% for STD.
>
> The total number of insured employees grew by 17% for LTD and 4% for STD.[26]

After selling the employer on the importance of this product, and working with the human resources area to determine communication strategy of the salary continuation program, you should work towards the opportunity to see as many employees as you can. Depending on the size of the firm, it is recommended that you meet with management people first to explain the disability income need.

In many businesses, employees will look toward their manager in an employee benefit situation to see what their immediate supervisor thinks of the offering. Thus, the management folks can influence results, even if they are not actively speaking for or against a product. By getting their buy-in as to what you are trying to accomplish with your interview, you will increase your participation rate among the rest of the employees.

There are a number of DI carriers that specialize in worksite marketing, and have an individual, voluntary, payroll deduction DI product for this purpose. There will be, in general, two types of individual product offerings:

1. Management/Key Employees: Depending on the outcome of your salary continuation plan discussion, there will probably be a need for a comprehensive DI contract similar to that discussed under the personal DI product section of this Part 3. Total and/or residual disability, higher monthly benefits to serve larg-

er incomes, and longer benefit period options will be the norm here. These employees will have a need for higher coverage levels to replace their incomes, and the salary continuation plan may already have singled out these individuals for more extensive benefits.

2. Rank-and-file employees: The majority of employees in almost any business are not management. They may be paid hourly, weekly, or bi-weekly. But just because their incomes aren't as high as exempt employees doesn't mean their income protection needs are any less important. DI insurers provide adequate coverage at reduced premiums to best fit this type of employee. The product is streamlined somewhat, with coverage for total disability only perhaps, and shorter benefit periods available like 12 or 24 months. But there are a number of appealing products that can fill this need. Some contracts, for example, will offer a 100% all-sources benefit that allows the employee to receive up to 100% of pre-disability income from any number of resources such as Social Security, Workers' Compensation and, of course, the payroll deduction DI policy itself.[27] Individual one-on-one meetings with each employee are a must, and many DI insurers have an enrollment program that can be set up on your laptop for everyone's ease.

> From 1997-2000, the number of women-owned businesses with 100 or more employees grew by 44%, and the number with $1 million-plus in revenue grew by 32%.[28]

With the product being streamlined to be able to offer it to as many people as successfully as possible, there is a good chance that the underwriting can be streamlined as well. That means no medical exam, a shorter application with less questions, and fast turnaround by the insurer in the interest of being able to retain the entire case.

This is good news for the agent. There is an opportunity for multiple sales at the same address, and products and applications are specifically designed to make the experience a positive one for all concerned.

Group Disability Products

While smaller firms are more likely to opt for the voluntary, payroll deduction approach, larger employers are apt to choose a group disability approach to their salary continuation funding needs. Group disability covers a wide range of people, and if the employer decides to pay the premium for it, all employees who are eligible for the plan will be covered. There's not much to the enrollment process in this case, with the employer completing the most important forms.

Group DI plans may be even more proactive about returning an employee to work following an injury or sickness. Employers understand that it is less costly to return an employee with a disability to work than to lose time and productivity training a new hire to do the same job.[29] Employees will be pleased to have the coverage without extensive paperwork and qualification.

For that reason, a majority of employers of all sizes tend to offer both short-term disability (STD) and long-term disability (LTD) coverage. In the larger employer market, more than 75% of employers offer disability benefit plans of this type.[30] Group DI sales numbers have been relatively steady even as the individual DI market has been battling its demons.

There are two primary group DI products:

1. STD: short-term, weekly benefits, payable for 13 or 26 weeks (sometimes 52 weeks), short elimination periods of 7 and 14 days (sometimes 30 days).

2. LTD: long-term, 90- and 180-day EPs (sometimes 365 days), monthly benefits, benefit periods to age 65 to 70.

New Group DI Sales Grow Faster than In-Force Revenue in 2003
Figures in Millions

	New Sales		In-Force Cases	
	Premiums	Lives	Premiums	Lives
LTD	$1,293	6.3	$7,382	34.2
STD	611	3.3	2,658	15.2
	Change from 2002			
LTD	+6%	+3%	+6%	+1%
STD	+11%	+10%	+7%	+3%

Source: 2003 U.S. Group Disability Market Survey, JHA, Inc.

To generate quotations from group DI carriers, you will have to obtain some preliminary data. This information will allow the group insurer to make the best possible bid for the business. Here is the essential information required:[31]

- full name and complete address of employer prospect,

- specific nature of the business (include 4-digit SIC, if known),

- current plan design with any plan changes made in the last 3 years,

- copy of existing group DI policy and certificate (if coverage currently held),

- definition of employee eligibility for coverage (classes of employees), and

- current census: gender, birth date or age, salary, occupation, and type of class.

For LTD cases where there are over 250 lives, experience rating may require additional data:

- paid LTD premium for the prior three years,

- paid claims for the last three years,

- covered lives for the last three years,

- rate history,

- open claims listing: age at disability, cause, prognosis if known, gross monthly benefit, and any offsets, and

- closed claim history.

As always, there may be more or less requirements depending on the insurer. The above listing should be sufficient in the majority of employer cases you have.

You should also specify what type of coverage you want—STD or LTD. As noted in this section and earlier in this book, there might be a need for both products based on how the salary continuation plan was established. STD may be put in place for all employees, while a certain class or classes of employees may be marked as eligible for LTD coverage in addition.

You can request STD from one insurer and LTD from another. Or, many agents are working with one DI carrier to cover both needs. This can even be done in one seamless package, where a combination STD/LTD plan pays weekly benefits for the initial short-term period of disability and switches over to monthly benefit payment for long-term disabilities.[32]

Such integrated group DI packages may be a cost-saver for the employer. In addition to avoiding two separate billings and doubled administrative work, there are incentives for the insurer to provide discounts for these plans. First, carriers are provided with early intervention possibilities because they also hold the STD policy. Second, carriers increase their revenue on each case because they are handling both coverage options. From the employee standpoint, working with one insurer guarantees a smooth transition from STD to LTD should the claim last that long.[33]

Group DI plans offered on a STD basis are generally streamlined for low pricing. An insurer's LTD contract, however, may be streamlined or could contain many of the comprehensive and competitive definitions seen in personal DI coverage such as an "own occupation" total disability definition and residual disability benefits. The more liberal the coverage, the higher the cost will be for the group DI policy.

Group DI insurers are always tinkering with their product offerings. Recently, one insurer introduced the possibility of extended LTD coverage for life under certain circumstances. At the expiration date of LTD benefits between age 65 and 70, this benefit would continue LTD payments if the individual met a more stringent test of disability. Like long-term care insurance definitions, this would involve the inability to perform two or more activities of daily living or the presence of a cognitive impairment like Alzheimer's disease.[34] This may become a trend.

There will also be the option of installing a base of group DI coverage and, for higher paid employees, adding individual personal DI on top. This gives the key employees broader and more complete coverage and, as an added bonus, individual coverage that they can take with them should they leave the business (not necessarily a selling point with the employer). Group STD and LTD are not portable products, although some may offer conversion privileges.

Individual DI insurers publish tables that indicate how much in personal DI monthly benefits is available when a group LTD plan is already in place.

Group disability is yet another product option for your work with a business, especially as a follow-up to your salary continuation or sick pay plan discussions.

CRITICAL ILLNESS

"Competence, like truth, beauty, and contact lenses, is in the eye of the beholder."

– Laurence J. Peter,
author of *The Peter Principle*

According to the American Heart Association, in the U.S. every 29 seconds someone suffers a coronary event, and every 45 seconds someone has a stroke. The American Cancer Society predicts nearly a million and a half new cases of cancer will be diagnosed each year. The odds of dying from a critical illness may be going down, but the odds of incurring one are rising all the time.[35]

A catastrophic disability creates a potential financial disaster for a family. With the numbers of uninsured people (those without health insurance) continually going up in the face of higher premiums and greater out-of-pocket responsibility, the need for cash at the time of a disability has increased to even higher levels.

Individual and group disability insurance provide some income protection, but these personal products are meant to assist with regular, ongoing expenses, not the overwhelming costs of surgeries, treatments, and hospital and doctor bills.

High earning individuals may also find themselves left short in terms of percentage of income covered by disability. Issue limit tables scale down as incomes increase, and maximum issue limits can leave these professionals in a financial quandary at time of a catastrophic disability.

> "For more than 50 years I have been a devoted husband. I have three children and 11 grandchildren. My wife Dolores and I were enjoying the pleasant peace that comes after the challenges of parenthood. At the height of this happiness, I went for my regularly scheduled physical and left the doctor's office with a diagnosis of cancer. My life as I knew it was over. The prospect of a relaxing retirement with the woman I love was replaced by debilitating surgery and a long, painful recovery. My medical expenses were enormous while my business continued to decline. Fortunately, my surgery was successful. Recuperating at home, I was discovering new hope and just being thankful my life was spared. Just as our life was returning to a manageable state, our peace was again shattered when Dolores had a severe stroke. Once again, I felt the pain of not being prepared for the misfortunes life can bring. If I had the opportunity years ago to purchase a critical illness policy, I would have bought it and had the financial security I needed. The emotional and physical pain associated with severe illness is bad enough. Why compound it with financial stress as well? If we had critical illness protection, our medical bills would have been completely covered. Unfortunately, precious time that should have been devoted to healing was, instead, spent on generating income. I recommend that whether young or old, protect yourself and your loved ones with the security available through critical illness insurance protection." [36]

This is, after all, what most people worry about most when forced to think about disability. It's not the broken leg or the flu that concerns the average individual. It's the heart attack, cancer, stroke, and other medical conditions for which the road to recovery is a long and perilous journey.

Supplementing an individual's DI policy with critical illness might make sense for some prospects. It would be like writing a combination payment method under a DBO policy. The DI plan would pay monthly benefits for the long haul, while a Critical Illness (CI) policy would provide a lump sum for immediate ease of the financial strain.

Who are the prospects for a Critical Illness insurance policy?

Critical Illness Prospects[37]

- Anyone with debt or financial obligations

- Single people who are often poor prospects for life insurance

- Anyone whose occupation makes him or her a poor disability insurance risk

- High income professionals to supplement DI coverage

  And[38]

- Families caring for children and aging parents

- Couples in their late 40s or 50s who are not yet ready to purchase long-term care insurance

Employers and employees have shown substantial interest in this type of product. In a 2004 Eastbridge study, 97% of those surveyed were highly interested in products that provided cash to cover deductibles and out-of-pocket expenses. A critical illness policy is one product that fits this need.[39]

What does a Critical Illness policy cover?[40]

• Heart attack	• Stroke
• Kidney failure	• Paralysis
• Loss of sight	• Loss of limb
• Loss of hearing	• Loss of speech
• Major organ transplant	• Alzheimer's disease
• Life-threatening cancers or heart bypass	• Angioplasty

You should check available policies to see if any other catastrophic-type conditions are covered. The ones detailed above are the most common medical situations addressed by these plans.

What does it pay? Insurers issue face amounts of coverage that can vary from $10,000 to $500,000 or more. It can be paid in a lump-sum amount upon diagnosis of any of the aforementioned medical events. Some of the conditions, like bypass surgery and angioplasty, will pay a percentage of the lump-sum (25%, for example) rather than the full amount.

Some insurers have a benefit for loss of activities of daily living, too. It is probably more restrictive than long-term care insurance, but a severe disability is likely to reduce the ability to perform several of these ADLs.

Coverage generally begins 30 days after the policy's effective date. After that time period, the policy then pays upon diagnosis of the covered illness, providing a needed cash infusion for the family. This money can be spent on whatever is necessary, be it out-of-pocket medical expenses, travel, and living expenses for long distance family members, or personal bills.

There is a waiver of premium feature on these plans for those individuals who might become totally disabled but not incur any of the stated conditions. This way, the policy would continue on in case of a future catastrophic event.

These policies are usually issued to age 60. There are often rate guarantees with the plans, but many are guaranteed renewable, meaning the rate for the plan could go up in the future if the entire policy class is approved for an increase by the state insurance department.

Here are some questions to ask when evaluating critical illness policies:[41]

- How many illnesses does it cover?

- Does the contract have stipulations about surviving illness before collecting benefits?

- Does the contract refund the premium if the insured dies without going on claim?

- Does the policy refund the premium if the person dies from, say, an accident, not the critical illness?

- Are the definitions of illness precise?

- What are the issue limits and financial criteria necessary for applicants to get issued at those limits?

Some plans also have an option available to purchase a *blanket health screening rider* that automatically provides $50 per calendar year for covered health screening tests. Obviously, it's in both the insured and insurer's best interest to encourage this wellness feature.[42]

Homeowners have become an increasing target for this type of insurance. The need to continue the mortgage payment following an accident or sickness is one of the centerpieces of any disability income discussion. There are about 72 million homeowners in the United States and about 45 million home mortgages. The U.S. has one of the highest homeownership rates in the world and a medical care industry that assures higher survival rates for critical illness victims. In a typical year, about 5 million new home mortgages are made for refinancing, first-time buyers, and a mobile population.[43] Protecting this asset is a high priority for people.

Critical illness insurance was introduced in the early 1990s in this country. As time has elapsed, some interesting hybrids of this product have taken shape.

Critical illness is being linked with disability income, life insurance and long-term care insurance via an optional benefit rider.[44] Even group term policies can carry a special Critical Illness rider to pay a portion of the face amount upon diagnosis of certain significant medical events.[45]

Critical Illness By Distribution Channels, U.S. Market, 2003[46]

Distribution Channels	Number of U.S. Insurers
Individual	18
Worksite	30
Group Employee Benefits	5
Internet	3
Direct Marketing	3
No longer writing product	4
Annuities	1
Other	

There are still a few regulatory hurdles to clear as states scramble to write statutory language for the plans in their jurisdictions.[47] But it's clear that, though off to a slow start, critical illness insurance seems destined to stay. For individuals, it's much easier to talk and relate to the potential financial disaster of a catastrophic illness. It's what many people fear, and critical illness insurance directly addresses these concerns.

As an adjunct to disability income protection, it's an excellent and appropriate partner.

FOOTNOTES

1. Brain J. Lauber, "Unbundled DI Products Fit Client Needs," *National Underwriter*, Life & Health/Financial Services Edition, Cincinnati, OH, March 5, 2001, p. 20.
2. Source: John Hewitt & Associates, 2003 U.S. Individual Disability Market Survey, published April 2004.
3. Jeffrey H. Rattiner, "Not Your Father's Disability," *Financial Planning*, March 2003, p. 73.
4. Lucretia DiSanto Jones, "Timing is Everything," *Advisor Today*, June 2004, p. 24.
5. Donald Jay Korn, "Cadillac Comeback," *Financial Planning*, April 2002, p. 59.
6. "Read the Fine Print," *Kiplinger.com*, web page, October 2002.
7. James Foley, "Look Beyond the Definition of Disability," *National Underwriter*, Life & Health/Financial Services Edition, Cincinnati, OH, July 29, 2002, p. 6.
8. John H. Sullivan, "Is it a Total or Residual Claim?" *Advisor Today*, August 2002, p. 54.
9. Source: U.S. Supreme Court, Case No. 02-469, Argued April 28, 2003, Decided May 27, 2003.
10. Richard A. Magro, FSA, CPA, and Joel Kastin, CSA, "Individual Income Protection," *Life Insurance Selling*, December 2002, p. 24.
11. Jeffrey H. Rattiner, "Not Your Father's Disability," *Financial Planning*, March 2003, p. 73.
12. Guy W. Bertsch, "Disability-to-LTC Conversion Policies Are Here To Stay," *National Underwriter*, Life & Health/Financial Services Edition, Cincinnati, OH, February 24, 2000, p. 11.
13. "New Packaged Concept in Disability Insurance Allows Policyholders to Change Coverage as Needed," *Business Wire*, October 4, 2000.
14. "Riders that Make Sense for You," *Smart Money.com* web page, October 2002.
15. Paul G. Wesling, "Use Riders to Present DI Scenarios to Prospective Clients," *National Underwriter*, Life & Health/Financial Services Edition, Cincinnati, OH, September 2, 2002, p. 14.
16. "UnumProvident Provides Social Security Assistance to Customers," *Business Wire*, March 27, 2002.
17. Linda Koco, "Disability Plans Emerge to Protect Retirement Contributions," *National Underwriter*, Life & Health/Financial Services Edition, Cincinnati, OH, May 19, 2003, p. 24.
18. Mark Ameigh, "Some Executive Worksite DIs Now Offer Retirement Benefit Protection," *National Underwriter*, Life & Health/Financial Services Edition, Cincinnati, OH, March 24, 2003, p. 8.
19. Ron Panko, "Insuring Retirement," *Best's Review*, May 2000, p. 113.
20. Source: John Hewitt & Associates, 2003 U.S. Individual Disability Market Survey, published April 2004.
21. Source: John Hewitt & Associates, 2003 U.S. Individual Disability Market Survey, published April 2004.
22. Linda Koco, "Mass Mutual Aims Its Buy-Sell DI at Small Businesses," *National Underwriter*, Life & Health/Financial Services Edition, Cincinnati, OH, June 12, 2000, p. 23.
23. Edward Tafaro, "Protecting Intellectual Capital," *Advisor Today*, September 2001, p. 94.
24. Dennis Mullen, "Prospecting for Supplemental Disability Income Insurance Sales," *Life Insurance Selling*, April 2002, p. 51.
25. "10 insurance policies you don't need," *Consumer Reports*, July 2004, p. 49.
26. Source: John Hewitt & Associates, 2003 U.S. Group Disability Market Survey, published March 2004.
27. Gregory Dulac, "To Excel With Worksite DI Products, Understand Differences Between Them," *National Underwriter*, Life & Health/Financial Services Edition, Cincinnati, OH, June 25, 2001, p. 8.
28. Source: Center for Women's Business Research, "Women Business Owners in Numbers" November 2002.
29. Steven Hulbert, "Ability-Focused Sales – Selling Disability Insurance in a Down Market," *Life Insurance Selling*, November 2001, p. 132.

30. John Barilla, "Expand Your Practice with Group Disability Insurance," *National Underwriter*, Life & Health/Financial Services Edition, Cincinnati, OH, January 5, 2004, p. 11.
31. Kevin Riley, "Where Has All the Data Gone?" *National Underwriter*, Life & Health/Financial Services Edition, Cincinnati, OH, September 22, 2003, p. 5.
32. Blaise DiFedele, "Integrated Disability Coverage: Seamless and Successful," *National Underwriter*, April 12, 2004, p. 17.
33. Andre C. Baillaregeon, FSA, "Developing a Successful STD/LTD Package Discount Program, *Disability Newsletter*, July 2000, p. 2.
34. "Standard Insurance Company Announces Launch of Its Lifetime Security Benefit," *Business Wire*, December 12, 2000.
35. Ken Smith, "Financial Plans Often Lack Critical Illness Insurance," *Life Insurance Selling*, April 2003, p. 59.
36. Paul Peter Magnaterra, Sr., "He Learned the Hard Way What Not Having CI Insurance Means," *National Underwriter*, Life & Health/Financial Services Edition, Cincinnati, OH, June 3, 2002, p. 17.
37. Sheila Matheson, "Unlocking the Market's Vast Potential," *National Underwriter*, Life & Health/Financial Services Edition, Cincinnati, OH, March 25, 2002, p. 4.
38. Jeffrey J. Morgan, Sr., "CI Insurance Has a Place on the Worksite Benefit Menu," *National Underwriter*, Life & Health/Financial Services Edition, Cincinnati, OH, June 16, 2003, p. 11.
39. "Eastbridge Study Finds Some Surprising New Trends in Voluntary Products," *PR Newswire*, June 15, 2004.
40. Jennifer M. Gangloff, "Critical Illness Insurance May Fill the Gap Between Life and Disability Coverage," *insure.com* website, July 2001.
41. Linda Koco, "Critical Illness Insurance: Real or Gimmick?" *National Underwriter*, Life & Health/Financial Services Edition, Cincinnati, OH, January 8, 2001, p. 11.
42. Neiciee Durrence, "Critical Illness Insurance: The Essential Cushion," *FAIFA Journal*, Spring 2002, p. 12.
43. Shelby Smith, "Linking Critical Illness Insurance to Reality," *Life Insurance Selling*, November 2001, p. 34.
44. Susan Kimball, FSA, MAAA, "CI Insurance Isn't Just a Stand-Alone Product Anymore," *National Underwriter*, Life & Health/Financial Services Edition, Cincinnati, OH, June 16, 2003, p. 14.
45. Linda Koco, "Group Term Policy Gets a CI Upgrade," *National Underwriter*, Life & Health/Financial Services Edition, Cincinnati, OH, December 3, 2001, p. 41.
46. Daniel R. Pisetsky, "CI Insurance Update: Market is Poised for Growth," *National Underwriter*, Life & Health/Financial Services Edition, Cincinnati, OH, June 16, 2003, p. 5.
47. Patricia Metzner, JD, "Critical Illness Insurance Faces Regulatory Obstacles," *National Underwriter*, Life & Health/Financial Services Edition, Cincinnati, OH, April 4, 2000, p. 23.

Part Four:
Knowledge is Power

"It has yet to be proven that intelligence has any survival value."

– Arthur C. Clarke

Key Concepts

1. The 1990s were a financial shock to DI insurers stung by overly generous policy provisions. The resulting market consolidation saw many companies leave the market or merge.

2. Annual growth rates in new individual DI annualized premium for the industry from 1989 to 1998 were mostly negative. 2001 saw the first strong increase in individual DI sales.

3. Women represent an increasingly high percentage of middle to high income earners in today's economy and a growing number of small business owners.

4. Asian-Americans are a promising target market with many high income earners and business owners.

5. Insurers are increasingly flexible in their approach to covering home-based business owners, a relatively untapped emerging market

6. The professional market is clearly different from two decades ago, with lower issue limits and less favorable disability definitions, but opportunities remain.

7. The vast majority of disabilities are due to illness rather than injury.

8. Obesity is leading to increased disability among the young.

9. Taxation of disability income insurance varies according to the source of premium payments and the policy beneficiary.

10. Many DI claims departments use a transferable skills analysis in evaluating a disability claimant.

If you have read this far, you have learned more information about disability income insurance than you would likely ever impart to one client. And yet there is so much more to study. This section of the book adds more topics to your understanding of this vital source of income and asset protection. It includes background on the product's history, additional product and market information, a handy tax reference, more on the Americans with Disabilities Act, and some additional statistical data. In a sales interview, you never know what might be important to the prospect, but being a student of the product line will have you prepared in the event the most unlikely of appealing features or questions springs front and center in the individual's mind. You know better than to prejudge people. If you apply that same lesson to the information in this book, you will enjoy tremendous success helping people carve out their financial destinies.

HISTORY OF THE DISABILITY INCOME WORLD, PART 1

"History is, indeed, little more than the register of the crimes, follies and misfortunes of mankind."

– Edward Gibbon

You don't have to be Alex Haley to understand the concept and the power of one's roots. The legacy of the past is often reflected in today's world. Disability income insurance is no different.

Roman history is more than the stabbing of Julius Caesar and Nero fiddling away while the glorious city burned. It is in this ancient culture that the first idea of disability income protection was born. Here, workers belonging to an artisan guild all contributed to a fund that was accessed and used to furnish cash payments to families of guild members who were injured or ill and could not conduct their practice.

The idea of "Greeks bearing gifts" may also have disability income implications. Grecian mariners taken ill on a sea voyage were rowed ashore to the nearest island—the Aegean Sea is full of them—and given lodging, candlelight, and an attendant to see to his needs until recovery. No cash like the practical Romans, but room and board and rehab, an equally important combination.

Personal disability policies today have a presumptive total disability clause in them. The earliest form of this provision involves the infamous Dutch mercenaries, soldiers of war who continue to ply their trade even today. In "renting" these warriors out in the 17th Century, the Dutch government bestowed on them insurance for the loss of sight or limbs, certainly a hazard in that line of work.

As we know, Lloyd's of London will take odds on almost anything from Phineas Fogg's balloon ride to James Cameron's search for the *Titanic*. Insuring people for a disability? No problem. From England, this idea of economic protection against medical misfortune was brought over to the colonies – us.

Insurance companies began appearing in the 18th Century in America. Disability coverage was first called "establishment funds" where cash payments went to employees who suffered an accident or sickness. Accident-only plans were created following the development of the railway system as Americans heeded the call to "go west."

As noted in Part 2 of this book, the Industrial Revolution, while a marvel of technology and progress, also took its toll on the workers who operated the earliest "time-saving" machines. Workers' compensation laws were eventually installed in the first decade of the 20th Century and included total and partial disability payments for such on-the-job occurrences. Shortly after, employers found reasons to insure the disability threat on a group basis for their employees, the genesis of group DI plans.

The Social Security Act initially made no provision for disability income until several years later, but that enhancement really brought disability coverage into the public eye. It also made people aware that this Social Security benefit needed a supplement, and individual DI sales took off.

During the Eisenhower administration, whilst suburban America grew and men in gray flannel suits went to work, insurers refined their disability insurance offerings. Out of this came the expansion of the total disability definition to include "own occupation" language that was a radical one-test approach to qualifying insureds for benefits.

This policy language would help to bolster new premium dramatically, but eventually would create its first claims crisis in the (when else)

1960s. It was a decade when America itself seemed on fire, and DI insurers had to break out the extinguishers themselves. It was a time of sweeping examination of the nature of disability claims and how policy language did (or did not) support what was happening most often to people following an injury or illness.

This analysis resulted in the introduction of a new individual DI policy benefit in the early 1970s. While President Nixon was waving goodbye to the White House, insurers were saying hello to this new feature that paid a portion of benefits to an individual based on the amount of income lost following a disability. Existing DI policies only addressed the return of an individual to his or her own occupation on a short-term (six months or less) basis. Yet claims results were showing the majority of policyowners operating at a financial debt for months and even years while recuperating at work. Residual disability suddenly plugged this gap.

But agents at that time didn't listen to this part of the story. At the same time insurers introduced residual language to the world, they also pulled back the "own occupation" definition of total disability. The one-test qualifier became a two-test either immediately, or after a short period of time. To those that had to sell these new policies, residual disability looked like a takeaway. Even the name "residual" implied something less than the whole, especially when your "whole" was long-term "own occupation" total disability coverage.

Rocky start, yes? All of the education and training in the world had difficulty putting the residual concept across as anything but second-best. It would take a few good claims years in the late 1970s – early 1980s before the majority of disability income insurers brought back "own occupation" and packaged it with residual disability to ease the suspicions of jaded insurance advisors. Within a short-time, however, residual disability with its many definitions and parameters became the benchmark by which a strong disability income portfolio was measured, sort of like artists whose work isn't appreciated until long after they are dead.

The 1970s also saw the election of Jimmy Carter, a milestone marked by a coincidental meteoric rise in inflation. Oil shortages led to lines at the gas pump longer than people waiting overnight to buy Bruce Springsteen concert tickets. Prices for nearly everything skyrocketed and double-digit inflation was suddenly a pocketbook concern for everyone. DI insurers responded to this with Cost of Living riders in the late 1970s that increased claim benefits each year, understanding that the value of the claim dollar would decrease over time.

The late 1970s also saw two other concerns addressed in the form of new product enhancements. It was becoming clear that the Social Security Administration was turning down a substantial majority of initial disability claims, and though some of these were eventually awarded, the appeals process was a lengthy, drawn-out affair, and it would be a year or two before much of this was settled. DI insurers' issue limit tables were taking Social Security benefits into account, an overly optimistic view that left many people underinsured when Social Security was using their "Denial" stamp with greater frequency.

The Social Security offset riders of the late 1970s gave DI purchasers a new opportunity to "guarantee" that if Social Security denied their claim, this rider would help bring benefit levels, when combined with base coverage, back up to amounts at which a family could maintain their former standard of living.

The other trend apparent in the late 1970s was the use of rehabilitation programs to help injured or ill workers return to work. These programs might help an individual go back to their original job, or be re-educated for a new one. There was a cost to them, of course, and having the DI insurer foot the bill was a positive incentive for the disabled insured. With residual disability coverage now paying a portion of benefits based on income loss following a return to work, rehabilitation provisions implemented in this creative product development period furnished the early incentive to start this process.

This array of new product achievement in the 1970s led to significant attention for the DI market, especially by agents eager to sell this type of income protection to a workforce who needed it. Some of the corrections to the product done in the early part of this decade to halt unexpectedly high claims losses was also paying off; a result some DI insurers would use as a reason to, in the words of the Roman soldier Maximus in the film *Gladiator,* "unleash hell."

History of the Disability Income World, Part 2

"History never looks like history when you are living through it."

– John W. Gardner

The disability income market had come a long way forward from the Roman Empire. It was important coverage, and by the 1980s a number of insurance agents were selling it on a regular basis. It still didn't enjoy the support and activity that life insurance, annuities, and—later in the "Greed is Good" decade—variable products and securities possessed.

Stop Making Sense

By the early 1980s, DI insurer profits were healthy beyond expectation. This was so encouraging to them that they transformed into game show hosts, their pockets bulging with cash, anxious to make their contestants happy and the studio audience crying for more.

The "own occupation" definition of total disability played its "Get out of Jail Free" card. In early 1980s DI product enhancement, carriers made it a one-test deal for lifetime, and would have insured the hereafter if they could price it. Short memories ruled, and the market's superstar was enjoying its comeback status. Agents were back on familiar ground.

Issue limits went from Mount Tom to Mount Everest. In 1975, $5,000/month in coverage was considered a substantial amount of coverage (and insurer liability). By the early 1980s, underwriters were approving $15,000, $20,000, $25,000 as if we were all sitting in an art auction. Much of this was issued with a lifetime benefit period, stretching insurer financial responsibility into the stratosphere.

Females had begun joining the workforce in record numbers, as Boomer women ignored the traditional childbirth rites and headed instead to the boardroom. By the time Reaganomics was in full bloom and the number of small female-run businesses multiplying, the DI industry began examining their customary pricing practices of setting female rates higher than their male counterparts.

While women experienced favorable results on the mortality (life expectancy) side of the actuarial ledger, this was not the case with the morbidity (disability) tally. Females simply had more disability claims then men. Now, in an effort to interest the increasing ranks of professional women in this income protection concept, insurers decided that this poor experience was probably due to the smaller sampling that represented sales to women over the last few decades. Today's "new" female, was different, they argued, and had even greater incentive than men to return to work following a disability to prove their mettle.

DI carriers began advertising "unisex" rates for their professional occupation classes, a few occupations reflecting the upper tier of past claims experience. The "unisex" label was a bit misleading, as many companies didn't average the male and female rates; instead, they calculated the "male" rate and set the female rate equal to it, an even more optimistic outlook than perhaps originally intended.

This had all the makings of a good idea and there was resulting good publicity from this revision in "old thinking." But in the 1980s, good ideas were churned up in a stampede for more premium dollars. With record profits in hand, carriers felt DI was the holy grail for this era.

So they super-sized the female rate reductions. They extended this practice of calculating male rates for both genders throughout the occupation classes. In addition, they removed "normal pregnancy" as an exclusion from the policy, extending DI coverage to this event that could only happen to one sex, excluding the Arnold Schwarzenegger film *Junior*. This meant expanded coverage to the female risk at a price significantly lower than had ever been charged.

This kind of gung-ho attitude permeated through the insurance company. Premium rates in general dropped to attract new business. Medical exam requirements were nearly outlawed, with strong reliance on attending physician's statements rather than current exam data up to $10,000/month.

With all the one-upsmanship going on, replacements ran wild. Why should a physician hold onto a $10,000/month policy with insurer A, when insurer B was offering the same $10,000 at a lower elimination period and longer benefit period for less money? It was "White Sale" days year-round at your friendly neighborhood DI insurer. Consumers felt like Thomas Jefferson after he completed the Louisiana Purchase.

Small Craft Warnings

The reason this shopping spree was so much fun is that it takes about 6-10 years for a DI portfolio to measure its success or failure by claims experience. DI liberalizations were easy to take because the impact on the bottom line was years away, and many were betting, with the resilience of those who play the Lottery every week, that it would never come at all.

But eventually the Reaper left a calling card. Claims liability and resulting reserves soared, and the toys had to be repossessed. Beginning in the late 1980s and continuing throughout the 1990s, the bottom fell out of the market for many DI carriers.

It didn't take a flurry of claims to accomplish this DI portfolio pillaging. After all, how many $35,000/month lifetime claims does it take to turn claims experience upside down? That's $420,000 in benefits just in the *first year*. The insurer smiles disappeared, and no amount of brushing with Pepsodent was going to help.

America loves to point fingers and everywhere people were looking for someone to blame. They fixed quickly on an unlikely target – physicians. Doctors had long been the sought after market, one of high premiums and low frequency of claims. But experience for this medical occupation was deteriorating to frightening levels. Managed care became the scapegoat, a health care delivery practice that cut down practitioners' incomes and apparently chased them onto disability claim, exacerbating any medical condition they had.

The reasons more likely lay with the high indemnity, benefit rich, low-cost policies that could pay out more than the national treasury of Argentina. It was good to sell DI until policyholders started filing claims with some regularity. The DI path to insurer riches had wandered far off course. Small craft warnings were issued. It was time to take drastic action.

The belts not only were tightened; they choked off circulation. A flurry of insurer exits was followed by drastic policy and rate changes. The female rate experiment was over. So were $35,000/month issue limits.

Occupational classifications changed overnight, with physicians dropped down several notches, their toehold at the top at an end.

Insurers began requiring tax returns with the applications to verify income. Medical exam requests came back in vogue and blood tests were routinely required, giving underwriters access to a bevy of current data, better even than an attending physician's report. Insurers swore off lifetime benefits and 30-day elimination periods, but like quitting cigarette smoking, some of the heavy damage had already been done.

At the front-end of the new business underwriting process, the 1990s brought these trends:

Changes by 1993	% of Insurers
Companies with geographic pricing	70%
Companies with limits on drug, alcohol or Mental/nervous disorders	48%
Companies with restrictions on MDs	39%
Companies with limits in California	35%
Companies with limits in Florida	22%
Companies with sex-distinct pricing	22%

Source: A.M. Best survey of 23 DI insurers

These were unprecedented moves to be sure. The Mental/Nervous disorder benefit limitation would eventually expand to all companies. Retirees may have loved Florida and California as a destination, but DI insurers would just as soon return them both to Spain. Physicians found themselves scrambling for coverage, and no longer able to cover even a third of their incomes in some cases.

On the back end, it was as if Boris Badenov and Natasha Fatale had taken over the claims departments. The insurers played strong arm hardball with that former marketing "darling" – the own occupation definition of total disability. This clause has always had more sales appeal than logical insurance credibility. But agents loved keeping the sales presentation short – "if you can't legitimately perform the main duties of your occupation, you'll collect total disability benefits no matter what else you choose to do and how much money you make." Never mind that this provision actually meant that someone could be potentially better off on claim than working, a paranoia DI carriers had been nursing for years. There was an objective to bring in the large premium numbers, and this policy provision was the easiest way to do that.

The explanation of this policy feature may have been simple, but in Claims Land, the ride was rocky with steep drops in the dark. Claims examiners, at times, seem to hang on the claimant's possible performance of any one duty of an occupation to dismiss policy eligibility. For example, a surgeon that could no longer perform surgery due to a medical condition was being denied "own occupation" benefits because he could still read ex-rays or confer with patients. It didn't seem to matter that no one was going to see this surgeon due to his inability to operate. What was said at sales time and what was happening during the claims review created a cottage industry of litigating attorneys and DI expert witnesses.

Residual disability fared little better. Claims examiners requested mountains of paperwork from the insureds, many of whom were forced to hire and pay for accountants to assemble the data. These demands ranged from convoluted expense breakdowns to patient logs, to be reviewed under the microscope by the newest members of the claim department family – CPAs. Claims handling had moved from stealth to stalemate.

The attorneys and DI specialists began publishing articles about how to fill in a claim form to lessen the ammunition a claims examiner might use against a disabled insured. There were different instructions if you had a policy that contained both total and residual disability. Agents were chastised in these articles for both not playing a larger role in the claims process or getting involved and then filling out the claim form to the client's detriment.[1] It was like the scene at the end of the film *Bridge on the River Kwai* where the camp doctor is wandering around in the aftermath of the explosion that sunk the bridge, saying, "Madness! Madness!"

Die Another Day

The 1990s was a financial shock to the system for DI insurers. The losses peaked in 1994 and have been slowly improving since then. Only a couple of DI carriers escaped the wrath of the "own occ" Gods. Trends in this decade included:[2]

1. Market consolidation, with many companies choosing to exit the market, while others merged together to form a stronger unit.

2. A substantial reduction in new premium being issued.

3. More restrictive products and underwriting practices; and

4. Greater sophistication and utilization of claim management resources.

Some insurers decided the best strategy was to sell their DI block (if they could) and move on. Others sought strength in numbers. Provident Life & Accident acquired Paul Revere Life uniting the two largest DI writers in a merger akin to combining the Yankees and the Red Sox. Provident then went to join forces with UNUM Corporation in June 1999. UNUM had already acquired payroll deduction DI king Colonial Life & Accident, so essentially the four largest DI writers were now operating under the same umbrella, christened UNUMProvident.[3] By 2001, two other DI giants – Guardian Life and Berkshire Life – had also decided to break bread from the same table, giving the industry its second monolith in a short period of time.[4] Some people had to wonder if the DI market would ever rebound.

For a while it seemed as if disability income was destined to be the Montreal Expos of the insurance industry, slated for contraction. But something happened on the way to Valhalla. As the 21st Century dawned, more than two centuries since the Romans paid DI benefits to infirmed members of the artisan guilds, the DI product line managed to rise from the ashes of controversy, burgeoning loss ratios and a sales slump to ride a strong resurgence and return to profitability.

Well, the market (and the need) never really went anywhere. It was the disappearing acts of agents and insurers that took this product line out of the positive limelight, leaving behind reduced benefit levels, questionable claims practices, higher rates, tighter underwriting, and, ultimately, working consumers, vulnerable to a loss of earning power. A number of disability insurance agents moved over to long-term care when the DI market dropped like the Tower of Terror elevator at Universal Studios Orlando. But now that the LTC industry is doing its own strutting and fretting on the claims stage, curiosity is bringing these sales people back to DI.

Sales growth had been dismal since 1989. Annual growth rates in new individual DI annualized premium for the industry from 1989 to 1998 was mostly negative. (See chart later on in this section.) The years 1999 and 2000 witnessed flat to slightly positive increases in new business.[5]

Then came 2001. U.S. individual disability insurers saw sales increases of 11%, according to the John Hewitt & Associates annual survey. Premium revenue from the sales of non-cancelable DI went up by 15%.[6]

Ironically, leading the way in the DI market today are several carriers who chose not to follow Alice down the rabbit hole in the 1980s game of competitive product enhancements that created policies that were too good to be true. Mocked at the time, even by their own field forces, these insurers chose to stay a practical course and have maintained their DI portfolios throughout the lean period of 1986 – 2000, when the individual non-cancelable industry consistently lost money year after year.

These companies kept benefit amounts at a reasonable and thus insurable level. They relied on disability definitions that were fair, and underwrote the risk properly, enabling them to grow their business even through the market downturn. They've explored new ways to write business, including providing coverage for the new at-home worker.

The 2001 news was a welcome respite for a beleaguered industry and came at a time of economic recession, as the roaring 90s gave way under the pressure of sustaining unreachable numbers. Historically, this type of national financial downturn has promoted floods of claims of relatively short duration. That this did not occur shows the movement towards longer elimination periods during the previous decade had greatly diminished this negative claims effect.[7] Of course, many DI carriers missed the monetary windfalls individuals and companies experienced during the 1990s, but many were just pleased to be taken off of life support.

The news seemed even better in 2002, with increases again. A Conning Research & Consulting study indicated that the individual DI market has shown signs of a sustainable recovery—the first time that had been said in over a decade.[8] Carriers had made their adjustments and come out ready to play again. On the sales end, newer agents to the business, unaware of the previous history of this product line, were also looking for education and training to sell this coverage to their clients.

This was good tidings for the insurers who have stayed front-and-center with this product through tough times. It's even better news for consumers who have gone unprotected from the threat of injury or illness. Working families today are living close to the edge, and college education expenses for the kids loom in front of them like white water on a canoe trip. They deserve to hear the DI story and, with more of us telling it, they might have the opportunity to add this important protection to their financial portfolios.

DI insurers seem to have crossed the Rubicon. Proper pricing, less liberal but exceedingly fair policy provisions, unbundled products for maximum flexibility, and a younger generation poised to move into their higher earnings years who have a stronger need for security than the Boomers did at their age, all point towards a better future. Thus, there are sales to make, people to help; and so, like James Bond, disability income insurance will just have to die another day.

Non-Can DI Financial Results

Item	1980	1981	1982	1983	1984	1985	1986	1987	1988
New Sales Growth	-	-	-	-	-	-	17.0%	12.6%	3.6%
Premium $(000)	$395.2	$454.7	$527.4	$611.4	$714.4	$836.0	$962.9	$1,129.8	$1,304.6
Premium Growth	-	15.1%	16.0%	15.9%	16.8%	17.0%	15.2%	17.3%	15.5%
Incurred Claims	43.5%	44.2%	46.5%	46.9%	48.1%	50.3%	56.5%	58.1%	64.1%
Increase in Policy Reserves	17.1%	16.8%	15.0%	12.9%	13.3%	9.9%	11.4%	12.3%	12.6%
Claims & Increase in Policy Reserves	60.6%	61.0%	61.5%	59.8%	61.4%	60.2%	67.9%	70.4%	76.7%
Commissions	22.2%	23.3%	24.0%	24.2%	24.9%	26.0%	26.4%	27.1%	26.1%
Expenses	22.7%	24.0%	25.7%	26.6%	27.4%	26.8%	27.8%	28.0%	27.0%
Tax, Licenses & Fees	3.3%	3.4%	3.5%	3.4%	3.6%	3.6%	3.6%	3.7%	3.5%
Commissions, Expenses & Taxes	48.2%	50.7%	53.2%	54.2%	55.9%	56.4%	57.8%	58.8%	56.6%
Net Investment Income	20.9%	21.4%	21.1%	21.8%	23.1%	24.4%	23.6%	23.6%	26.9%
Margin	12.1%	9.7%	6.5%	7.8%	5.8%	7.8%	-2.2%	-5.5%	-6.4%
Margin/Total Revenue (Premium & Net Investment Income)	10.0%	8.0%	5.4%	6.4%	4.7%	6.3%	-1.8%	-4.4%	-5.0%

Non-Can DI Financial Results (cont'd)

Item	1989	1990	1991	1992	1993	1994	1995	1996
New Sales Growth	6.3%	3.0%	3.0%	-1.3%	-8.6%	-5.2%	-12.0%	-23.5%
Premium $(000)	$1,503.6	$1762.5	$1981.2	$2163.6	$2314.3	$2466.8	$2594.7	$2687.1
Premium Growth	15.3%	17.2%	12.4%	9.2%	7.0%	6.6%	5.2%	3.6%
Incurred Claims	63.7%	64.7%	69.1%	77.1%	79.9%	91.1%	96.0%	103.7%
Increase in Policy Reserves	11.9%	12.4%	12.3%	12.1%	13.4%	13.5%	12.7%	10.3%
Claims & Increase in Policy Reserves	75.6%	77.1%	81.3%	89.2%	93.2%	104.6%	108.8%	114.0%
Commissions	25.0%	25.0%	23.7%	22.0%	22.6%	20.9%	20.5%	17.7%
Expenses	27.5%	25.9%	25.0%	23.6%	21.6%	19.2%	17.3%	16.0%
Tax, Licenses & Fees	3.4%	3.3%	3.2%	3.2%	3.2%	3.1%	2.9%	2.8%
Commissions, Expenses & Taxes	55.8%	54.3%	51.9%	48.8%	47.4%	43.2%	40.7%	36.5%
Net Investment Income	27.7%	26.9%	28.7%	30.3%	32.1%	32.5%	34.7%	37.1%
Margin	-3.7%	-4.5%	-4.5%	-7.7%	-8.5%	-15.3%	-14.8%	13.4%
Margin/Total Revenue (Premium & Net Investment Income)	-2.9%	-3.5%	-3.5%	-5.9%	-6.4%	-11.6%	-11.0%	-9.8%

DI MARKET INFO UPDATE

"Money was never a big motivator for me, except as a way to keep score. The real excitement is playing the game."

– Donald Trump

The markets for disability income have long centered on the professional risk. Those with a substantial educational investment – doctors, lawyers, CPAs, architects, pharmacists, engineers – were—and for the most part, still are—the types of insureds DI companies want to attract.

Non-Can DI Financial Results (cont'd)

Item	1997	1998	1999	2000	2001	2002	AVG.
New Sales Growth	-10.1%	-9.3%	-2.3%	-3.5%	12.0%	5.3%	-0.8%
Premium $(000)	$2702.4	$2673.8	$2692.4	$2771.7	$2770.7	$2788.0	-
Premium Growth	0.6%	-1.1%	0.7%	2.9%	0.0%	0.6%	9.3%
Incurred Claims	101.0%	108.3%	101.6%	103.8%	107.8%	114.6%	75.7%
Increase in Policy Reserves	11.2%	9.3%	7.5%	6.5%	3.1%	1.7%	11.3%
Claims & Increase in Policy Reserves	112.3%	117.6%	109.0%	110.2%	110.9%	116.4%	86.9%
Commissions	15.0%	13.7%	13.0%	11.5%	11.5%	11.4%	20.8%
Expenses	17.9%	19.9%	21.0%	18.9%	18.6%	18.8%	22.9%
Tax, Licenses & Fees	2.9%	2.7%	2.5%	2.6%	2.8%	2.6%	3.2%
Commissions, Expenses & Taxes	35.8%	36.4%	36.5%	33.0%	32.9%	32.8%	46.9%
Net Investment Income	42.7%	49.4%	49.8%	51.8%	58.6%	59.6%	33.4%
Margin	-5.4%	-4.5%	4.3%	8.6%	14.9%	10.4%	-0.4%
Margin/Total Revenue (Premium & Net Investment Income)	-3.8%	-3.0%	2.8%	5.6%	9.4%	6.5%	-0.3%

This has changed some over the last few years. DI insurers spent the 1990s looking into the abyss, and what they saw were other market opportunities. Professional risks only make up about 20% of the DI market, and someone finally did the math and decided to focus on selling to the rest of a large, underserved working population. Middle income earners ($25,000 - $75,000) were the new targets. Benefit levels would naturally be lower, as these amounts are based on income, keeping the overall financial liability lower for the carrier.

Other markets started to emerge, and older groups that had dropped out of favor were re-tooled, as the 21st century brought renewed vigor to this important product line.

Women

Females have always been a willing listener to ideas about financial security. They have a stronger sense of their own vulnerability, and have long been the voice of reason in the family when considering disability income coverage. Women represent an increasingly high percentage of middle to high income earners in today's economy.

A 2004 study recently released would seem to confirm that females should remain high on the priority list for insurance agents and advisors discussing disability protection. Financial independence is their primary goal, and women are more involved today than ever in personal and household financial decisions, including purchasing or managing various products that help grow and protect wealth.[10] Other key results of the Prudential Study on the Financial Experience and Behaviors among Women:

> More than 80% of women polled indicate they need some level of help when making financial decisions.
>
> Women are in agreement that it is good judgment to review financial plans and financial topics, and more than half of those polled said they prefer a financial professional to other channels or information sources.
>
> Among seven major financial goals, 40 to 50 percent of women polled are not confident they have sufficiently prepared to meet their objectives.
>
> Source: Prudential Financial, Inc.

Noted earlier in this book is that women represent a growing number of new small business owners, a position they are intent on protecting. This opens the door for talks about personal disability income, business overhead expense, and even disability buy-out coverage.

Asian-Americans

Did you know that 22% of Asian-American households earn $100,000 or more annually? Or that between 1990 and 2000, the Asian-American population grew by 72%, far outpacing the U.S. total population growth of 13%? Or that more and more Asian-Americans are becoming business owners, many of whom are running very profitable companies?[11]

No? Here is a promising target market, growing at a phenomenal clip. These are high earners, business owners – exactly the type of prospect you are looking for to talk about disability income protection. Insurers are starting to realize that this is a potentially strong market for their products and some have developed language-specific information aimed at this audience.

You might consider pairing up with Asian-American agents in your approach to this market. They will have the contacts and the credibility in this market, while you can provide the technical back-up necessary to properly identify a need for disability income protection.

Population of Major Asian-American Groups (in millions)

Chinese	2.9
Filipino	2.4
Asian Indian	1.9
Korean	1.2
Vietnamese	1.2
Japanese	1.1

Source: LIMRA International

Asian-Americans who have been in the United States for many years tend to have a large influence on recent immigrants.[12] Nurturing an effective center of influence here will also assist you in DI market penetration.

Nail salons, hotels, and grocery stores are all businesses where Asian-American ownership is high. Study your occupational guide and financial underwriting information from your DI insurer(s) to see what type of coverage can be written. Approach this as you would any other target market by learning as much as you can about this emerging DI prospect group. It can pay off handsomely for you and provide crucial income protection to an underserved group.

Home-Based Businesses

Most of America's 11 million home-based businesses do not have proper business insurance coverage, according to an Independent Insurance Agents & Brokers survey. More survey results:[13]

- One in 10 U.S. households operates a full or part-time home-based business. However, nearly 60% of these businesses do not have insurance coverage.

- Nearly 40% of home-based business owners say they thought they were protected by other coverage.

- 30% say their businesses are too small to insure; nearly 20% could not give a reason for not having insurance.

It is important to remember that insuring home-based businesses is still relatively new for DI insurers. But, as the years have passed, more experience is improving carrier confidence in this prospect-filled market.

It's clear from these 2004 survey results that there is a need for education in the insurance area for these (likely new) business owners. Since many may have started their home business as a result of a layoff at the firm in which they worked, the insurance protection side of running your own company is brand new territory for these folks.

Insurers are increasingly flexible in their approach to writing the home-based business owner. It's another emerging market that is relatively untapped. Check out the local home-based business association in your area and begin your target market work today.

The Professional Market

Today's professional market in disability income is clearly different from two decades ago. Issue limits are well below their old levels. The "own occupation" total disability definition is more of a rarity, and only a few professionals can obtain this type of contractual language today. Lifetime benefit periods have been largely eliminated, and are available in truncated forms now.

That doesn't mean there are not opportunities here. Executives, engineers, architects, and pharmacists are some of the professional occupations often overlooked during the write-the-doctor/attorney sweepstakes of the 1970s and 80s.

There are some things to remember as you continue to work in this market.[14]

1. Existing coverage owned by these risks is, in all likelihood, a piece of gold. It should be placed in the family vault and only brought out on special occasions. The premiums, definitions, and coverage are probably untouchable.

2. Some prospects may have maximized their issue limit capabilities in the individual market. But there is still additional coverage that may be added through their professional associations. You might look to see if there is an opportunity to write group LTD if the business has a sufficient number of employees. It may be worth paying the premium for a few workers to obtain additional benefits through this route. There is also critical illness coverage that can supplement the individual DI protection. You may have to be creative, but the possibilities to serve the prospect are there.

3. If the insured has room to add some more individual DI coverage, check the DI market thoroughly. There are quality individual policies available with better definitions, but be sure to survey what's available through a disability brokerage firm to ensure you are providing the best in available benefits today.

4. Evaluate fully what definition of disability will be most suitable here. For many professionals, the "own occupation" language is still desired and appropriate. You may also add residual disability benefits to cover all eventualities. Since professional risks can often afford both definitions, it is a comprehensive package you can easily assemble. If premium is an issue, then select, with the prospect's help, the definition that best fits the likely claim scenario.

STATISTICS TO WORK BY

"USA Today has come out with a new survey – apparently three out of every four people make up 75 percent of the population."

– David Letterman

The use of statistics should be kept to a minimum in a sales interview. However, this data is a great way to learn more about disability insurance and perhaps help you focus on the task at hand – to see and tell the DI story to as many people as you can.

Impairments by Percentage of Claim

Only 13.4% of all disabilities are due to injury. The vast majority are illness-related. Here is a breakdown:[15]

Impairment	Percentage of All Claims
Back disorders	18.2%
Emotional/psychiatric	12.7%
Neurological	11.3%
Extremities	9.0%
Cardiovascular	4.1%
Diabetes	3.6%
Substance abuse	3.3%
Hearing	2.9%
Vision	2.6%
Blood disorders	2.6%
Cancer	2.3%
Asthma	1.7%
Other	25.7%

Obesity Leading to Increased Disability Among the Young

Debuting at the Sundance Film Festival in January 2004 was a documentary called *SuperSize Me*, about director Morgan Spurlock's 30-day binge at McDonald's restaurants. He was spurred onto this project by a judge's rejection of a lawsuit filed by two teenage women against the fast food giant (43% of the market) that alleged eating at McDonald's created obesity and health problems for them. Spurlock had his own health problems in the making of this documentary, including weight gain, cholesterol increase, and, even more dangerous, declining liver functions.

The 2004 National Health Interview Survey looked for disability trends among people age 18-69 from 1984 to 2000. What they discovered should be interesting to disability income sales people:[16]

- From 1984 to 1996, the sharpest increases in incidence of disability were amongst the 30-39 age grouping.

- Among those aged 50 to 59 years, disability rose only among those that were obese.

- Obesity accounts for about half of the increased disability among those age 18-29, about one-quarter for those age 30-39, and about one-tenth for those age 40-49.

- The percentage of U.S. workers who are obese has skyrocketed over the past 40 years and is leading to a surge in disability claims among workers. It's not just the weight: obese workers suffer from diabetes, heart disease, back pain, and other health problems due to their weight and eating habits, and recovery rates from these disabilities are far lower.[17]

This may lead to the necessity of using group STD and LTD in firms as many of these workers will not meet even the generous weight requirements for an individual DI policy. A typical weight chart looks like this:[18]

A paramedical exam is required if the client's weight exceeds the limit in the table below:

Height	Weight	Height	Weight
5'0"	159	5'11"	211
5'1"	163	6'0"	218
5'2"	166	6'1"	222
5'3"	171	6'2"	229
5'4"	176	6'3"	235
5'5"	181	6'4"	242
5'6"	186	6'5"	248
5'7"	191	6'6"	255
5'8"	196	6'7"	261
5'9"	201	6'8"	268
5'10"	207		

While these can be considered very fair weight limits before some adverse medical underwriting may occur, it is an increasing challenge to have some prospects stay under these minimums. This may open up the group market more, as many group cases are sold without underwriting requirements, depending on the number of employees involved.

Disability Sales Surpass Life Insurance

For the first time ever, in 2002 disability sales overtook life insurance sales, increasing 35% since 2001, according to a recent study of worksite marketing carriers. The Eastbridge Consulting Group found, in its fourth such study that disability income and life insurance remain the "lead" products for worksite marketers.19 Any time DI product activity outperforms life insurance in any area of the market is a cause for some celebration for lifelong DI marketers. It shows that, if mentioned, there can be an acceptance of using DI as a resource for income protection.

More on the ADA

"The most valuable function performed by the federal government is entertainment."

– Dave Barry

The Americans with Disabilities Act was passed in 1990 and intended to give people with medical handicaps better opportunities for jobs and benefits. It has led to a wave of lawsuits against employers. While there has been some progress in the area for which it was originally intended, such as making reasonable accommodation to try and bring a disabled worker back, it has been seen by many as a potential monetary windfall.

Defining disability continues to be a prevalent issue in cases filed under the ADA. What exactly does it mean to have a disability under the law?[20] This is not much different than insurers trying to apply their disability definitions in their policy to determine claims eligibility.

What did Congress originally intend nearly a generation ago? Much of this has been decided in court, of course; and the U.S. Supreme Court has seen its share of work in this regard.

**Statistics on EEOC Enforcement of the ADA
1990 – 1999**

ADA charges received: almost 126,000
Resolution favoring plaintiffs: 18,694
Benefits obtained: $261 million
Average award per person: $13,407
Lawsuits filed: 416
Lawsuits resolved: 314
Percentage of ADA cases comprising EEOC caseload: 21 percent

Source: Equal Employment Opportunity Commission, February 2001

As noted in Part 1 of this book, the Supreme Court has generally narrowed the scope of the law, giving some relief to employers. One of their primary decisions was to reduce the ability of individuals with physical impairments that are correctable with medication or assistive device to sue under this law.

The primary contribution of the ADA for disability insurance purposes has been to raise the level of awareness about disability and its nature to consumers. Disability is a very real risk to the working individual and disability income protection can be a surer bet as a financial option than taking one's chances with a successful lawsuit under the ADA.

TAXATION

"The avoidance of taxes is the only intellectual pursuit that carries any reward."

– John Maynard Keynes

The following chart will clarify the various tax treatments of disability income insurance:[21]

Disability Insurance and Federal Taxes

Organization Form	Coverage for	Premium Paid by	Owner/ Beneficiary	Tax Treatment Premium	Tax Treatment Benefits
Individual	Individual	Individual	Individual	Not deductible (IRC Sec. 213 and IRC Sec. 262)	Tax-free (IRC Sec. 104(a)(3))
Sole Proprietor	Sole Proprietor	Sole Proprietor	Sole Proprietor	Not deductible business expense (IRC Sec. 213 and IRC Sec. 262)	Tax-free (IRC Sec 104(a)(3))
	Employee	Employer	Employee	Deductible business expense. Not taxable income to employee (IRC Sec. 162 and IRC Sec. 106)	Benefits reported as income (IRC Sec. 105)
	Employee	Employer	Employer business expense (IRC Sec. 265)	Not deductible sole proprietor (IRC Sec. 104(a)(3))	Tax-free to
Partnership	Partner	Partnership	Partner	Not a deductible business expense (IRC Sec. 262 and IRC Sec.162)	Tax-free (IRC Sec. 104(a)(c))
	Employee	Employer	Employee	Deductible business expense. Not taxable income to employee (IRC Sec. 162 and IRC Sec. 106)	Benefits reported as income (IRC Sec. 105)

Disability Insurance and Federal Taxes (cont'd)

Organization Form	Coverage for	Premium Paid by	Owner/ Beneficiary	Tax Treatment Premium	Benefits
	Employee	Employer	Partnership	Not deductible business expense (IRC Sec. 265)	Tax-free to partnership (IRC Sec. 104(a)(3))
C Corp	Employee	Corporation	Employee	Deductible business expense. Not taxable to employee (IRC Sec. 162 and IRC Sec. 106)	Reported as income (IRC Sec. 105)
	Employee	Corporation	Corporation	Not deductible business expense (IRC Sec. 265)	Tax-free to corporation (IRC Sec. 104(a)(3))
	Employee	Employee funds received through executive bonus	Employee	Executive bonus is tax deductible to the business and is reported as income to employee	Tax-free (IRC Sec. 104(a)(3))
S Corporation	More than 2% Shareholder	Employer	More than 2% Shareholder	Entity deductible expense (IRC Sec. 162) Individual Income taxable (IRC Sec. 61)	Tax free (IRC Sec. 104(a)(3))
	Employee or 2% or less Shareholder	Employer	Employer	Entity deductible expense	Benefits reported as income (IRC Sec. 105)
	Employee or 2% or less Shareholder	Employee funds received through executive Bonus	Employee	Executive bonus is tax deductible to the business and is reported as income to the employee	Tax free (IRC Sec. 104(a)(3))

Disability Overhead Expense

Organization Form	Premium Paid by	Owner/ Beneficiary	Tax Treatment Premium	Benefits
All forms of Eligible Business	Sole proprietor or business	Sole proprietor or business	Tax-deductible (Rev. Rul. 55-264, 1955-1 CB 11)	Reportable as income. However, overhead expenses which are deductible as ordinary business expenses will, to the extent deductible, offset the reportable benefits.

These illustrations should not be considered legal advice. The facts of a particular situation may change the results indicated by these general illustrations.

Used with permission of The Union Central Life Insurance Company. ©2005, The Union Central Life Insurance Co.

> "Big business never pays a nickel in taxes, according to Ralph Nader, who represents a big consumer organization that never pays a nickel in taxes."
>
> – Dave Barry

This book has well-documented the plight of some high earning professionals today as they try to purchase as much DI benefit as possible to cover the greatest percentage of their income, helping to ensure the maintenance of their standard of living after a disability. For individuals earning $500,000 today, for example, a $15,000/month benefit represents only 36% coverage of gross income.

If group or association coverage or critical illness insurance doesn't get the job done, this would seem to leave these upper tax bracket practitioners in an income shortage situation if a disability strikes. Let's face it. Regardless of the level of earnings, people tend to carry a similar debt-to-income ratio. While $15,000/month in coverage is fine for most of us, the wealthier individuals may have a couple of mortgages that come close to that amount.

Some planners are advocating the use of an Equity Disability Trust (EDT) to supplement the individual DI policy. The EDT is a simple vehicle to set up, with no ERISA oversight and no tax filing necessary. It allows these high earners to put a substantial amount of money aside in this supplemental trust on a tax-deductible basis in the event of disability. The benefits will be taxable as income, but the funding should be sufficient (if done properly) to cover the individual's needs.[22]

For example, a 40-year-old whose company contributes $100,000 annually into an EDT for 10 years could have over $3 million in account value by age 60 assuming $94,000 of it goes toward account growth at an 8% return annually. It can even be set up with a premium refund option, meaning it can also act as a retirement supplement (withdrawals can even be taken before the customary age 59? on qualified plans).

It probably works best with a small firm as employees must benefit as owners do, but for a tax deduction and additional money for disability, and possibly retirement if disability benefits are not used, it might just be the thing for your wealthy client or prospect.

As always, check with your tax advisor as tax-favorable programs can easily fall in and out of favor with the IRS.

DI Product Info, Part 1

"You can't have everything. Where would you put it?"

– Steven Wright

Stand-alone disability insurance can be expensive to purchase, especially for workers earning less than $40,000 annually. This doesn't mean the person lacks the need for the coverage, only that the routine DI benefits route is not a financially viable solution.

One way to mitigate the price problem is to consider alternative ways to purchase DI. There are insurers who have developed a DI rider that can be added to a life insurance policy. While it may lack some of the pricier features of an individual DI plan, it does provide some basic total disability coverage for at least a 2-year benefit period.[23]

This has the effect of solving a couple of needs at once. It may not be as comprehensive an answer to the funding problem, but the alternative – leaving it uncovered – makes less sense. The $40,000 income and under worker may not have ample life insurance benefits either, and this approach helps address the total income protection the family needs.

The annuity market has been in a boom phase over the last decade, sold not only by traditional insurance agents but by stockbrokers and bankers as well. With disability an undersold product, some insurers are taking advantage of the annuity boom by tying a DI option to it.

Annuities address the concern of living too long. Disability income is also a hedge against a medical condition that isn't fatal. To package them together makes some sense, and the parallel can be drawn easily for a prospect.

Initially, the packaging trend was limited to the offering of enhanced death benefits or guaranteed minimum income or minimum cash value riders with variable annuity contracts.[24] But this has now expanded to the type of DI rider packaged with life insurance plans as noted above.

Also on the rider front, critical illness insurance is now being tested as an accelerated death benefit option on life insurance policies. Traditionally, the accelerated rider was primarily for terminal illnesses and began paying out all or a portion of the life insurance policy face amount in advance of one's relatively imminent death.

Critical illness, of course, pays upon the diagnosis of a catastrophic condition like a heart attack, stroke, or cancer. These are not necessarily terminal situations, but do create a need for money. That is the purpose of this policy language.

Again, cost savings can be a factor here. When realized as an accelerated rider on a mainstream, fully-underwritten life policy (rather than as a stand-alone product), per policy expenses shift from high to marginal, and claim costs drop due to the value of the underwriting, as well as the efficiencies between the two benefit triggers. The result can be a 30 to 50% reduction in critical illness premiums relative to the stand-alone version.[25]

These options are creative ways to address the need and are better alternatives for most than self-insuring the disability risk.

There are also "all-in-one" type products that cover a variety of needs, including disability. This is not to say that this is an optimum comprehensive solution, as the product must streamline all of the protection in each area, or risk it being price-prohibitive.

That said, it might work for some, especially if packaged and sold at the worksite level. These policies can include benefits for life, supplemental health needs, disability, and a discount savings card.[26] It's an alternative program for those that have difficulty affording the usual stand-alone plans, and with the number of uninsured workers edging ever higher, it may be the option that can bring those alarmingly high numbers down.

DI Product Info, Part 2

"Age to me means nothing. I can't get old; I'm working. I was old when I was twenty-one and out of work."

– George Burns

It is becoming more evident that the Boomer generation will work long beyond the traditional retirement age of 65. One reason is legislated: full Social Security benefits won't be available to Boomers until age 66-67. Another is practical: they need the money, having fallen far behind in adequate retirement planning through spending binges when younger and a late call to parenting. And then there is the emotional: the Boomer identity has long been associated with their working persona.

One of the reasons a person purchases disability income protection is for a sense of security. This has long been the reason DI buyers opted for lifetime benefit periods in the past. The nature of disability is such that it doesn't know when age 65 or 66 or 67 has arrived; it continues to be a problem for the individual. Income needs are still high for as long as the person lives. Given the advances in medical technology, that could be for a long time.

So, there are two issues here: issue age and benefit period length. With respect to issue age, traditional issue for DI policies ends at age 60. Beyond that, the disability options are miniscule. Long-term care insurance, while a necessary purchase by that time, does not provide one with much straight income; most of the benefits are paid to facilities or other providers. With respect to benefit period length, benefit periods backed up big time in the face of the DI crash in the late 1980s – early 1990s. Lifetime coverage was seen as an unwanted luxury by those insurers who had to post mammoth reserves too often for comfort.

There may be signs of loosening on both fronts. Insurers understand the work trend. It's never made sense to me to tell people that are age 65 "thanks for the memories, have a good game of golf." We've tossed aside a lot of valuable experience with this attitude. Many seniors end up returning to the workforce in another capacity due to boredom, need for money, or for self-esteem.

Projected Growth in Senior Labor Force (1982 to 2012)[27]
Number of Workers (thousands)

	1982	1992	2002 Estimated	2012 Projected	Projected Change 2002-2012
Ages 65-74	2,566	2,932	3,665	5,411	48%
75 +	464	542	804	1,000	24%
All Ages	110,204	128,105	144,863	162,269	12%

The numbers above reveal the extent of growth expected from what is thought of as the "gray" labor force. It's a trend DI insurers should not ignore.

The problem of course is pricing. How much do you charge a consumer, age 68 that wants to buy first-time or additional DI coverage? There are more chronic conditions present in older workers, so perhaps DI insurers will look to a different definitional language more along the lines of loss of Activities of Daily Living (ADLs) rather than occupational duties. It is a more restrictive definition, but probably more appropriate for the older worker.

Insurers might also recognize the general health improvement in the older Boomer worker today. The 50-something Boomer is in much better health overall than his or her parents were at the same age. This makes the risk slightly more palatable for the carriers who might see this as a growing market.

Carriers may offer more limited benefit periods to the older buyer. Some insurers modify the benefit period down to two years for those who are writing workers (generally on a group basis) in their 60s.[28] Look for more interest on the part of DI insurers in addressing this group of prospects in the future.

On the benefit period front, insurers may also be recognizing that a longer need beyond age 65 is necessary. While not willing en masse to bring "lifetime" back off the shelf in its unlimited form, a well-known DI carrier has recently introduced new benefit periods of age 67 and 70.[29] The theory is to address the later retirement ages and eligibility for Social Security in addition to the financial obligations such as a child's college education that may arise in one's 60s.

Many feel that age is just a number. DI carriers may soon be coming around to that way of thinking.

DI Product Info, Part 3

"I'm astonished by people who want to know the universe when it's hard enough to find your way around Chinatown."

– Woody Allen

Group disability sales are a tricky business. Group long-term disability (LTD) could be sold on its own. It can be sold in conjunction with group short-term disability (STD), group life insurance, or even individual disability insurance. All of these will have an effect on the pricing of it.

Whereas individual DI coverage has a specific rate that is filed with each state, group LTD has a range of rates that provide more flexibility to reward better case potential with a lower rate. It's not necessarily an exact science.

Interest rates have an effect on LTD pricing. Actuaries use interest rate assumptions in the pricing of disability insurance, be it individual or group. Since group carries a lower rate, and potentially lower margin, it is important to keep pace with market results. The last few years have seen lower interest rate returns and assumptions should be adjusted accordingly. Interest returns are part of the assets that back up LTD claims and thus carry significant importance.[30]

LTD insurers do experience rate as well, relying on past LTD data for a group that it is considering for new business. With pricing margins minimal, group insurers need to be as accurate as they can. Some of the ways that insurers can improve their accuracy in pricing can be useful for the insurance agent selling this type of protection to understand:[31]

1. Collect an accurate, up-to-date census from in-force and potential customers.

2. Develop accurate manual rates that underwriters can trust to represent the basic underlying risk on the case.

3. Underwrite the real reason why a case should or could run differently than the manual rates. For instance, examine financial underwriting; communicate with the claims department about

how the employer is impacting risk results; and obtain experience on more subjective types of claims.

4. Track differences between sold rates and manual rates.

While this type of experience rating will most likely be done with larger cases, one shouldn't ignore the smaller employer. Not all of these firms are better candidates for voluntary, individual coverage. There may be opportunities to install a group STD and/or LTD plan for the smaller size business.

> Combined group disability in-force premium grew approximately 6 percent in 2003, with LTD in-force premium growing about 6 percent and STD in-force premium up about 7 percent. These growth rates are up slightly compared to results for 2002.[32]

Like it or not, with or without significant resources, we know that the small employer is going to have to address future disability situations. We know there will be savings ultimately for the employer that plans ahead. Insured STD/LTD programs have built-in return-to-work methodologies to help place disabled employees back in their jobs as soon as possible. This also aids the small employer who, by having workers return to their positions, will save in reduced workers' compensation costs, reduced costs for other insurance programs, fewer training costs for replacement workers, tax incentives and deductions, and increased productivity.[33] Do not miss out on this small employer market.

The future of group LTD would seem bright. There is a push being made to make DI insurers more risk managers than just disability evaluators. This is a major shift in emphasis, not something a carrier does lightly.

Instead of focusing solely on determining whether employees are eligible for disability benefits, insurers and administrators could work with the in-place health care plan to coordinate early risk identification efforts, wellness services, case management services, rehabilitation services, and more. Managing income benefits could become a secondary objective to maximizing employees' productivity.[34] This focus on wellness could be the next generation of LTD product, where having benefits tied to keeping employees well rather than simply reacting to their sickness would make a great story to tell an employer prospect.

Transferable Skills Analysis

"Always read stuff that will make you look good if you die in the middle of it."

– P.J. O'Rourke

The evaluation of a disability claim is important for the insurance agent and advisor to understand. This is, after all, what you are selling. You deliver a policy today, but it is the promise to pay future benefits that is the true commodity here.

With definitions that have moved away from broader "own occupation" coverage and more towards a return to work emphasis with residual disability benefits, the role of a transferable skills analysis takes on greater importance. What can disabled workers do today and what talents do they possess that can be utilized in other occupational capacities? If returning to their prior profession is not possible, but there is an ability to do other work, how is this evaluated?

Many claims departments use a transferable skills analysis. Skills are identified by knowledge of an industry, skills learned for a specific job, or skills acquired by hobbies or interests that can be utilized for a new job. Reprinted below are the basic aspects of this evaluation process, a vital practice for your client that it is helpful for you to know.

Name _____

Age _____ Telephone _____

Has transportation _____ Yes _____ No

Limitations (if not known, project probable limitations based on injury):

    Lifting: _____ lbs
    Standing: _____ minutes
    Sitting: _____ minutes
    Bending: _____ times/hour
    Walking: _____ minutes

Financial requirements:

    Salary at time of injury/illness: $ _____
    Expected salary: $ _____

Licenses:

    Driver's license: _____ Yes _____ No
    Other licenses: (include certifications or certificates) _____
_____
_____

Union affiliation:

Belongs to union: _____ Yes _____ No
Name of union: _____
Contact person: _____

Employee resources:

Name of family or friends working in jobs client would like to do:

Name: _____ Job: _____ Company: _____
Name: _____ Job: _____ Company: _____
Name: _____ Job: _____ Company: _____

Personal interests and abilities:

How did client spend spare time before injury/illness? _____
_____
_____

Spends time now? _____
_____

List all hobbies and skills needed to do same:

Hobby	Skills
_____	_____
_____	_____
_____	_____
_____	_____

Which would client rather do? (Check one)

1. Work with people _____ or Work with machines _____ ?
2. Work with hands_____ or Work with brainpower_____ ?
3. Work indoors _____ or Work outdoors_____ ?
4. Be in charge _____ or Have a good boss _____ ?
5. Know what is expected _____ or Plan own work_____ ?
6. Meet deadlines _____ or Do job at own pace _____ ?
7. Make few mistakes _____ or Make no mistakes _____ ?
8. Get help fixing errors _____ or Figure out errors by self _____ ?
9. Have job security _____ or Chance for advancemen _____ ?
10. Work with children_____ or Work with adults _____ ?
11. Have regular hours _____ or Change hours as needed _____ ?
12. Make new things_____ or Fix things _____ ?
13. Work at same place _____ or Work at different place_____ ?
14. Travel in job _____ or No travel in job _____ ?
15. Do paperwork_____ or Talk to people_____ ?
16. Learn in class_____ or Learn on the job_____ ?

Skills analysis:

Education:

    High School Diploma?: _____ Yes _____ No   GED? _____ Yes _____ No
    If "No" – Last grade completed _____ Average grade? _____
    Other Education? (include colleges and armed forces training)_____
_____
_____

Reading & comprehension:

    Client reads: Books? _____   Other? _____
                                Magazines? _____   Nothing? _____
                                Newspapers? _____   Can't read?_____

Checks newspapers for want ads? _____ Yes _____ No
Can read and understand application for jobs? _____ Yes _____ No
(If not sure, have client read application to you)
Can fill out application? _____ Yes _____ No

Mathematics ability:

Can make change? _____ Yes _____ No
Can do simple problems? _____ Yes _____ No
Has a checking account? _____ Yes _____ No
Who in family handles family budget? _____
Does client help with shopping for family? _____
Does client help make decisions re: home management? _____

Interpersonal skills:

Appearance: Needs improvement? _____ Yes _____ No
Use of language: Easily understood? _____ Yes _____ No
Comprehension: Understands directions? _____ Yes _____ No

Other:

Has own transportation or can get to jobs? _____ Yes _____ No
General health is good? _____ Yes _____ No
Motivated to return to week? _____ Yes _____ No

Job seeking skills:

Can identify prospective employers? _____ Yes _____ No
Needs help with interviewing skills? _____ Yes _____ No

Additional information:
_____
_____
_____

Expanded work history:
(include part-time jobs, student jobs, and work done in Armed Forces)

Job Title: _____
Tools used: _____
Skills needed _____
Liked best about job: _____
Liked least about job: _____

Job Title: _____
Tools used: _____
Skills needed _____
Liked best about job: _____
Liked least about job: _____

Job Title: _____
Tools used: _____
Skills needed _____
Liked best about job: _____
Liked least about job: _____

Job Title: _____
Tools used: _____
Skills needed _____
Liked best about job: _____
Liked least about job: _____

Occupational categories:

Circle the industry and job in which the client has had experience:

Accounting jobs:

Bookkeeper
Cashier/teller
Billing clerk
Timekeeper
Accountant
Other _____

Machine trades:

Metal working
Paperworking
Printing
Wood machining
Textile
Other _____

Sales jobs:

Real estate/insurance
Food
Apparel/notions
Chemical/drugs
Furniture/appliance
Equipment Retail
Telephone
Rental
Building materials
Sporting goods
Other: _____

Processing jobs:

Metal plants
Ore refining
Food
Tobacco
Paper
Petroleum
Chemicals/rubber

Clerical jobs:

Secretary
Typist
Receptionist
Inventory/stock
Shipping clerk
Receiving clerk
Copy machine
Other _____

Agriculture jobs:

Groundskeeper
Animal care/grooming
Park attendant
Other _____

Service jobs:

Domestic
Food & beverage:
  server
  bartender
  cook
  dishwasher
Desk clerk
Other Hotel job
Cosmetology
  hair stylist
  manicurist
  make-up
Recreation attendant
  movie house
  bowling alley
  golf course
  restroom
  other _____
Guide
Apparel
  dry cleaning

Processing jobs:

Wood/stone/glass
Leather/textiles
Other _____

Bench work jobs:

Metal products
Medical products
Watches/clocks
Electrical
Computer
Painting/decorating
Wood products
Sand/stone products
Clay/grass products
Textile/leather
Electronics
Other _____

Miscellaneous:

Motor freight
Transportation
Packing/materials
Minerals/logging
Utilities
Motion picture
Other _____

Service jobs:

laundry
shoe repair
Protective Services
   bridge tender
   crossing tender
   security guard
   corrections officer
   other _____

Professional jobs:

Architecture/engineering
Medical/health
Education
Library/museum
Law
Writing/art
Entertainment
Managerial
Administrative
Other: _____

Summary of Transferable Skills:

The client has had job experience in the following industries:

1. _____
2. _____
3. _____

The client has acquired the following skills:

1. _____
2. _____
3. _____

These other resources are available:

1. _____
2. _____
3. _____

Taking into account limitations of _____
_____
_____

This client should be able to have a primary job goal of: _____
_____
and may also qualify for these other jobs: _____
_____
_____

This client will also require: (check all that apply)

Assistance with job search _____
Job readiness counseling _____
Possible on-the-job training _____
Possible specialized training _____
Other _____

Comments: _____
_____
_____
_____
_____

CLAIMS-RELATED INFORMATION

"People who work sitting down get paid more than people who work standing up."

– Ogden Nash

There is, of course, more to claims handling than just a transferable skills analysis. Disability is the vaguest of claims, making it the hardest to adjudicate. Automobiles get dents; humans get ulcers. One is easy to see; the other is not, nor is it simple to judge how it affects a person's ability to work. Some people are fragile health-wise; others are more stoic. Attitudes concerning work will also affect an individual's return to the job.

As has been pointed out earlier in this book, disability definitions are subjective and their vagueness is intended to give some latitude to allow for differences between individuals trying to recover from the same medical condition. One only hopes, as an agent and an insured, that common sense will reign over the whole process.

Nothing is clear cut, as evidenced by the cases noted below. Yet DI insurers turn down only a fraction of the claims submitted each year. Following 9-11-2001, several DI insurers noticed a slight uptick in the number of disability claims paid, with a healthy percentage of these being nervous disorders, including a person from a city other than New York who developed a fear of returning to work in the high-rise building of the business.[35] A claims examiner's job is not, sometimes, for the faint of heart.

California: A state Superior Court in California reversed an Appeals Court's decision to permit an insurer to deny coverage despite an incontestability clause. In its decision handed down, the Los Angeles Superior Court reviewed the effect of a standard incontestability clause and decreed the lower court erred in permitting the insurer to deny coverage for the insured's disability, caused by AIDS, because the insured tested positive for antibodies to HIV before the policy was issued. They held that the policy's incontestability clause bars the insurer from denying coverage for the disability, whether or not the causative sickness first manifested itself before the policy's date of issue. It also cited a prior case where a court had established that an incontestability clause does not condone fraud but merely establishes a time line within which it must be raised.

The claimant had tested positive for HIV antibodies in June 1987, applied for a disability policy in July, 1988, and filed claim in 1994. The application did not specifically ask about HIV testing, although it did ask about any pre-existing conditions.[36]

New York: In 2002, a New York state court upheld a jury verdict against an insurer that awarded $2.8 million in past and future disability benefits and legal costs to a dentist, injured in 1988. The original jury agreed with the plaintiff that the insurer had acted in 'bad faith" when it terminated the claimant's benefits. But it rejected allegations of deceptive trade practices. It may be the first NY case where the award included attorney's fees and lump-sum *future* benefits. The concern for insurers is that the risk of losing such a case *was* to have to pay past benefits in a lump sum, but the assumption was that future benefits would return to its initial regular monthly payouts.[37]

California: An Orange County, California jury took the unusual step of awarding $800,000 in punitive damages to an insurance company involved in a fraud verdict involving a disability claim. The case involved a 1989 claim filed by a Laguna Beach developer who claimed his asthma condition prevented him from doing his job. The DI policy had been purchased in 1987. The insurer paid out $623,000 in benefits from 1989 to 1996 when they received reports that the insured was actually still working. Subsequent videotapes showed the developer walking around construction sites and engaging in other activities he claimed he was unable to perform. The jury took the extra action because they felt the developer should be punished as fraud drove everyone's premiums higher.[38]

Welcome to the Wide World of Disability Insurance!

FOOTNOTES

1. Gregory L. Denes, Esq., "Beware the Own-Occ Claims Minefield," *Advisor Today*, February 2000, p. 104.
2. Robert W. Beal, FSA, "M&R's Survey of the Individual Disability Income Market Trends During the 1990s," *Disability Newsletter*, March 2000, p. 3.
3. Barbara Bowers and Ron Panko, "Profit Slide," *Best's Review*, December 2000, p. 95.
4. "Guardian, Berkshire to Merge – Combined Entity to be a Top Five DI Carrier," *HIU Magazine*, October 2000, p. 58.
5. Robert W. Beal, FSA, "Putting the United States IDI Market on the Road to Recovery in 2001," *Disability Newsletter*, March 2002, p. 1.
6. Allison Bell, "Individual Disability Sales Were Up 11% Last Year," *National Underwriter*, Life & Health/Financial Services Edition, Cincinnati, OH, June 24, 2002, p. 47.

7. Mark S. Seliber, FSA and W. Duane Kidwell, FSA, "Double Digit Gains! Non-Can DI 2001 Financial Results," *Disability Newsletter*, July 2002, p. 1.
8. "Conning Research: Individual Disability Insurers Rebound After Decade of Disaster," *PR Newswire*, November 5, 2003.
9. Source: Milliman USA, August 2003.
10. "Prudential Financial's 2004-2005 Study on the Financial Experience and Behaviors among Women," *Business Wire*, June 17, 2004.
11. Nilufer Ahmed, "Higher Education, High Incomes Make Asian-American Market Attractive," *National Underwriter*, Life & Health/Financial Services Edition, Cincinnati, OH, April 21, 2003, p. 8.
12. Marcella de Simone, "Tailor Your Approach to the Generation," *National Underwriter*, Life & Health/Financial Services Edition, Cincinnati, OH, April 21, 2003, p. 4.
13. Facts and Figures: Home-Based Business Owners, *Advisor Today*, May 2004, p. 30.
14. Bob Herum, CLU, ChFC, RHU, REBC, LTCP, "The Professional DI Market," *HIU Magazine*, May 2004, p. 40.
15. John Newell, CLU, ChFC, "How's Your Disability Awareness?" *Life Insurance Selling*, April 2004, p. 64.
16. "Obesity Leading to Increased Disability among the Young," *HIU Magazine*, April 2004, p. 40.
17. Allison Bell, "Group Disability's Weight Problem," *National Underwriter*, Life & Health/Financial Services Edition, Cincinnati, OH, May 10, 2004, p. 12.
18. Source: Principal Financial Group underwriting guide.
19. "Study finds disability sales surpass life insurance," *Employee Benefit Advisor*, September 2003, p. 47.
20. Bernice Caldwell, "Courts Consider Effect of Mitigating Measures in Disability Cases," *Employee Benefit Plan Review*, February 2001, p. 22.
21. Source: Union Central Life Insurance Company.
22. Roccy DeFrancesco, "The Ability of Disability," *Financial Planning*, December 2002, p. 57.
23. Vincent DeMarco, "DI Cost an Issue? Look at a Life/DI rider," *National Underwriter*, Life & Health/Financial Services Edition, Cincinnati, OH, March 5, 2001, p. 10.
24. Norse N. Blazzard and Judith A. Hasenauer, "Get Ready, Annuity/DI Packages Are on the Way," *National Underwriter*, March 5, 2001, p. 19.
25. Chris Shanahan, "CI Insurance Will See True Market Test as an Accelerated Life Rider," *National Underwriter*, Life & Health/Financial Services Edition, Cincinnati, OH, June 7, 2004, p. 26.
26. Linda Koco, "Worksite Plan Targets Uninsured Workers," *National Underwriter*, Life & Health/Financial Services Edition, Cincinnati, OH, March 6, 2000, p. 25.
27. Source: Mitra Toossi, Bureau of Labor Statistics, Washington, D.C. 2004.
28. Allison Bell, "Extend the Reach of Disability Insurance," *National Underwriter*, April 26, 2004, p. 29.
29. "The Principal Broadens Spectrum of Custom Solutions with Enhanced Disability Income Insurance Product," *Business Wire*, June 1, 2004.
30. Daniel D. Skwire, FSA and Charles Waldron, FSA, "Questions to Ask About Your Long-Term Disability Business," *Disability Newsletter*, April 2003, p. 6.
31. Andre C. Baillaregeon, "Some Pointers on Pricing Large Case LTD for Profitability," *National Underwriter*, Life & Health/Financial Services Edition, Cincinnati, OH, May 13, 2002, p. 12.
32. Source: JHA, Inc. 2003 U.S. Group Disability Market Survey, published March 2004.
33. James Conway, "The Right Perspective for Group Disability Sales," *Life Insurance Selling*, April 2004, p. 50.
34. John Wiggin," A Rehab Plan For Group Disability," *National Underwriter*, Life & Health/Financial Services Edition, Cincinnati, OH, May 10, 204, p. 17.
35. Christopher Oster, "Insurers Brace for Disability Claims Tied to Sept. 11," *Wall Street Journal*, November 8, 2001, p. A12.

36. Catherine Arnold, "California Disability Case Favors Insured," *National Underwriter*, July 3, 2000, p. 3.
37. Allison Bell, "Disability Insurer Loses Court Decision in New York," *National Underwriter*, Life & Health/Financial Services Edition, Cincinnati, OH, January 7, 2002, p. 3.
38. Trevor Thomas, "DI Fraud Verdict Gives Insurer Punitive Damage Award," *National Underwriter*, Life & Health/Financial Services Edition, Cincinnati, OH, March 3, 2000, p. 42.

Glossary of Terms

Accident: Accidental bodily injury for which benefits under a disability policy are paid.

Account Balance: In a Business Overhead Expense claim calculation, this figure is the total of the policy monthly benefit plus any unused benefits not previously paid out.

Americans with Disabilities Act: Legislation passed by Congress in 1990, intended to create greater opportunity for the disabled in the workplace.

Association Coverage: Disability income insurance available to an individual as part of a benefit package due to membership in a professional organization.

Attending Physician's Statement: A report utilized by the underwriting and claims departments of an insurer, completed by a physician that documents current and prior health history.

Automatic Indexing: Usually a standard policy provision, it increases the monthly disability benefit annually by either a pre-determined amount or the Consumer Price Index change without evidence of either medical or financial insurability for a limited period of time.

Avocation: Unusual and risky hobby for the insured like parachute jumping or scuba diving that could affect a standard issuance of the DI policy be the insurer.

Balance Sheet: An itemized listing of an individual or company's assets and liabilities that gives a snapshot of one's current financial position.

Benefit Period: The length of time for which disability benefits will be paid under a policy, such as 5 years or to age 65.

Blood Profile: A lab test requested on most disability applicants today to give the underwriter a current reading of a number of medical measurements, such as cholesterol and triglycerides.

Business Disability Coverage Form: A document used to obtain an overall picture of a business applicant's ownership, financial, and medical information to properly identify needs.

Business Overhead Expense: A business disability insurance policy that reimburses a business owner for his or her share of covered business expenses during a qualifying disability.

Business Interest Value: The actual amount a business owner's interest is worth after a calculation based on a valuation formula.

Buy-Sell Agreement: Or Buy-Out Agreement, this legal document details the specific procedures to follow and the qualifying events that would trigger the purchase of business owner's interest by either the other owners or the entity itself.

Cafeteria Plan: An employee benefit arrangement under Internal Revenue Code Section 125 whereby an individual is allowed to select among certain employee benefits, including disability income, to be paid for with pre-tax rather than post-tax dollars.

Capital gains tax: In a Disability Buy-Out policy, payment of proceeds that exceeds the insured's investment in the business may be subject to a tax on the profit made on the sale.

Carryover Account: A calculation during a Business Overhead Expense claim that tracks both unused policy benefits and unreimbursed business expenses.

Cash Sickness: A short-term state disability benefit program available in New York, New Jersey, Rhode Island, California, and Hawaii for off-the-job disabilities and that affects individual issue limits in those states.

Conditionally Renewable: Found primarily in Disability Buy-Sell and Key Person disability policies, under this provision, the insurer agrees to renew the insurance contract providing the insured meets certain qualifications.

Conversion: A policy provision for all business disability plans enabling the insured to exchange the business DI contract for personal disability protection should business circumstances change. In a personal DI policy, this is the opportunity to convert to a long-term care (LTC) contract, usually at an advanced age.

Cost of Living Rider: An optional benefit that increases the policy monthly benefit annually during a claim by the percentage change in the Consumer Price Index.

Covered Expenses: These are a business owner's expenditures that may be reimbursed under a Business Overhead Expense policy. Examples include rent or mortgage, employee's salaries and benefits, and telephone.

Critical Illness Policy: A disability-based insurance plan that pays a lump-sum benefit out upon the diagnosis of a specified number of catastrophic-type medical conditions such as stroke or cancer.

Cross-Purchase Agreement: A type of buy-out arrangement where each business owner is responsible for purchasing the interest of the disabled individual owner.

Current Earnings: During residual disability, this is the amount of money a disabled insured earns upon return to work following a disability.

Disability Income: A monthly benefit paid to an individual in the event of an accident or sickness to help replace earnings lost.

Disability Income Fact-Finder: Form used to accumulate data about an individual for the purpose of identifying personal disability income needs.

Disability Buy-Out: Also called Buy-Sell, this is a type of business disability insurance policy that insures the value of an owner's interest in the firm.

Elimination Period: The number of days an insured must be disabled before becoming eligible for benefits under a disability income insurance policy.

Employer-paid issue limits: A chart by which one can determine the amount of monthly disability income coverage an individual can purchase when the employer is paying the premium. This amount is higher than if the insured was paying the premium as claims benefits will be taxed upon receipt.

Entity-Purchase Agreement: A type of buy-out arrangement where the business itself is responsible for the purchase of a disabled owner's interest. It is generally used when there are more than two business owners.

Exclusions: This policy provision names several circumstances where the disability policy will not pay any benefits. These include war, self-inflicted injuries and normal pregnancy.

Field Underwriting: The process by which an insurance agent helps to evaluate the prospect through the completion of an application for insurance, detailing financial and medical history.

Financial Underwriting: A method by which an underwriter evaluates data relevant to earned income, unearned income, net worth, fringe benefits and other compensation elements to determine the amount of policy monthly benefit for which the applicant is eligible.

Gainful Occupation: A test applied under the policy definition of total disability that measures the ability of the disabled insured to perform work that is commensurate with one's education, training, experience and prior earnings.

Gross Earnings: An individual's income, after business expenses are deducted, but before taxes are applied.

Group LTD: A type of disability income contract issued to an employer to provide benefits to employees in the event of a long-term disability. It has a minimum elimination period of 90 days and benefits are usually payable to age 65 or 70.

Guaranteed Renewable: A type of policy renewal provision under which the insurer agrees to continue the policy as long as premiums are paid on a timely basis by the insured. The insurer reserves the right to raise premiums on a class basis, but cannot change any policy provisions.

Guarantee of Insurability: An optional benefit available with most disability policies that enables the insured to add more coverage to the initial amount issued with only evidence of financial insurability.

Income Statement: Also called a Profit/Loss statement, this document is used in the business valuation of a company in a Disability Buy-Out policy to help determine the coverage available for issue. It lists revenue and expenses for the business over a specified period of time.

Indemnity contract: Disability insurance policy that pays a stipulated amount of money if a person becomes disabled.

Installment Option: In a Disability Buy-Out contract, this is an option to pay out the proceeds under the policy once the buy-out has been triggered. It pays a monthly benefit amount over a specified number of months.

Issue limit: The maximum amount of disability monthly benefit that can be issued based on an individual's income or, in business cases, on the amount of expenses or the value of the interest in the business.

Key Person: This is a business disability policy that directly reimburses the business for its financial loss during the loss of a key employee in the firm.

Limited Condition Rider: In health underwriting, this is an offer to extend some coverage to a specified medical condition rather than completely excluding it from any benefits, such as "covered after 180 days of disability for twenty-four months."

Loss of Earnings: A percentage used in the calculation of a residual disability benefit that measures current earnings against prior earnings during a return to work following disability.

Lump-Sum Payment: This is the primary method used for the distribution of policy proceeds to the disabled business owner under a Disability Buy-Out insurance contract after satisfaction of the elimination period.

Maximum BOE Benefit: Under a Business Overhead Expense policy, this is the total policy value calculated by multiplying the monthly benefit times the number of months in the benefit period.

Medical Underwriting: The process of an underwriter's evaluation of an applicant's health history to determine eligibility for a disability income policy, using medical exams, blood profiles and attending physician's statements among other tools.

Mental/Nervous Disorder Benefit Limitation: An optional benefit or sometimes a policy provision that reduces the benefit period under a disability income contract to 24 months for certain medical conditions.

Minimum Benefit: Under a residual disability policy, this is the least amount the insurance contract will pay in the first six months of a return to work, usually 50 percent of the total disability monthly benefit.

Money Provisions: In a disability policy, these are the policy clauses that an insurance agent can quantify in dollars that could be paid out during a disability claim.

Monthly Benefit: The amount of coverage in a disability policy that is paid regularly during a claim. During a residual disability claim, a percentage of this amount is paid.

Net Worth: The total non-business assets of an insured that are part of the financial underwriting evaluation to determine eligible issue amount. In a Disability Buy-Out policy, this is the amount used in the valuation of the business.

Non-Cancelable: A type of renewal provision that states the insurer cannot modify the policy in any way, raise the premiums or not continue the policy until insured's age 65 as long as the policy premiums are paid on a timely basis.

Non-Covered Expenses: In a Business Overhead Expense policy, these are the business expenditures that are not reimbursed during a claim. These include the owner's income and income of associates in the firm performing the same work as the insured.

Occupation Class: A category of insurance risks based on specific job duties that are used to determine the type of policy and amount of premiums an individual would pay for disability income coverage.

Optional Benefit: Extra coverage choices that can be added to the base policy to help personally design the income protection program to cover an individual's needs. Examples include Cost of Living and Guarantee of Insurability benefits.

Own Occupation: A definition used in total disability that only has one test that is applied to determine eligibility for policy benefits, that of the ability of the insured to perform the duties of one's own job.

Personnel Replacement Benefit: An optional benefit under a Key Person DI policy, this feature reimburses the business for the expenses associated with searching for and hiring a replacement for the disabled key person.

Policy Schedule Page: This is the section in a disability insurance policy that specifies the details of the policy data such as premium, monthly benefit, elimination and benefit periods and optional benefits chosen.

Pre-Existing Condition: This policy provision, usually found under the Exclusions language that defines when an illness or injury that existed before the policy was issued and that may not be covered for a certain period of time after the policy is issued.

Prior Earnings: In the calculation of the residual disability benefit, this is the amount of income the insured is determined to have made before disability began. There is usually a choice of time periods to use to arrive at this number.

Presumptive Total Disability: A disability policy provision that waives the normal tests of disability for certain losses like sight, speech, hearing, or the loss of two limbs, and also waives the elimination period to begin paying the policy monthly benefit.

Programming: The process of calculating the disability need and identifying the additional coverage that can be written taking into account all existing disability benefits.

Public Disability Coverage: These are disability funding sources, such as Social Security and Workers' Compensation, that an individual might be eligible for following an injury or illness.

Railroad Retirement Act: Public benefits program for railroad workers that includes some disability income coverage.

Recurrent Disability: A provision in a disability income policy that defines when an accident or sickness will be considered continuous despite a short period of recovery when the insured is not considered disabled under the policy.

Regular Care and Attendance of Physician: A secondary part of the definition of total disability under a contract requiring that the insured be under the care and attendance of a physician for the injury or illness that is the cause of disability.

Rehabilitation: A policy provision under which the insurer agrees to reimburse the disabled insured for expenses associated with a program that will assist in returning the individual to work.

Reimbursable contract: A disability insurance policy that pays benefits based on specific expenses that have been incurred, like a Business Overhead Expense plan.

Renewability: This policy provision outlines the conditions under which a disability policy can be continued. Examples include non-cancelable and guaranteed renewable.

Residual Disability: A key policy provision or optional benefit that pays the disabled insured a percentage of the policy monthly benefit based on the percentage of earnings lost during a disability.

Retirement Benefit Protection: An optional rider that specifically replaces retirement plan contributions during a disability.

Return to Work: A policy definition under the Residual Disability provision that allows the benefit to still be calculated for a period of time to determine if there is a loss of earnings even though the insured is back to work on a full-time basis.

Salary Continuation Plan: Also called "Sick Pay Plan," this is a tax-favored program to ensure that the business can deduct any income paid to a disabled employee as an ordinary business expense.

Sickness: The language in a disability income contract that defines an illness or disease that first makes itself known to the insured at any time following the issue date of the policy. Sickness covers both mental and nervous disorders unless specified otherwise.

Social Security: A federal government program that includes disability benefits for which most working Americans are eligible. The disability definition is restrictive, requiring the individual's disability to be expected to last at least 12 months or be terminal.

Social Security Offset Rider: An optional benefit where the amount of coverage is coordinated with any benefits received under the Social Security disability program and sometimes under any public government program.

Substantial Loss of Earnings: A definition under the Residual Disability benefit specifying the amount of earnings loss, usually 75 or 80 percent, whereby the full total disability benefit would be paid rather than doing the residual calculation.

Substitute Salary Expense Rider: An optional feature under the Business Overhead Expense policy that provides funds to pay for a replacement worker brought in to assist with the business following an owner's disability.

Total Disability: The primary definition in a disability policy that qualifies an insured for benefits following an injury or sickness.

Transfer privilege: In a Disability Buy-Out policy, this policy provision allows the exchange of one insured for another when business ownership interest is changed.

Transferable Skills Analysis: Claims process that identifies the disabled insured's primary talents to evaluate future occupational and rehabilitation possibilities in an effort to change the disability status from total to residual or recovered.

Treatment of Injuries: Available as either a policy feature or optional benefit, the payment of medical expenses due to an accident when the disability is not eligible for any other policy benefits.

Trigger point: This date marks the end of the elimination period under a Disability Buy-Out policy when a buy-out of a disabled business owner's interest begins.

Unbundling: The current fad in disability income insurance to offer many DI policy features on an optional basis to provide more flexibility and affordability to the average consumer.

Unearned Income: Passive income that will continue to be available to an individual during a disability, this affects the amount of coverage a person can purchase in a disability policy.

Valuation: In a Disability Buy-Out policy, this is the method used in calculating the worth of the business that helps to determine the amount insurable and payable under the contract.

Voluntary DI Benefits: Disability insurance offered as an option at a worksite that employees can either accept or refuse that may or may not have an employer contribution to the premium payment.

Waiver Form: A document used in the solicitation of disability income insurance that an individual signs if not wishing to obtain disability coverage as the funding vehicle for income protection needs.

Waiver of Premium: A policy provision that allows a disabled insured to continue a disability income policy without the requirement of paying the premium for it.

Workers' Compensation: A public program that provides, among other coverage, disability income benefits for on-the-job injuries or illnesses.

INDEX

A
Accident 162, 248-249
Accounting Fee Benefit 201, 210
Americans with
    Disabilities Act 22-24, 251-252
Asian Americans 245-246
Association Coverage 67-68
Attending Physician's Statement 134
Automatic Indexing 175-177
Avocations 137-138

B
Baby Boomers 15-17
Balance Sheet 205
Bankruptcy 4
Benefit Modifications 138-139
Benefit Period 62, 108, 114, 214
Blood Profile 105, 134
Business Overhead
    Expense 124-126, 192-204
Business Ownership
    Interest 204-205, 208
Business Valuation 208
Buy-Sell Agreement 126-128

C
Cafeteria Plan 122
Carryover Account 194-195
Cash Sickness 69-70, 84
Claims 140-144, 268-269
COBRA 9
Conditionally Renewable 162, 208-209
Conversion 180-181, 200-201, 209, 214
Cost of Living Rider 62, 188-190
Counteroffers 138-140, 146-147
Covered Expenses (BOE) 199-200
Critical Illness Insurance 30-31, 222-226, 256
Current Earnings 170-171

D
Death Benefit (BOE) 201
Disability Income Fact-Finder 58-59
Disability Buy-Sell 126-128, 204-211
Disability Risk 5-6, 22, 41, 93-94

E
Elimination Period 62, 107, 113, 125, 174, 206, 213-214
Equity Disability Trust 254
Exclusions 138, 181-182, 202, 210
Existing Coverage 59, 63-68, 86-89, 99, 102-103, 114-115

F
Fact-Finding 58-64
Field Underwriting 103-104
Financial Underwriting 136-137
Foreign-born Workers 56
Future Income Option 62, 114

G
Government Employees 55, 60
Group DI 28-29, 48, 63, 65-67, 121-122, 137, 219-222, 259-260
Guaranteed Renewable 160, 197
Guarantee of Insurability 183-185, 202, 210

H
Health Savings Accounts 118
Health Screening Rider 225
HIPAA 136
Home-Based Businesses 12-14, 54, 246-247
Illness 162-163, 248-249

I
Income Statement 205

283

Injury 162, 248-249
Installment Option 206-207
Issue Limits 45-47, 50

K
Key Person 212-213
Key Person DI 128-129, 211-216

L
Legal Fee Benefit 201, 210
Limited Condition Rider 138
Liquid Assets 50-51
Loss of Earnings 171
Lump-Sum Payment 206-207

M
Maximum BOE Benefit 193-194
Medical Underwriting 61, 103-106, 134-136
Mental/Nervous Disorder Benefit
   Limitation 178-179
Middle Income Workers 8-10
Minimum Benefit 171-172
Multi-life Underwriting 137

N
Net Worth 49
Non-Cancelable 161-162, 197, 214

O
Occupation Class 51-52, 60
Optional Benefits 62, 182-183, 214, 255-256
Own Occupation 165, 183

P
Personnel Replacement Benefit 215
Pre-Existing Condition 181
Professional Market 56-57, 247-248
Prior Earnings 49-50, 169-170
Premium Cost 96-98
Presumptive Total
   Disability 174-175, 202
Public Disability Coverage 68-86

R
Railroad Retirement Act 76-77, 85
Rating 138
Recurrent Disability 179-180, 202
Regular Care and Attendance
   of Physician 172-174, 202, 214
Rehabilitation 177-178, 202
Reimbursable contract 193
Renewability 159-160, 197, 214
Residual Disability 53, 62, 167-172, 198-199
Retirement Benefit
   Protection 50, 190-191
Return of Premium 63
Return to Work 172

S
Salary Continuation Plan 20, 123
Self-Insuring 43-44
Sick Pay Plan 20, 123
Sickness 162-163, 248-249
Small Business Owners 18-22, 54, 109-115, 117-123
Social Security 77-84, 86, 88, 101
Social Insurance Offset
   Rider 46-47, 62, 88, 185-188
Substitute Salary Expense
   Rider 203

T
Taxation 115-116, 126, 214, 251-254
Total Disability 53, 164-167, 197-198, 209, 214
Transfer Privilege 209-210
Transferable Skills Analysis 261-267
Treatment of Injuries 180

U
Unbundling 157-159
Unearned Income 49

V
Voluntary DI Plans 216-218

W

Waiver Form 132
Waiver of Premium 32, 179, 202, 214
Weight 135, 249-250
Women 10-12, 245
Workers' Compensation 70-75, 85, 101
Worksite Marketing 28-30, 122, 216-222
Young Professionals 56-57